ROLLERCOASTER

ROLLERCOASTER

THE INCREDIBLE STORY OF THE EMERGING MARKETS

GILL TUDOR

Published by **Pearson Education**

London / New York / San Francisco / Toronto / Sydney / Tokyo / Singapore
Hong Kong / Cape Town / Madrid / Paris / Milan / Munich / Amsterdam

PEARSON EDUCATION LIMITED

Head Office:
Edinburgh Gate
Harlow CM20 2JE
Tel: +44 (0)1279 623623
Fax: +44 (0)1279 431059

London Office:
128 Long Acre
London WC2E 9AN
Tel: +44 (0)20 7447 2000
Fax: +44 (0)20 7240 5771
Website: www.business-minds.com

....

First published in Great Britain in 2000

The right of Gill Tudor to be identified as author
of this work has been asserted by her in accordance
with the Copyright, Designs and Patents Act 1988.

ISBN 0 273 65009 2

British Library Cataloguing in Publication Data
A CIP catalogue record for this book can be obtained from the British Library

10 9 8 7 6 5 4 3 2 1

Typeset by Pantek Arts Ltd, Maidstone, Kent
Printed and bound in Great Britain by Biddles Ltd, Guildford and King's Lynn

The Publishers' policy is to use paper manufactured from sustained forests.

ABOUT THE AUTHOR

GILL TUDOR reported on the 1997–99 crisis at first hand for Reuters as a London-based Emerging Markets Correspondent. She has covered developing countries for more than a decade, both as a reporter and as a political and economic analyst for an independent think-tank. Educated at Cambridge and London University's School of Oriental and African Studies, she joined Reuters as a trainee journalist in 1987 and has held postings in Johannesburg, New Delhi and Abidjan. She is currently taking a break from day-to-day reporting to train other journalists.

For Mum and Dad,

for Jenny,

and for Chloe, who may read it one day.

CONTENTS

ACKNOWLEDGEMENTS

First and foremost, a huge thank you to all the Reuters journalists around the world who covered every aspect of the most recent emerging market crisis, and the Mexican crash before it. Their work forms the backbone of this story, and provides a large part of the flesh; without it, the book would simply not have been possible. I have tried to give credit as often as I can by naming names; apologies to those whose contributions remain anonymous.

In particular, I must thank all my colleagues on the London Capital Markets desk, past and present, for their encouragement and help. Mike Dolan, who knows more about the global markets than I ever shall, made time to read my drip-fed manuscript and offer invaluable feedback; I owe him a very large debt, payable in Guinness. Andy Priest sacrificed the comfort of his sick bed to explain the intricacies of the LTCM affair. John Paul Rathbone and David Chance bounced ideas around and helped keep me in touch with a rapidly changing market while I sweated in my ivory tower. Thanks to everyone for their guidance and camaraderie.

Izabel Grindal and Elaine Herlihy had faith in my ability to produce something rather longer than Reuters' usual 800-word limit, and backed me up with generous enthusiasm. Corrie Parsonson and Mike Tyler whipped up the charts, for which Greg Clark dug out some of the more inaccessible market data. Peter Blake and his technical team breathed life into an injured computer at the crucial moment. Keith Stafford showed impeccable understanding when book-time sometimes impinged on training time. Thanks to all – and to the Reuters photographers whose pictures bring the text to life.

My gratitude to Martin Drewe at Pearson Education for providing calm advice and encouragement in the face of mounting authorial stress; and to Nikki Bowen for handling some extensive late amendments with patience and aplomb.

Thanks too to all the emerging market traders and analysts who have spared time in an often frenzied world to talk to me, both for this book and for the Reuters file. Many are named here; others have sometimes preferred to remain anonymous, but their off-the-record insights and candour are no less appreciated for that.

Last but not least, thanks to Jenny Larsen, not only for her constant support and professional editing eye but also for her considerable tolerance during the writing of this book – a period that can politely be described as "brief but intense".

A couple of apologies. First, I may have given short shrift to aspects of the story on which some readers would have preferred more detail. I can only say that cramming a story of such broad historical and geographical scope into a book of this size has inevitably meant simplifying or glossing over some details – not, I hope, to the detriment of accuracy. Second, for speed and simplicity the word "dollar" refers here to the US currency unless otherwise indicated; apologies to residents of Hong Kong, Singapore, Canada, Australia, Zimbabwe, Jamaica and the many other nations whose own currencies share that name.

Quotations or key data taken from sources other than Reuters are acknowledged in the text or footnotes. All others are from Reuters stories or my own interviews and communications. Any errors are, of course, my fault. Any unattributed opinions expressed in the book are also my own, and are quite separate from the neutral stance required on the Reuters file.

ON THE BRINK

AS DIPLOMATIC LANGUAGE GOES, the note passed to Japan's "Mr Yen" from the US camp didn't mince its words.

"Eisuke, the world is going to hell," it said. "We've got to co-operate."

The recipient was Eisuke Sakakibara, Tokyo's outspoken vice finance minister for international affairs, whose nickname reflected his heavy clout in global currency markets. The note came from US Deputy Treasury Secretary Lawrence Summers, a major mover in Washington's dealings with the developing world. It was Monday, September 14, 1998, and the Group of Seven (G7) leading industrial nations was meeting in London to discuss the international shock waves from Russia's financial meltdown.[1]

In a rousing speech the same day in New York, US President Bill Clinton said the world was facing its worst financial crisis for half a century, with a quarter of the global population hit by falling or negative economic growth. In Beijing, China and Japan were trying to thrash out a joint approach to Asia's year-old economic crunch, amid stern warnings from the Chinese that Tokyo was not doing its bit to salvage the region.

The tidal wave of debt, currency collapse and stock market panic that had engulfed the much-feted Asian Tiger economies in mid-1997 was still roaring round the globe, crashing over Russia and foaming on towards Latin America. A month earlier, Moscow had given up trying to defend its embattled rouble against an onslaught of market speculation – but only after pouring some $9 billion of its foreign reserves down the drain in a futile attempt to prop up the currency. Now the rouble was twitching around wildly at roughly half to a third of its previous value, and the Russian stock market was on the floor. The banking system was in tatters, prices were escalating, and ordinary Russians were battening down the hatches for a grim winter. Morose savers were queueing in the rain for hours outside locked banks in the faint hope of retrieving their cash. Store shelves had been stripped bare of basic foods – flour, salt, vegetable oil – and importers were in no hurry to part with precious dollars to buy in more supplies.

There were dark predictions of unrest on the streets, and fears of a political vacuum in the former superpower. Russia's ailing and increasingly erratic president, Boris Yeltsin, had just backed down in a bitter power struggle with the Communist-led parliament over who would head the government. He was holed up in his dacha outside Moscow while the new compromise prime minister, former spymaster Yevgeny Primakov, struggled to create a cabinet capable of working together.

In Asia the crisis had plunged an estimated 100 million people into the kind of poverty not seen for 30 years, despite modest signs that at least some of the battered economies were starting to stabilize. Four national leaders had lost their jobs, including Japanese Prime Minister Ryutaro Hashimoto and Indonesia's frail but tenacious President Suharto. Fresh riots had just broken out across Indonesia as protesters and looters raged at rampant inflation that had tripled the cost of rice. The Indonesian government said at least 17 million families were facing food shortages, and in some areas more than half the population could afford only one meal a day.

In Kuala Lumpur the Commonwealth Games, originally planned as a showcase for Malaysia's headlong rush to join the rich world, had turned into more of a distraction from the gloom than a symbol of success. Mercurial Malaysian Prime Minister Mahathir Mohamad, never slow to blame the Asian crisis on "robber" currency speculators, had pulled down the shutters by slapping capital controls on foreigners' local stock market holdings and pegging the value of the ringgit firmly to the dollar. Investors were licking their wounds and muttering that Malaysia could say goodbye to any more cash for a very long time.

On the other side of the globe Brazil was fighting to support its real, the new currency that had successfully killed off chronic hyperinflation just a few years earlier. The São Paulo stock market had suffered one of its worst beatings ever, plunging nearly 16 percent in a single day. Desperate to persuade investors to keep their money in Brazil, the central bank had cranked up interest rates from 19 percent to a crippling 50 percent in less than a week. The government, treading a political tightrope ahead of the October presidential elections, had chiselled about $5 billion off its spending plans. But dollars were still gushing out of the country at up to $2 billion a day, and the astronomical cost of borrowing was squeezing the economy dry.

The so-called emerging markets, the Wild West of 1990s global capitalism, had suddenly turned very sour. For little more than a decade, enthusiasts had drooled over the world's less developed capital markets from Beijing to Buenos Aires, from Almaty to Zagreb, which offered bigger risks but potentially far bigger rewards than dull old European blue-chip stocks or cast-iron US government bonds. The buzzword was globalization: communism was dead, world trade was booming, and the Asian Tigers were in full roar. Invest in Indonesia! Buy Brazil! Take a punt on Poland!

Hundreds of billions of dollars had poured into stocks, bonds and bank loans in countries that many investors would have been hard pressed to find on the map. But when the bubble of confidence in one or two economies burst, fortunes sluiced straight back out again. Investors who saw the Thai baht drop like a stone in July 1997 started to wonder whether it was such a good idea to keep their money in South Korea, or Malaysia. Pretty soon they started getting nervous about Russia, or South Africa, or Argentina – or anywhere that didn't look like a nice, safe bet. And even if they did keep their nerve, many were forced to sell good assets to offset losses on the bad.

> ❝ The so-called emerging markets, the Wild West of 1990s global capitalism, had suddenly turned very sour ❞

The rouble's plunge was frightening enough for emerging market investors. What really shook them was Russia's simultaneous default on some $40 billion worth of rouble-denominated government bonds. A country would not default on its domestic debt, they had thought as they loaded up their portfolios with the high-yielding paper; after all, it can always print more money to pay it off. They were wrong, and the way things were going it looked as though Russia might default on some of its foreign currency debt, too. Credit rating agency Fitch IBCA warned that foreign investors could lose more than $100 billion on their Russian debt holdings alone – the single biggest credit loss ever imposed on private-sector creditors.

The Russian collapse set off fresh turmoil across the emerging market map, and currency speculators set their sights on Brazil's increasingly shaky real as the next target for attack. Why Brazil? Well, like Russia, it had a heavy load of short-term debt coming due and dwindling foreign reserves to pay it. Besides, with Asia and Russia down and other emerging markets falling like dominoes, could Latin America be far behind? Once markets are spooked, their fears have an unnerving way of becoming self-fulfilling prophecies. And if Brazil crashed, the logic went, its neighbour and trading partner Argentina would be next. And if Argentina were forced to discard its ultra-stable currency board, Hong Kong would be in for trouble, for the purely psychological reason that it shared the same type of exchange rate system. And if Hong Kong fell, maybe China would forget its promise not to devalue the yuan, and the whole of Asia would get caught up in a fresh bout of competitive devaluations in a desperate race for export markets.

Panic was mounting. "Not so much emerging markets as submerging markets" became the weary joke. In financial centres around the world, emerging market traders, analysts and sales staff were glancing nervously over their shoulders and wondering if they still had a job.

But by now the major markets were also tasting fear. Japan, mired in its worst recession for four decades after its stocks and real estate bubble had burst at the turn of the 1990s, had already seen its weak glimmers of recovery snuffed out by the wider Asian crisis. The Japanese economy had shrunk for the third quarter running, the banking system was crippled by bad debts, and the Tokyo stock market was close to a 12-year low.

Stocks in other major industrial countries had been reaching record peaks as recently as July 1998, but now they too were on the slide, led by shares in banks that looked increasingly vulnerable to emerging market losses. One of Wall Street's leading investment banks, Lehman Brothers, was forced publicly to deny market rumours that it faced imminent bankruptcy. In just two months New York's Dow Jones Industrial Average had fallen more than 16 percent, London's FTSE-100 index was down 17 percent, and Germany's DAX had shed 23 percent. Spain was even worse hit because of its close Latin American business ties, with the Madrid market dropping a cool 30 percent.

To make matters worse, market talk had it that a high-flying, high-stakes US hedge fund with two Nobel prize winners among its partners was on the skids after losing nearly all its capital as the Russian crisis turned world bond markets on their heads. If the unfortunately named Long-Term Capital Management (LTCM) went under, not only would the banks that invested in or lent to LTCM make huge losses but the unwinding of the fund's highly leveraged market positions, amounting notionally to more than $1.4 trillion, could rattle Wall Street to its foundations.

By the time the International Monetary Fund (IMF) and World Bank held their yearly get-together in early October, an estimated $4.3 trillion had been wiped off the value of the world's stock markets[2] – more than the annual economic output of Germany, France and Spain combined. Britain's *Observer* newspaper reckoned the slide had slashed an average of £4,000 off the net wealth of every person in Britain through its impact on pension funds, popular share savings schemes and so on.[3] The IMF virtually halved its 1999 forecast for world growth to just over 2 percent.

Fears were growing that not just Asia and Russia but the whole world was heading for a credit crunch in which wounded banks would become increasingly reluctant to lend to *anybody*, from the Brazilian government to the corner shop. Businesses would be starved of funds, defaults and bankruptcies would escalate, and economic downturn could accelerate into full-blown slump. Jobs were already disappearing in Britain and other developed countries as Asian manufacturers that had expanded proudly in the glory years shut down factories or shelved expansion plans. Demand for both raw materials and finished goods would slip, prices would fall, consumers would save rather than spend, and the whole cycle would gain momentum. For nearly three decades, governments had been bent on stamping out inflation; now they were staring at the prospect of equally damaging deflation. It had already happened in Japan in the 1990s – and worldwide in the 1930s.

Urgent calls were circulating for interest rate cuts in the United States and other major industrial nations, to try to stimulate growth and take some debt-service pressure off countries such as Brazil. Clinton's New York speech and a simultaneous G7 statement both seemed to be hinting at rate cuts, in virtually identical language: the "balance of risks" in the world economy had shifted away from inflation and the new priority was growth.

But the signals coming out of central banks in Washington, London, Frankfurt or Tokyo were far from clear, and to many on the financial scene the leaders of the world's most powerful countries were too preoccupied with their own domestic worries to pay much attention to the big picture. Clinton was wading through a sex-and-lies scandal that threatened an ignominious end to his stay in the White House. Japan's government was wrangling with opposition parties over plans to clean up the shambling banking sector, a cornerstone of its recovery hopes. Germany was in the thick of a general election campaign, and most of the European Union was fretting about keeping a tight rein on monetary policy before launching the euro at the start of 1999.

> **Few would have thought a spot of currency bother in a moderately sized South-East Asian country could have set off such a massive chain reaction around the globe**

Few would have thought a spot of currency bother in a moderately sized South-East Asian country could have set off such a massive chain reaction around the globe. It was no coincidence that in mid-September 1998 *The Economist* ran a background piece on the Great Depression of the 1930s. The question on many lips was: "Is it happening again?"

NOTES

1 Story recounted by Eisuke Sakakibara in *Yomiuri Shimbun*, August 4, 1999.

2 *Independent*, October 3, 1998.

3 *Observer*, October 11, 1998.

1

HISTORY LESSONS

If you owe your bank a hundred pounds, you have a problem; but if you owe it a million, it has – Attributed to John Maynard Keynes

HOW TO SPOT AN EMERGING MARKET

On the face of it, "emerging markets" are easier to define by what they are *not* than by what they *are*. They are what's left when the world's major, developed markets – New York, London, Frankfurt, Tokyo, Paris, Milan, and so on – are taken away. But of course that is an oversimplification. Few people would suggest that Somalia, for example, was an emerging market country just because it's not as rich as Spain. At the other end of the spectrum, Greece – an upstanding member of the European Union with an economy bigger than Ireland's – is often found in emerging market portfolios.

The truth is that "emerging" is in the eye of the beholder. There are probably almost as many different lists of emerging markets as there are investors in them, yet everybody seems to know well enough by intuition what the phrase means. It is a useful shorthand way of saying "financial markets in developing countries and the former Eastern Bloc, offering a reasonable range of investments open to foreigners", or some such mouthful. "I've been investing around the world for more than

30 years, and I never knew that there was such a thing as an 'emerging market'," said retired Wall Street whizz-kid Jim Rogers. "But there is always a compelling case for investing in a market where things are low and things are going to get better – whether it's Germany or Ethiopia." [1]

The phrase itself was coined in the early 1980s by the International Finance Corporation (IFC), the World Bank's private-sector lending arm, when it started encouraging developing countries to build up their rusty or new-born capital markets as part of a wider shift to a market-based economy. The IFC's general definition is extremely broad: "The term 'emerging market' can imply that a process of change is under way, with stock markets growing in size and sophistication, in contrast to markets that are small and stagnant. The term can also refer to any market in a developing economy, with the implication that all have the potential for development." [2]

But the IFC also had to settle on more selective criteria for including countries in its benchmark emerging stock market indices (since taken over by credit ratings agency Standard & Poor's), which are used widely by fund managers as a gauge for judging their own investment perfor-mance. Originally, the key factor was purely the size of a country's economy: if its annual gross national product (GNP) per head fell into the World Bank's low- or middle-income categories – defined in 1999 as below $9,656 – its stock market was regarded as emerging. By the mid-1990s the IFC decided there was more to it than that, particularly as dollar-based GNP figures could fluctuate wildly as a result of exchange rate movements, and in 1999 it came up with a new set of criteria for joining or leaving the list. New entrants must now qualify as low- or middle-income in at least one of the past three years. To "graduate" from the emerging market fold, countries must not only be in the World Bank's high-income range for three years running but also show a ratio of investable capitalization (the total value of all the shares that a for-eigner can invest in without serious restrictions) to gross domestic product (GDP) near the developed market average for three years.

The IFC's definition is far from binding, and investors often categorize coun-tries as much by gut feeling as by fundamentals. The IFC indices do not include Hong Kong or Singapore, two territories with high per capita income and liquid, sophisticated markets. Yet most investors would instinc-tively regard both of these as an integral part of the emerging markets scene, particularly in light of the events at the end of the 1990s. Saudi Arabia is rich, but the fact that its stock market is fairly small and illiquid, and heavily restricted for foreigners, prevents it from joining the ranks of the major world markets. Taiwan has high per capita income and a very active market, yet it too places restrictions on foreign access. Israel meets the World Bank's high-income criterion but few investors, whatever their politics, would see it as stable enough for major market status. Portugal and Greece are members of the European Union – the former is even part of the euro zone – yet Portugal only "graduated" from the IFC indices in 1999, and Greece is still covered. (Another provider of benchmark stock market indices, Morgan Stanley Capital International, said in March 2000 it would decide by the end of November whether to designate Greece as a developed market.)

Even trickier is defining the cut-off point at the "bottom" of the list. Few people would disagree that countries such as Thailand, Poland, South Africa and Brazil are mainstream emerging markets, but what about Ukraine? Or Vietnam? Or Kenya? Some investors differentiate between fully fledged emerging markets and "frontier", "pioneer" or "embryo" markets, which are less developed, less liquid, a little riskier, even more Wild West. The borderlines can prove fluid – investors in Japan in the 1960s were considered courageous pioneers – and those with the steeliest nerves are always trying to get in at the bottom of the next boom market.

> 66 A market will be "emerging" only if foreign investors, as a group, decide to see it as such 99

Ethical considerations – a country's record on equality or human rights, a company's stance on work conditions or pollution – seldom enter the equation. And the emerging market label is one that can be imposed or awarded only from outside. Kenyans and Vietnamese may decide they would like their countries to be thriving emerging markets, hoovering up investment capital, but they cannot force the pace; they can only try to make their markets as attractive as possible. A market will be "emerging" only if foreign investors, as a group, decide to see it as such.

PLUS ÇA CHANGE – THE EARLY EMERGING MARKETS

Of course, there is nothing particularly new about the idea of investing in emerging markets, apart from the label itself. The more adventurous (and sometimes the more gullible) investors have always been ready to take a punt on distant places that looked as though they were on the up and offered a lucrative payback. Some countries that are now regarded as developing have come down in the world; at the turn of the 20th century Argentina was one of the top seven economies, and the phrase "rich as an Argentine" was common in Europe. Others, such as the United States or Japan, were once every bit as "emerging" as Brazil or Thailand today. In 1800, GNP per head in North America was lower than in Latin America, although it was already higher than in Western Europe.[3] Japan, now the world's second-biggest economy despite a decade-long economic trough, did not industrialize until the late 19th century, and even in the 1960s it was still perceived as a poor and risky place to invest.

There is certainly nothing new about financial crises, either. The history of the markets is littered with cautionary tales of boom turning to bust in the twinkling of an eye, ruining investors who failed to leap early enough off the crashing bandwagon. Time and time again, from the Dutch tulip-buying frenzy of the mid-17th century, through the run-up to the 1929 Wall Street crash and "Black Monday" of October 1987, investors have succumbed to what veteran political economist J. K. Galbraith calls "financial euphoria":

Some artifact or some development, seemingly new and desirable – tulips in Holland, gold in Louisiana, real estate in Florida, the superb economic designs of Ronald Reagan – captures the financial mind or perhaps, more accurately, what so passes. The price of the object of speculation goes up. Securities, land, objets d'art, and other property, when bought today, are worth more tomorrow. This increase and the prospect attract new buyers; the new buyers assure a further increase. Yet more are attracted; yet more buy; the increase continues. The speculation building on itself provides its own momentum ... Something, it matters little what – although it will always be much debated – triggers the ultimate reversal. Those who had been riding the upward wave decide now is the time to get out. Those who thought the increase would be forever find their illusion destroyed abruptly, and they, also, respond to the newly revealed reality by selling or trying to sell. Thus the collapse. And thus the rule, supported by the experience of centuries: the speculative episode always ends not with a whimper but with a bang.[4]

Two of the earliest financial crises on record centred on European-based companies that promised fabulous rewards on the basis of their operations in far-flung lands. In late 1719 French investors scrambled to buy shares in the Compagnie d'Occident, or Mississippi Company, which purported to be prospecting for gold in North America. The old Paris bourse was "the scene of the most intense, even riotous, operations in all the history of financial greed".[5] Trading had to shift to a less cramped location; demand was so desperate that women offered their bodies in exchange for the right to buy shares. The whole shaky edifice was undermined by two awkward facts: first, the company had not lifted a pickaxe in North

America, much less found gold, and second, the escalating shares were paid for by near-worthless paper notes printed hand over fist by the very bank that had set up the Mississippi Company in the first place. The bust came in mid-1720 with a run on the bank; 15 people were killed in the crush.

In the same year Britain fell prey to the famous South Sea Bubble. The ambitious London-based South Sea Company claimed trading rights with the whole of South America, despite the fact that Spain held an effective monopoly over all trade with the region. (On top of that, the company also hatched an exotic plan to privatize Britain's national debt.) Stocks in the firm rocketed to more than 100 times their face value, fuelled not only by high hopes in the company itself but by fevered speculation on the share price. The crash was even swifter, with share prices ending the year lower than they had begun it.

> 66 The history of the markets is littered with cautionary tales of boom turning to bust in the twinkling of an eye 99

Opportunities to invest directly in developing countries multiplied as most of Latin America threw off the colonial yoke in the 1820s, a decade that saw a bonanza of mainly British investment in the region. Newly independent Latin American governments pumped out some £20 million in bonds, and shares worth £36 million were floated in mining, commercial and other companies.[6]

So enthusiastic was the demand in London that a Scottish conman, Gregor MacGregor, successfully launched a £200,000 bond issue for the fictional country of Poyais, situated on the Caribbean coast of Central America. Styling himself Gregor I, Cazique of Poyais, he also sold chunks of territory and commissions in his non-existent army. The fraud took a tragic twist when 200 would-be settlers sailed for the territory, to which MacGregor had gained a dubious concession from the local Mosquito Indian ruler. Instead of the opulent capital city, fertile land and mineral wealth they had been promised, they found nothing but swamp, jungle and unfriendly locals. Many died of hunger and disease, others drowned trying to escape, and one cobbler shot himself. Of the 200, fewer than 50 made it back to Britain. MacGregor vanished to France.[7]

Investors in genuine Latin American countries did not fare much better. By 1829 nearly £19 million of the bonds were in default, and most of the shares were worthless. The debtor countries were frozen out of the international capital markets for decades to come; it was not until 1886, for example, that Mexico reached a settlement with creditors to restructure its 1820s debt.

The bankers eventually returned with open wallets, only to be stung by a fresh wave of Latin American defaults in the 1870s and 1890s. In 1890, the Bank of England had to bail out the renowned merchant bank Baring Brothers after it dabbled disastrously in loans to Argentina. The episode sounds uncannily familiar to modern ears: the bank had overextended itself, while a drop in commodity prices meant the Argentine government was unable to repay the loans when they fell due. As Galbraith comments: "No one should suppose that the modern misadventures in Third World loans are at all new."[8]

The first Barings crunch is also a fine example of how crisis can prove contagious. Financial historian Charles Kindleberger noted that it "brought a sharp decline in British lending worldwide and precipitated or contributed strongly to economic crises in South Africa, Australia and the United States down to 1893".[9] Nevertheless, in the late 19th and early 20th century European capital poured into a gamut of shares and bonds in the Americas, Russia, China and Turkey, as well as European colonies in Africa, Asia and the Middle East. Finance for big infrastructure projects, particularly the railways and the Panama and Suez canals, was particularly popular, capturing the romantic ambition of the age. Some investments earned a good return, others did not.

Sometimes investors were overtaken by political events. Purchasers of a £100, 4½ percent bond issued by the Russian South-Eastern Railway Company in 1914 would no doubt have been reassured by its proud statement that it carried the "absolute guarantee of the IMPERIAL Russian Government for the payment of interest and principal". The bond certificate today is both a snapshot of Russian history and a lesson in political risk for emerging market investors. Until 1917, the attached paper coupons representing the six-monthly interest payments have been carefully snipped away; the rest, from 1918 to 1924, remain intact and unclaimed.[10] British investors who lost their shirts on the repudiated Tsarist bonds had to wait nearly 70 years before London and Moscow agreed a modest compensation deal; French bondholders waited 80 years. Few of the original buyers were still around to reap the skimpy benefit.

THE MONEY BAZAAR – BANKS, OIL AND
THE EUROMARKET

World War One brought the old global economic certainties to an abrupt end, and a further bout of Latin American bond fever in the 1920s was snuffed out by the 1929 Wall Street crash and subsequent Great Depression. More than one-third of countries that had international bonds outstanding between 1930 and 1935 fell into default,[11] leaving stung bankers and investors with little appetite for fresh lending to any developing country – even those that had kept a clean record on debt payments.

The years after World War Two were marked by an ideological shift away from private foreign investment; Eastern Europe and China were sealed off behind the Iron and Bamboo Curtains, and many other developing nations adopted socialist or inward-looking, nationalist policies. The governments of the industrialized world came to view aid as the main weapon against Third World poverty, with the useful side effect that it furthered their geopolitical influence and bought Cold War allies.

It was not until the early 1970s that economic conditions led to a fresh flurry of lending to what were then called less developed countries, or LDCs. A drop in US interest rates at the start of the decade encouraged an exodus of dollar deposits to banks outside the United States, where they could earn higher returns. This swelled what was known as the Euromarket, a pool of dollars and other major currencies held outside their countries of origin under the control of international banks.

The Euromarket was born in the 1950s, when the hardening frost of the Cold War persuaded the Soviet Union and other Eastern Bloc countries to shift their dollar holdings from US to European banks to reduce the risk of having them frozen. Dominated by offshore branches of the main US banks, and adopting London as its biggest centre, the market grew steadily, and in the 1970s it came into its own. Its blinding attraction was that it operated beyond the reach of central banks and was free of tough US and other national restrictions on bank lending. From $8 billion in 1960, the net stock of Eurocurrency deposits (excluding money that had already been relent) burgeoned to $110 billion in 1972[12] – and it was on the lookout for lucrative new lending opportunities.

The catalyst was the 1973 oil shock, when the Organization of Petroleum Exporting Countries (OPEC) squeezed supply and forced up world crude prices fourfold in a matter of months. Suddenly oil producers, especially the desert nations of the Middle East, had more money than they knew what to do with. Their relatively small economies literally could not absorb all the petrodollars flowing their way, so they deposited the excess in Western banks, which then had to find something to do with the cash. At the same time, developing countries that were not fortunate enough to be sitting on oil wells were feeling the pinch of much higher prices for their energy imports. They were in the market to borrow. The banks were in the market to lend.

A circular flow of money developed – encouraged by Western governments and the IMF – in which oil profits were recycled through the Euromarket to the oil importers, and then back into the exporters' coffers in exchange for further oil supplies. Interest rates were low or sometimes even negative (below the rate of inflation), so that far from paying for loans, countries actually made money out of borrowing. It seemed poor countries would be mad not to take advantage of dirt-cheap money to fund their budget deficits and get a leg-up in the development stakes, and many oil producers, such as Mexico and Nigeria, also jumped on the borrowing bandwagon. What was more, unlike lending from international institutions such as the IMF, which was invariably tied to strict policy conditions, the bank finance came with few or no strings attached. "We raise a few routine questions about their economy, then we ask them what their borrowing programme is, and then we lend them money," one international banker said.[13] Even communist Eastern Europe got in on the act, with countries from Poland to Yugoslavia borrowing to fund their state-run industries.

> 66 The banks played a profitable game of pig-in-the-middle, raking in deposits and re-lending as fast as they could 99

The banks played a profitable game of pig-in-the-middle, raking in deposits and re-lending as fast as they could. Setting aside the lessons of history, they viewed sovereign borrowers (even poor ones) as a rock-solid credit – particularly as the preferred mode of operation was now the syndicated loan, in which several banks shared the risk in each deal by dividing up the lending between them. The chairman of Citibank, Walter Wriston, became famous for asserting that "countries don't go bankrupt". The banks' confidence was further boosted by a change in lending practices away from fixed-interest bonds to floating-rate loans, shifting the risk of future rate moves on to the borrower's shoulders while guaranteeing the banks a steady premium or "spread" over benchmark market rates.

More and more capital poured into the Euromarket, with net deposits hitting $250 billion in 1975 and then almost doubling by 1978 to $485 billion. The second oil shock in 1979, sparked by the turbulence of the Iranian revolution, threw more fuel on the flames. (In 1971, a barrel of crude had cost less than $2; a decade later it was around $35.) By 1982 net Euromarket deposits had reached a massive $940 billion – two-and-a-half times the total official reserves of the non-communist world.[14]

The syndicated loan market quickly dominated the financial scene, and commercial bank lending became a major source of external capital for developing countries. Some loans were to governments themselves, others to parastatal bodies such as railways, utilities or development banks, but they were invariably state-guaranteed. In 1973, loans from private creditors accounted for some 38 percent of the total foreign debt owed by LDC governments; by 1982 the proportion was 55 percent. For countries on the doorstep of the powerful US banks, the rise was even starker. Bank loans to Latin America accounted for 58 percent of the region's public external debt in 1982, while in the Caribbean the total was an overwhelming 77 percent.[15] A 1978 survey in London financial industry magazine *The Banker* showed Brazil was the world's second-biggest borrower in the Euromarket during the mid-1970s after Britain, with Mexico following closely in third place.[16]

The banks were falling over each other to lend, and threw caution to the winds. "International bankers … formed into roving bands of money gypsies, descending on any town where there was a whiff of borrowing need," journalist Darrell Delamaide wrote in 1984. "Certain borrowers or groups of borrowers enjoyed a vogue, and the money bazaar moved in."[17]

Syndicated loans as big as $1 billion were arranged in a matter of days, and as many as 500 banks or more could be involved in a single major deal. Eager for a piece of the action, hundreds of small, local banks got into the market. They had little clue about financial conditions in the countries they were lending to, but relied on the skill and expertise of the big international banks that set up the loans. The foreign loans portfolio of one Ohio-based bank exploded from zero in 1979 to more than $1 billion in 1983; another bank in Indianapolis increased its foreign loans fifteenfold in the same period.[18] The novices stuck close to the herd: if it was good enough for Citibank, it was good enough for them.

Chucking $1 million or $10 million into $100–200 million syndicated loans became a matter of routine. So many proposals came along that bankers could not possibly have enough time to study them all in the detail such deals would usually merit. Besides, even the big banks had precious little access to vital economic data on the countries concerned. Loans were passed for indeterminate use, or for projects that were still on the drawing board. Individual promotion prospects depended less on the reliability of future returns than on churning out as much money as possible in fresh loans; in any case, highly mobile international careers meant the bank officials who set up the loans were seldom around to carry the can if problems arose later.

One young banker who plied the loan trade during the 1970s later described a business full of "bright but hopelessly inexperienced lenders in their mid-twenties [who] travel the world like itinerant brushmen, filling loan quotas, peddling financial wares and living high on the hog".[19] Bankers became not only blasé but scared of missing out on any hot new chance that might come along. "It was what I call 'receptionist banking'," another banker later told Delamaide. "When you went out for lunch you could tell the receptionist to watch the telex and take $5 million of any deal offered."[20]

The few voices of caution were drowned out in the clamour. A 1974 article in *The Banker* stated confidently that "contrary to the panicky rumours that have been put about from time to time, there seems no reason to believe that the debt is unmanageable".[21] The foreign assets of US banks rose fivefold between 1965 and 1980[22] and the weight of commercial LDC debt came to far outstrip the capital of the big international banks themselves.

Unfortunately, the borrowed cash was not always well spent. Vast sums were frittered away in what radical economics writer Susan George calls "mal-development" – a combination of misguided industrialization, corruption, militarization, grandiose white-elephant projects, and spending on day-to-day consumption. Rich elites used the cash to buy luxuries rather than to fund productive investment, or salted it away in foreign bank accounts.

Mexico squandered much of its bank borrowing on lavish consumer imports and a headlong rush to develop the oil industry at the expense of other sectors. Brazil poured money into an extravagant industrialization drive, but the resulting "Brazilian miracle" had spluttered to a halt by the end of the 1970s. The Philippines borrowed enthusiastically under late president Ferdinand Marcos, whose wife's vast shoe collection became a byword for corruption and self-aggrandizement. One of its more unnerving bank-funded projects, a $2.1 billion nuclear power plant at Bataan, was built at the foot of a volcano in the middle of the Pacific Rim earthquake zone. Happily, it was never used; the elected government that replaced Marcos after the 1986 "People Power" revolution swiftly mothballed the plant and took US construction company Westinghouse to court for bribery and shoddy workmanship. (A $100 million out-of-court settlement was finally agreed in 1995.)

By the time Mobutu Sese Seko, dictator of the former Zaire, fled into exile in 1997, he had amassed such a vast personal fortune in cash and world-wide real estate that diplomats reckoned he could have paid off at a stroke the entire debt of the country he had raped for 32 years. Nigeria threw cash into large-scale agriculture projects, iron and steel plant, and a new capital city, none of which brought much in the way of returns, while the country sank steadily into a swamp of corruption. Billions of dollars of oil revenues and loan capital did nothing for ordinary Nigerians; by the early 1980s the country's GDP per capita was lower in real terms than it had been in 1973.

COMING TO A CRUNCH – THE 1980s DEBT CRISIS

The turning point came in late 1979, when the United States declared war on the rampant inflation triggered by the oil shocks and began cranking interest rates sky-high. Other developed countries followed suit. Committed to variable- rather than fixed-rate loans, borrower countries suddenly saw their debt-service costs escalate. Short-term US interest rates virtually doubled from just over 8 percent in 1978 to nearly 16 percent in 1981; the London Interbank Offered Rate (LIBOR), the benchmark Euromarket rate for many of the bank loans, did similar acrobatics to reach nearly 17 percent. This meant debtor countries were paying closer to 19 percent a year, once banks had added their spread on to these basic rates.

Oil importing countries suffered a double blow from higher crude prices and debt-servicing costs, but oil producers were not cushioned for long. The oil shocks had spurred increased investment in production and exploration, either to cash in on the boom or to provide an alternative to OPEC's near-stranglehold on supplies. New sources, such as the North Sea, were coming on-stream, and world crude output rose. At the same time, high oil costs and rising interest rates tipped the industrial nations into recession and damped down global oil demand. From 1981 crude prices started falling, along with prices for most major commodities, which had also been riding high in the 1970s. Developing countries that had borrowed at rock-bottom interest rates, when their oil and commodity exports were fetching healthy world prices, were suddenly pinched between soaring debt costs and plunging export earnings. As Victor Bulmer-Thomas of London University's Institute of Latin American Studies put it, the region's debt-service ratio – the proportion of export earnings needed to cover interest and principal payments – "jumped from a feasible 26.6 percent in 1975 to an impossible 59 percent in 1982".[23]

66 The United States declared war on the rampant inflation and began cranking interest rates sky-high 99

By early 1982 fresh bank lending was tailing off as concern spread that borrowers might not be able to keep servicing their debt. There had already been warning signs as one country or another ran into payment problems, but the sums in question were generally too small to call the whole circus into question. In 1975 Zaire, under Mobutu's rapacious rule, had stopped paying any principal or interest on $700–800 million of commercial bank debt. Attempts to restructure the debt dragged on for years, but the sums involved were relatively small. Most banks gave up any hope of getting their money back, and wrote off their Zaire loans.

Peru also ran into problems during the 1970s, but the then booming world prices for its copper and other commodity exports gave the impression that a rescue plan worked out by the banks and the IMF had been successful. Costa Rica and Nicaragua hit payment problems, but relatively few people noticed. A $2.5 billion restructuring of Turkish debt in the late 1970s caused bigger ripples, but it was only when Poland announced in March 1981 that it was unable to pay any interest or principal on some $24 billion of official and commercial debt that serious jitters started setting in. After tortuous talks, a rescheduling agreement with the banks was signed in April 1982.

The real crunch came in August that year when Mexico, the banks' second-biggest customer in the developing world with net debts of $49 billion, announced it did not have enough foreign exchange to meet impending debt obligations. Soon afterwards it declared a 90-day moratorium on principal repayments.

Suddenly, loud alarm bells rang in Washington. US banks were up to their necks in Mexican debt, and a default would threaten the entire financial system. Mexico's economy was also at risk, and the last thing the United States wanted was chaos on its southern border. The US government swung quickly into action, drumming up a package of emergency credits that would allow Mexico to keep up its debt-service payments while it negotiated a standby agreement with the IMF. With this breathing space, Mexico managed to negotiate a deal to restructure its debt, under which the banks reluctantly agreed to lend the country even more money to tide it over.

But Mexico's near-default opened the floodgates. Argentina and Brazil soon followed suit, requesting IMF help and bank debt rescheduling, and it became clear the world was facing an unprecedented credit crisis. Virtually every continent had its problem cases but Latin America was overwhelmingly the biggest headache, to the extent that the whole episode is often referred to as the "Latin American debt crisis". At the end of 1982 Latin American countries owed just over $200 billion to commercial banks – nearly two-thirds of total bank exposure to developing countries.[24]

Not only did Latin America owe far more than any other region, but three-quarters of its total debt was at floating interest rates, compared to only one-third in Africa (with the exception of Nigeria) or Asia. Numerous African countries were running into debt crises of their own as commodity prices plunged, but by world standards they were mainly small beer, although the eventual impact on local people was no less devastating. Most African debt was owed to governments or international financial institutions rather than to banks; only Nigeria, which had guzzled down commercial loans in the oil boom years, gave bankers sleepless nights.

> 66 Latin America threatened disaster for the big international banks. Liquidating Argentina was not an option 99

East Asian borrowers such as South Korea and Taiwan were better equipped than Latin America and Africa to weather the storm, mainly because they had been developing large export industries for some time and were less reliant on commodity prices. The debt-service ratio of East Asian middle-income countries barely flickered from a tiny 6.7 percent of export earnings in 1970 to 8.6 percent in 1982.[25] Only the Philippines ran into serious repayment problems.

Latin America threatened disaster for the big international banks. Sixteen out of the top 18 US and Canadian banks had lent more to that region than their total shareholder equity,[26] and despite the scatter-gun frenzy of the syndicated loan race, most of it was concentrated in a handful of countries. Citicorp alone had lent more than $10 billion to Mexico, Argentina, Brazil, Venezuela and Chile. British banks were also heavily exposed, with Latin American debts amounting to more than two-and-a-half times the capital of Lloyd's Bank and more than three times that of Midland Bank.[27]

Citibank's Wriston may have been technically correct that countries do not go bust in the same way that companies do, but they can certainly do a very good imitation of bankruptcy. (Wriston offered a more subtle analysis just after the Mexican crisis broke, writing in *The New York Times*: "Any country, however badly off, will 'own' more than it 'owes'. The catch is cash flow.") The snag is that although governments can in theory print more cash or raise taxes to pay debts in their own currency, they cannot spirit foreign exchange out of thin air. And foreign banks cannot repossess a railway or take a controlling stake in a revamped Brazil Inc. Liquidating Argentina was not an option. A few missed interest payments would not in themselves have broken the banks, but the fact that they were halted would mean the loans would legally have to be declared "non-performing" – banking-speak for a washout. No shareholder likes to see too many non-performing loans on a bank's balance sheet, so the risk of a crisis in confidence and a wholesale banking share sell-off looked very real. If just one small bank in a syndication called in its cash, the entire loan would have to be called into default. With the banks so heavily exposed, two or three major defaults could have mortally wounded the entire banking system.

With one country after another pleading penury, an emergency group of banks, creditor governments and international financial institutions was formed to try to find a way out of the crisis. Bankers and bureaucrats scurried from one tense meeting to another. Because the crisis was seen as a problem of cash flow rather than overall solvency, the solution seemed to be to lend more money up-front to tide the debtor countries over – and crucially, from the banks' point of view, to allow them to stay up-to-date on their debt payments. The IMF took a leading role, orchestrating complex financial rescue packages in which both the banks and the official creditors agreed (often reluctantly) to increase their lending and accept repayment of existing debts over a longer period. In return, the debtor countries agreed to a fairly standard set of economic reforms including more realistic exchange rates policies and belt-tightening to cut their burgeoning fiscal deficits.

The negotiating process was agonizingly complicated. Delamaide recounted: "Mexico's proposal to the banks arrived on a telex 19 feet long. Transmission took one hour, so that it took several machines two-and-a-half days to send the rescheduling proposal to the 1,300-odd creditor banks. Argentina's proposal was 18 feet long."[28]

LOOKING FOR ANSWERS – THE BAKER AND BRADY PLANS

By 1983 more than a dozen Latin American nations had reached some sort of debt rescheduling agreement and another dozen developing and Eastern European countries had started debt talks. As well as straightforward rescheduling, which overhauled the timetable for repayments, a number of novel, market-based solutions were tried out. "Exit bonds" were created, which allowed some of the smaller banks to pull out of the mess by parcelling their Latin American debt into bonds that could be sold on to third parties at less than face value. The banks took a paper loss but could then wash their hands of the crisis; the purchasers gambled on getting back the full face value of the bond from the debtor country at some future date, or else reselling the bond for more than it had cost. A secondary market in bank debt was born, in which the discount to the face (or par) value of the bond reflected the perceived likelihood of repayment. Bonds from a country that looked fairly creditworthy might sell at, say, 70 cents on the dollar, while apparently no-hope Liberian or Sudanese debt was priced at less than a tenth of its face value. Other innovations included debt conversions, in which external debt was converted to domestic debt that could more easily be serviced in local currency, and debt–equity swaps, which converted debt into assets in local companies.

But the rescue packages did not solve two crucial problems. First, world commodity prices remained stubbornly low, so debt-service payments continued to swallow up around one-third of Latin America's depleted export earnings every year. Although the region's debt was trading at well below its face value on the secondary market, debtor countries were still bound to pay interest on the full amount. Second, Latin America was losing far more in capital transfers, in the shape of debt service and profits remitted by foreign-owned companies, than it was gaining in fresh lending and investment. As in earlier decades, banks were proving reluctant to cough up more lending for countries they now viewed with understandable wariness. Even at the start of the 1980s the region had still been enjoying a net capital inflow of around $13 billion a year, but in 1982 the flow turned sharply negative and by the middle of the decade the annual outflow was around $30 billion – equal to approximately 4 percent of Latin America's GDP.[29]

The haemorrhage was aggravated by capital flight as rich Latin Americans packed off as much hard currency as they could into foreign bank accounts. In 1983 alone, an estimated $12 billion or more of flight capital leaked out of Argentina, Brazil, Chile, Mexico and Venezuela.[30] In other words, yet more capital from developing countries was looping back into the banks in the form of private deposits. "The most aggressive banks, such as Citibank, have probably accumulated almost as much in assets from poor countries as they have loaned to them," economist James S. Henry wrote in *The New Republic* in 1986. "Their real role has been to take funds that Third World elites have stolen from their governments and to loan them back, earning a nice spread each way."[31]

By mid-1985 it was clear that existing debt relief plans were not working. The Big Three – Mexico, Argentina and Brazil – were all slipping on the terms of their IMF agreements. Mexico, in particular, was reeling from the cost of coping with two earthquakes and a dramatic oil price plunge, which slashed the cost of crude from around $30 a barrel in November 1985 to under $12 in less than five months. Meanwhile, Peru elected a new president, Alan García Pérez, who promptly declared the country would not pay more than 10 percent of its export earnings on debt service.

As the biggest creditor, the United States finally stepped in with a proposal that became known as the Baker Plan after incumbent Treasury Secretary James Baker. Presented at the annual IMF and World Bank meetings in October 1985, it stressed the need for growth and called for the injection of a further $30 billion into the 15 (later 17) most heavily indebted countries, of which $20 billion would come from the banks and $10 billion from the international financial institutions. Even this was insufficient to turn the tide, and net capital flows to the debtor countries remained stubbornly negative, yet creditor governments kept up the polite fiction that the Baker Plan was working.

It wasn't, and in February 1987 Brazil dropped a bombshell by unilaterally suspending interest payments on its $110 billion in medium- and long-term debt, including some $83 billion owed to foreign banks in loans, trade credits and money market deposits. Other countries followed, and in May Citibank (no longer chaired by Wriston) finally admitted what was increasingly obvious but was not uttered in polite company: it was never going to get back all its loan capital. The bank announced it was making loan-loss provisions of $3 billion, covering up to 30 percent of its Latin American lending. Far from damaging Citibank, however, the announcement boosted the bank's share price as the stock market welcomed an end to some of the uncertainty surrounding the debt crisis. By now the banks had had time to spread their capital base more widely, diluting the impact of Latin American losses, and soon other banks were following in Citibank's footsteps.

Brazil's debt problems were bandaged over with a 1988 rescheduling and IMF agreement that quickly proved unsuccessful. More and more countries started to build up debt arrears, and the banks stepped up pressure on the United States to help sort out the mess. In early 1989 Baker's successor as Treasury Secretary, Nicholas Brady, made a surprise speech recognizing what Citibank had implicitly acknowledged two years previously: Latin America's debt simply could not be repaid in full. Like it or not, the way out of the crisis would have to involve some kind of debt forgiveness, and the banks would have to take a share of the pain.

The practicalities of what became known as the Brady Plan were initially vague, and it was Mexican technocrats who put flesh on the bones. Mexico became the first beneficiary in mid-1989, with the restructuring of $48.5 billion in medium- and long-term debt. The basic principle was that outstanding bank loans would be replaced by bonds involving some form of reduction in the sum owed, and giving the debtor more time to pay. These so-called Brady Bonds were denominated in dollars and came in a range of flavours according to the country involved and the options offered to creditors. The most common formula was either to discount the face value of the debt (typically by about 35 percent) or retain the face value and cut the interest rate. Most significantly, the recipe included a special sweetener for bond purchasers: most Brady Bonds were backed by US government Treasury bonds put up by the debtor country and lodged with the Federal Reserve, the US central bank popularly known as the Fed. In other words, even if a country defaulted completely on its Brady debt (which was widely regarded as highly improbable), the bond-holders would still be left with solid US Treasuries.

> 66 Latin America's debt simply could not be repaid in full. Like it or not, the way out of the crisis would have to involve some kind of debt forgiveness 99

So the bond purchasers got some kind of payment guarantee, the creditor banks got some of their money back, and the debtor countries got to pay back less of their original debt. In return, the debtors had to sign up for more conditions, including policy reforms acceptable to the IMF and the United States. A host of other countries followed Mexico over the next few years, including not only the Latin American giants (Brazil negotiated a Brady deal in 1993) but several other sizeable debtors such as Nigeria, Bulgaria, Poland and the Philippines.

Critics argued that the Brady Plan made relatively little dent in debt-service ratios and might encourage debtors to think they could profit from reneging on their debts – the key banking and insurance concept of "moral hazard", which says that financial players have a weaker sense of responsibility for their actions if they know they are insured against the consequences. But crucially, the plan restored confidence both in the world financial system and in the countries whose debt was restructured. The mere news that a country was embarking on Brady Plan talks could be enough to buck up the economic mood. Capital that had fled the country started to return, local interest rates could be brought down, and a Brady deal on commercial debt was often met by a more accommodating stance from creditor governments on official debt. At the same time the element of debt relief helped to mollify political activists within the debtor countries who had been pressing for repudiation of the loans, arguing that the money had been foisted willy-nilly by irresponsible banks on incompetent or venal governments.

In 1991 the net flow of capital transfers to Latin America crept back into the black for the first time in ten years. Panic over – at least for the time being.

BANKS COUNT THE PROFITS; SOCIETIES COUNT THE COST

After the shouting from Wall Street and the City of London had died down, some analysts began to point out that the banks had not done so badly after all. For a start, making loan loss provisions is not the same thing as making actual losses; it just ensures a bank's books are prudently adjusted to take account of *potential* write-offs. Citibank and other banks were careful to make clear they would still require full repayment of the loans, with interest, and even the subsequent Brady Plan did not cut those debt-servicing costs to a huge degree.

A report in 1990 by IBCA Banking Analysis estimated the banks' world-wide losses from LDC lending would end up at something over $100 billion, calling it "the largest commercial bank mistake in history".[32] But several analysts have highlighted the banks' very high overall returns from LDC loans over the years, setting these losses in perspective. Many international banks raked in record earnings in the good years, fuelled largely by lucrative premium interest rates charged on LDC loans. Journalists Sue Branford and Bernardo Kucinski estimated that Britain's Midland Bank alone would have been gaining a return of roughly 49 percent a year on its loan capital at the start of the 1980s.[33] Even after the crisis had exploded, banks continued to pull in decent money; indeed, the more they were unwillingly roped into further lending under various restructuring deals, the more they felt justified in charging not only premium interest rates but extra commission too. "In terms of the net transfer of resources, the debt has already been repaid several times over, even allowing for inflation and for the payment of what in the 1970s was considered a 'normal' rate of interest," Branford and Kucinski argued.[34]

Figures from the Organization for Economic Co-operation and Development (OECD), an economic forum of mainly rich countries, show LDC debt-service payments to the commercial banks averaged around $77 billion a year between 1982 and 1989 – enough in just 15 months to offset the losses estimated by IBCA. "[S]ince the debt crisis broke in 1982, and however much they may whine and claim the opposite, banks have received extremely generous returns on their outstanding loans in less developed countries," wrote George. "In other words, the banks *as a group* were never in genuine danger on their aggregate Third World portfolios although many individual banks – US and British ones in particular – were in deep trouble vis-à-vis individual debtors, especially in the early 1980s."[35]

The banks also had reason to be grateful for a helping hand from governments in the rich and poor world alike. First, it became clear that Northern governments would, in Bulmer-Thomas's words, "take a generous view of the fiscal implications" of the crisis and allow tax relief on their losses.[36] Second, the dead weight of the debt shifted slowly and subtly from private to official creditors; debtor countries tended to devote more of their scant resources to paying the banks rather than Northern governments, which were better disposed to postpone debt service, and public-sector lenders tended to cough up a disproportionate share of new finance under the restructuring deals. (In Mexico's 1986 rescheduling, for example, more than three-quarters of the country's debt was owed to private banks, yet they had to stump up only half of the $12 billion in new funds that would essentially serve to keep Mexico's interest payments on track.[37])

> **“ Even after the crisis had exploded, banks continued to pull in decent money ”**

Northern taxpayers were not the only ones footing the bill. Stephany Griffith-Jones of the Institute of Development Studies at Sussex University noted that debtor governments often provided the banks with what amounted to retrospective public guarantees on debts that were originally taken on by private companies. "[W]hen acting as borrowers of last resort, LDC governments were to an important extent showing themselves more concerned with the stability of international banks than with their own economic growth," she wrote.[38]

In fact, many analysts have argued that the whole thrust of the US and IMF approach to the debt crisis was to protect the banks. "Commercial banks have weathered the debt crisis, while many debtor countries remain in economic paralysis or worse," Harvard economists Jeffrey Sachs and Harry Huizinga wrote in late 1987.[39]

The crisis may have been over as far as the banks and the IMF were concerned, but debtor countries would continue to bleed money to Northern creditors for years to come. Both Latin America and Africa effectively exported net capital to the developed world on a massive scale for most of the 1980s, amounting to around 3–4 percent of their GDP, as a result of servicing debts to private and official creditors. When they were unable to pay on time, arrears piled on to the original sum borrowed. Between 1982 and 1990, total debt-service payments from the poor to the rich world came to more than $1.3 trillion, while capital inflows amounted to just over $900 billion – a gap of more than $400 billion.

As part of the conditions for restructuring any debt, commercial or official, the IMF and the World Bank held debtor countries to tough austerity measures that became known as "structural adjustment", a phrase that would cast a long shadow over the development field for years to come. In their simplest form, the steps required typically involved belt-tightening across the state sector (including budget cuts and the removal of subsidies and price controls), devaluation to curb unnecessary imports and encourage exports, and tight monetary policy to clamp down on inflation. Extra ingredients crept into the mix: lifting trade barriers, liberalizing investment regulations, privatizing state-owned industries, and generally deregulating the economy.

66 If the United States was bruised, debtor countries were beaten to a pulp 99

Falling Latin American imports had a knock-on effect on the economies of the rich world. The United States, the region's single biggest trading partner, saw its exports to the region wilt by about one-third, from cars to soybeans. An estimated 1 million American jobs evaporated. "US workers and farmers have lost jobs and markets while banks have continued to profit from Latin American loans," Democratic Senator Bill Bradley wrote in 1987.[40]

If the United States was bruised, debtor countries were beaten to a pulp. In theory, the purpose of structural adjustment was to wrench shambling economies on to a more even keel, for the good of the nations and their creditors alike. The process was aimed, in the World Bank's words, at establishing "a market-friendly set of incentives that can encourage the accumulation of capital and more efficient allocation of resources".[41] In practice, the removal of subsidies usually meant poor people faced significantly higher bills for food, fuel and other essentials. Privatization tended to involve job losses, and it was often health, education and other welfare services that felt the pinch in the spending cuts. Money that might have gone into development went instead to pay off the debts. The United Nations Children's Fund (UNICEF) estimated in 1993 that governments in developing countries had been devoting on average only about 10 percent of their annual budgets to nutrition, water supply, primary health care, primary education and family planning. "This means that many governments of the poor world have been spending less on meeting human needs than on meeting military bills and debt-servicing obligations," it said.[42]

Latin America's income per head fell by 9 percent in real terms between 1980 and 1985. As the World Bank would point out much later, the number of people living in poverty in Mexico alone surged from just under 21 million in 1984 to 30 million in 1989 – up from 28 percent of the population to 36 percent. Declining nutrition drove up infant and pre-school mortality, and educational standards for the poor were chiselled away.[43]

Whether the money was owed to banks or governments, the picture for debtor countries was much the same. In Zambia the number of children dying below the age of five escalated by 25 percent between 1980 and 1991, despite falling infant mortality in most developing countries.[44] In both Latin America and Africa the 1980s became known as the Lost Decade, and the legacy of the debt crisis in terms of poverty and hardship would drag on into the next century.

NOTES

1 *The Wall Street Journal's Central European Economic Review*, May 1999.

2 IFC, *Emerging Stock Markets Factbook*, 1998, p. 2.

3 Bairoch and Lévy-Leboyer (eds), *Disparities in Economic Development Since the Industrial Revolution*, Tables 1.6 and 1.7.

4 Galbraith, *A Short History of Financial Euphoria*, pp. 2–4.

5 Galbraith, p. 38.

6 Dawson, *The First Latin American Debt Crisis*, p. xi.

7 Dawson provides a much fuller account of the Poyais story.

8   Galbraith, p. 54.

9   Kindleberger, *Manias, Panics and Crashes*, p. 121.

10   Bond certificate in author's possession.

11   *Euromoney*, November 1998.

12   Branford and Kucinski, *The Debt Squads*, p. 58.

13   Quoted by Keegan, *The Spectre of Capitalism*, p. 49.

14   Branford and Kucinski, p. 58.

15   Griffith-Jones, "International financial markets: a case of market failure", in Colclough and Manor, *States or Markets?*, p. 105.

16   *The Banker*, January 1978.

17   Delamaide, *Debt Shock*, p. 44.

18   George, *A Fate Worse Than Debt*, p. 36.

19   S.C. Gwynne, "Adventures in the loan trade", in *Harper's Magazine*, September 1983, quoted in George, *A Fate Worse Than Debt*, p. 30.

20   Delamaide, pp. 44–45.

21   Robert Moss, "Brazil: No break in the boom", *The Banker*, May (1974).

22   Delamaide, p. 43.

23   Bulmer-Thomas, *The Economic History of Latin America Since Independence*, p. 364.

24   ECLAC, *External Debt in Latin America: Adjustment policies and renegotiation*, p. 52.

25   World Bank, *World Development Report 1983*, table 2.14.

26   Bulmer-Thomas, p. 369.

27   Branford and Kucinski, pp. 123 and 129.

28   Delamaide, p. 99.

29   Bulmer-Thomas, p. 373.

30   Bulmer-Thomas, p. 373.

31   Quoted in George, *A Fate Worse Than Debt*, p. 20.

32   Quoted in George, *The Debt Boomerang*, p. 84.

33   Branford and Kucinski, p. 128.

34   Branford and Kucinski, p. 1.

35   George, *The Debt Boomerang*, pp. 85–86.

36   Bulmer-Thomas, p. 375.

37   George, *A Fate Worse Than Debt*, p. 210.

38   Griffith-Jones, in Colclough and Manor, p. 112.

39   Sachs and Huizinga, *U.S. Commercial Banks and the Developing Country Debt Crisis*, p. 54.

40   Bradley, "Resolving the debt crisis: a U.S. perspective", in Pastor (ed.), *The Debt Crisis: A financial or a development problem?*, p. 70.

41 World Bank, *Adjustment in Africa*, p. 2.

42 UNICEF, *The Progress of Nations 1993*, p. 3.

43 World Bank, *Global Economic Prospects 2000*, p. 52.

44 UNICEF, p. 12.

2

LIFT-OFF

The investment industry creates euphoria and panic. It moves astonishing amounts of cash around the world at startling speed with shocking results. Then it pays itself fantastic amounts of money – P.J. O'Rourke, *Eat the Rich*

FREE-MARKET FRENZY –
THE WASHINGTON CONSENSUS

You might have thought the 1980s debt crisis would have given investors enough of a jolt to put them off emerging markets for another few decades. But just as the whole restructuring drama was being played out, a matrix of historical forces, both political and economic, was setting the stage for a new LDC investment frenzy that would dwarf the previous booms. Capitalism was in, communism was out. The Asian Tigers were on the prowl. The world was getting smaller and faster. And the way the debt crisis was resolved – at least from the banks' point of view – was an integral part of those forces.

The early 1980s brought a sea change in the prevailing economic orthodoxy that would recast the roles of the state and the private sectors in economic development. In 1944 the Bretton Woods conference, which created the IMF and the World Bank, had mapped out a future in which governments would play a central part in raising the living standards of their citizens and regulating the markets. "Optimally, the visionaries of the postwar world economy looked forward to enlightened governance of peoples by officials of international organizations rather than by the well-heeled denizens of world financial markets," wrote political economist Jonathan Story. "Short-term capital movements were to be kept, figuratively, under lock and key, and currencies were to be fixed."[1]

The poor countries of the South – the term increasingly preferred over "Third World", which had acquired connotations of hopelessness, or "less developed", which smacked of inferiority – tended to favour statist policies and planning in which the government was the prime economic mover. Fearful of domination by the rich North, they largely turned their backs on international markets, which they saw as a highly uneven playing field. They maintained trade barriers, regulated capital flows, and restricted foreign investment. Import substitution, rather than export growth, was the name of the game.

The first oil shock in 1973, the result of unprecedented co-operation between oil-producing nations, spurred talk of a new "commodity power" in which poor countries could force better prices for their raw materials and a fairer share of the world's resources. For the rest of the decade the United Nations rang with calls from the South for a "New International Economic Order", an ambitious blueprint for global wealth redistribution that would attack protectionist trade barriers in the North, shift more aid and technology to developing countries, and give them a greater say in global decision making through the IMF, the World Bank and other international financial institutions. The 1980 Brandt Report caught the mood; produced by an international commission headed by former West German Chancellor Willy Brandt, it urged a major transfer of resources from rich to poor countries. The motivation for the North, it argued, should be not only an abstract sense of justice but practical self-interest, so that the world's "haves" did not live in permanent fear of the "have-nots".

But most of the North was not listening, the South proved too diverse to keep up a united front on its demands, and by the early 1980s hopes of commodity power were sagging along with the price of oil. The turning point was the election in swift succession of right-wing governments in Britain, the United States and Germany, which drove a final nail into the coffin of the supposed new order. Foreign aid budgets were cut and a new ideology took root, based on liberalization, free markets and private capital. This laissez-faire ethos was not new – it had underpinned the Industrial Revolution and the flowering of world trade in the mid-19th century – but it re-emerged with a vengeance. Its intellectual under-pinning came from the monetarist theory of Milton Friedman at the University of Chicago, who argued that tight control over the money supply was the key to economic stability. Its political force came from the populist conservatism of Ronald Reagan and Margaret Thatcher. And the 1980s debt crisis gave it its big break on to the world stage.

The conditions that were attached to debt rescheduling deals from Mexico City to Manila gave the rich world an unprecedented direct hold over economic policy in independent developing countries, and the free-market agenda spread around the globe. The main tool for enforcing the new paradigm was the IMF, which was originally set up to ensure the smooth functioning of the international monetary system, but which rapidly took on a much wider set of economic policing duties. Although the amount of money the Fund itself contributed to rescue packages was rela-tively small, no deal could go ahead without

66 A new ideology took root, based on liberalization, free markets and private capital 99

its seal of approval. The IMF's sister organization, the World Bank, also became heavily involved in the reform process, expanding its financing remit from specific development projects to much broader, policy-based lending programmes.

The policies promoted by the two Bretton Woods institutions echoed the new orthodoxy of the Reagan and Thatcher governments: to pull the government's fingers out of the economy. Market forces alone would work their magic, and previously inward-looking economies would be integrated into the international capitalist system through structural adjustment. And since their most influential proponents – the Reagan administration, the US Congress and Federal Reserve, the IMF, the World Bank, and a cluster of influential think-tanks and economists – were based in the US capital, the underlying philosophy became known as the "Washington Consensus".

So prevalent was the consensus in official circles that by the end of the 1980s more than 70 developing nations had embarked on IMF or World Bank reform programmes. "[The] once vibrant debate about develop-ment all but disappeared as the consensus took on almost religious qualities," wrote two economists familiar with the Washington scene in the 1980s. "Converts to the cult of the consensus spread far beyond the Beltway, as with other religions, through a combination of the appeal of its simplicity, proselytizing by its believers, and outright coercion."[2]

Supporters of this free-market development model maintain that governments across the South quickly saw the light, abandoned failed, statist policies, took enthusiastically to the new way and saw their growth rates surge. Opponents say its terms were foisted cynically on an unwilling South in a thinly disguised attempt to raise export earnings for debt repayment, made little convincing difference to growth, and paid no heed to the human suffering caused by resulting unemployment and the erosion of welfare provisions. By the mid-1990s even the World Bank was admitting that the human cost of structural adjustment had been higher than expected and the economic gains less clear-cut than they were often made out to be. But there seemed little realistic alternative. "[I]deologically speaking, there is no more mint chocolate chip, there is no more strawberry whirl, and there is no more lemon-lime. Today there is only free-market vanilla and North Korea," wrote *The New York Times* columnist Thomas Friedman.[3]

Voluntarily or not, governments beset by the debt crisis set about transforming their economies along strict market lines. Across Latin America, young, US-trained technocrats enthusiastically took up the refrain, and by the early 1990s the region's major economies were in full reformist flow. Mexico sold off state enterprises, opened its arms to foreign investors and made the huge psychological leap of throwing itself open to free trade with the United States and Canada through the North American Free Trade Agreement (NAFTA). Argentina and Brazil took radical steps to overhaul their currency systems, snuffing out chronic hyperinflation. In Asia, Philippines President Fidel Ramos declared: "We must deregulate and decontrol as much as possible."

TIGERS ON THE PROWL – THE RISE OF ASIA

By the early 1990s, however, the debt-stricken Philippines was something of an anomaly in its own neighbourhood. The Washington Consensus was not the only game in town for export-led growth; most of East Asia was already enjoying astonishing growth rates as a result of its own, longer-standing reform drive, pulling off the fastest industrial revolution the world had ever seen.

Japan kicked off with a postwar development drive that transformed a semi-agricultural economy with a reputation for shoddy manufactured goods into a paragon of high technology and the world's second-biggest economy. In 1960, Japan's share of the world's GDP was 1 percent; by the mid-1990s it was a commanding 18 percent – more than that of Germany and France combined. Its take-off was followed in the 1960s by what came to be known as the four original Asian Tigers: Hong Kong, Singapore, Taiwan and South Korea. By the early 1990s these four countries alone were exporting twice as many goods as the whole of Latin America. Behind them came a trio of new South-East Asian Tigers: Thailand, Malaysia and Indonesia. By 1995, East Asia, excluding Japan, accounted for 12 percent of the world's manufacturing output, compared to 3 percent in Latin America and just over 2 percent in the former Soviet countries.[4] The Asian Miracle was in full swing.

Between 1965 and 1990 eight East Asian economies (Japan, Hong Kong, South Korea, Singapore, Taiwan, Thailand, Malaysia and Indonesia) collectively notched up average GDP growth of more than 5.5 percent a year – more than twice as fast as any other region, including the rest of Asia, the major Western economies and the oil-rich Middle East.[5] Several countries regularly achieved annual growth of 7–8 percent or more. In 1965 Indonesians were poorer per head than Nigerians, and Thais poorer than Ghanaians; three decades later, Indonesians were on average nearly five times better off than Nigerians, and Thais some eight times richer than their Ghanaian counterparts.[6]

Economist Paul Krugman of the Massachusetts Institute of Technology puts the extraordinary speed of the transformation into perspective.[7] In the first 50 years of the 19th century, in the midst of the Industrial Revolution, Britain's income per head grew at a "hitherto unprecedented" rate of 1.3 percent a year. The United States improved on this with booming annual per capita growth of 2.2 percent between 1870 and 1913. Cut to Japan between 1953 and 1973, with annual growth per head of 8 percent. Then came South Korea's marathon run of 7 percent growth per person between 1963 and 1997 – "a ninefold increase in little more than one generation". "[I]n 1963 South Korea was probably poorer than Britain had been in 1800 – poorer, perhaps, than Britain had been since the 17th century," Krugman noted. "By 1997 the Koreans had reached more or less the per capita income of Britain in the early 1960s."

Then came the biggest of them all: China, whose per capita income quadrupled in less than two decades. "Never in human history have so many people experienced so rapid an improvement in their material status," wrote Krugman. Between 1975 and 1995 the Chinese economy grew by an annual average of nearly 9 percent, exploding in some years by more than 13 percent. The country went from being the world's 32nd largest exporter in 1978 to its tenth largest in 1994. By the late 1990s China's economy was the seventh biggest in the world, just behind Italy and ahead of Canada or Spain.

While keeping an iron hand on China's communist political system, paramount leader Deng Xiaoping quietly started ditching socialist economics from the end of the 1970s and put out the word that "to get rich is glorious". The authorities still prefer to speak of a

66 By the early 1990s there seemed little doubt that the centre of gravity in the global economy was shifting eastwards 99

"socialist market economy with Chinese characteristics", but it is full-throttle capitalism that now spins China's economic wheels. In 1993 the Hong Kong-based *South China Morning Post* reported that the People's University, a venerated Communist Party institution, had scrapped unpopular courses in basic Marxism and the history of the international communist movement to make way for classes in marketing, international business management, investment economics and real estate.[8]

What was more, Asia's rapidly transforming countries managed to distribute their new-found wealth far more equitably than in most other parts of the world. "The pay differential between a production-line worker for Samsung, Korea's largest company, and its president is ninefold," *The Economist* noted approvingly in a late 1991 survey on the Asian Tigers. "At any American company of a comparable size, the differential would be closer to 100."[9]

By the early 1990s there seemed little doubt that the centre of gravity in the global economy was shifting eastwards, and that the world was on the threshold of a new "Pacific Century". "Assuming that Asia's supercompetitive economies keep growing two-to-three times faster than the older industrial economies, by 2000 the average Taiwanese will be richer than most New Zealanders and catching up fast with most Australians," *The Economist* predicted. "Hong Kongers will be richer than their erstwhile colonizers, the British, and Singaporeans better off than Italians. South Koreans, the poorest of the Tigers' people with GDP per head of just over $6,000 a year, will be as wealthy as the Irish. By the middle of the 21st century there will have been a shift in economic power away from Europe and North America to the western side of the Pacific Rim."

The mystery was why such a diverse set of nations, from fiercely homogeneous Japan to sprawling Indonesia, from vast mainland China to the tiny city-states of Hong Kong and Singapore, should share such sudden prosperity. Shelves of books and articles were written about the superiority of the "Asian system" and the triumph of "Asian values", summed up by Singapore's veteran former prime minister, Lee Kuan Yew, as "belief in hard work, thrift, filial piety, national pride". These qualities were usually filed together under the label of Confucianism, conveniently fudging major cultural differences between, say, mainly Moslem Malaysia and Buddhist Thailand, and ignoring a striking similarity to the old-fashioned Protestant work ethic of the West.

Other commentators claimed the Asian transformation was prime evidence for the success of the market-oriented policies being applied elsewhere under the influence of the Washington Consensus. The Asian Miracle nations, they argued, had created a stable macroeconomic framework rooted in high domestic savings and high private investment, in which export-oriented industries could thrive. Prices were not controlled, inflation was moderate, and governments kept a tight rein on budget deficits, while investing in education to build a skilled and literate workforce. Great emphasis was placed on acquiring foreign technology, either through direct foreign investment or through licensing agreements with foreign firms. (Japan played a key role in spreading know-how across the region by forging ahead with increasingly high-tech industries while progressively farming out production of less sophisticated goods to its poorer Asian neighbours, who then climbed up the value-added chain in Japan's wake – a development model often referred to by the visual metaphor of "flying geese".)

On closer examination, however, there were important differences. Asia's policies were indeed market-friendly, but they certainly did not involve rolling back the frontiers of the state; on the contrary, all the Miracle nations (even mainly laissez-faire Hong Kong) tinkered with market forces to some extent. Many of them were run by deeply authoritarian governments that brought all their powers to bear on the challenge of development, giving rise to talk of the "Asian developmental state". Most actively promoted export-oriented industries through government incentives ranging from subsidies to tax breaks. Some, notably Japan and South Korea, protected their fledgling industries until they were strong enough to stand up to international competition. Several held down domestic interest rates to encourage investment, and used capital controls to keep their currencies undervalued and boost their international competitiveness. In its now notoriously bullish 1993 study, *The East Asian Miracle*, even the World Bank agreed somewhat grudgingly that at least some of these government interventions had contributed to economic growth (although it stressed that "pragmatic adherence to the fundamentals [i.e. the Washington Consensus] is central to success").[10]

The successful Asian countries shared another feature: a cosy co-operation between big business and the state that originated in Japan and was emulated across the region. This went a great deal further than the usual consultation in the West between governments and major companies or employers' organizations. In Japan, for example, it was the Finance Ministry that directed bank lending to the chosen growth industries in an "iron triangle" of government, an elite civil service, and business. Japan, South Korea, Malaysia and Singapore established formal councils for discussion between the government and the private sector, in which business could have a say in policy making. (Malaysia trumpeted its public–private forums with the slogan "Malaysia Inc.".) Huge business networks and conglomerates – Japan's *keiretsu* and South Korea's *chaebol* – held massive power; Taiwan's large private businesses were widely known to have close links to the ruling Kuomintang. Public–private ties were nurtured at every turn. In *The Economist*'s words: "There are numerous institutions for consultation between bureaucrats and business – what else are golf courses for?"

This model too won warm praise from proponents of the Asian way. The World Bank declared that some high-growth Asian countries had gone beyond plain Western notions of market-based competition "by creating contests that combine competition with the benefits of co-operation among firms and between government and the private sector";[11] it argued that the deliberation councils helped to avoid murky lobbying. Later, these snug relations between state and business would come under fire under a less flattering label – "crony capitalism".

THE WALL FALLS – COMMUNISM COMES A CROPPER

Along with the Washington Consensus, the Asian Miracle had the effect of opening up large areas of the developing world to international business and investment. Asia did not dismantle all its barriers to foreign capital overnight, but there were plenty of openings for outsiders keen to cash in on the region's impressive growth. Then came a third huge historical shift: in 1989, the Berlin Wall was hacked down and communism crumbled across Central and Eastern Europe. Within two years the Soviet Union had disintegrated.

With the zeal of religious converts, most of the countries that had languished behind the Iron Curtain set about transforming themselves into market economies. They were not short of Western advisers, most of whom saw the collapse of the command economies as vindication of the Washington Consensus. Unlike Latin America or Asia, most of the new "transition economies", as they became known, were not dragging themselves up from impoverished and overwhelmingly rural roots. Most already had some sort of industrial framework, however rusty, and had assured at least the basic needs of the majority of their citizens. But the challenges they faced were breathtaking – it was not just a question of changing a few policies but of creating entirely new financial institutions and a completely fresh system for generating and allocating economic resources.

In 1990 a new regional development bank, the European Bank for Reconstruction and Development (EBRD), was set up in London "to foster the transition towards open market-orientated economies and to promote private and entrepreneurial initiative in the central and eastern European countries committed to and applying the principles of multiparty democracy, pluralism and market economics". The EBRD's first annual *Transition Report* in 1994 neatly defined the ethos of transition: "In summary, the argument is that individuals freely pursuing their interests and interacting in the marketplace together provide a more efficient, dynamic and creative economy than one based on centralized commands."[12]

66 With the zeal of religious converts, most of the countries that had languished behind the Iron Curtain set about transforming themselves into market economies 99

Yet the EBRD stopped short of the more extreme anti-state positions prevalent in some circles, stressing that in certain circumstances markets could fail, and that governments still had a vital part to play in covering for those failures, assuring provision of health, education and other basic services and providing a legal framework for business. "It is fundamental to an understanding of the market economy to recognize that the role of the state is not eliminated in the transition but is transformed," it said. "Instead of directing output and resources, the role of the state is to set, supervise and enforce 'the rules of the game'."[13]

It was a note of caution that was not always heeded in the headlong, free-market scramble. The transition economies plunged into immense political and economic upheaval from which most have still to emerge fully, and their track record on both reforms and human welfare has been mixed. The end of communism brought political freedom, a vast array of consumer choice and the chance of wealth, but it also brought rising corruption, unemployment, poverty and inequality in societies that had previously seen relatively little contrast between rich and poor. Most people behind the Iron Curtain had not been well off, but they were not destitute either. The World Bank reported that the proportion of Poles living below the poverty line doubled to 12 percent between 1987–88 and 1993; in Bulgaria it rocketed to 33 percent and in Russia to 38 percent.[14]

Much of Central Europe managed to steer a reasonably steady course through the turmoil, and began to enjoy greater prosperity. But Russia, in particular, was gripped by an unbridled, freewheeling brand of capitalism, red in tooth and claw. Far from enforcing the rules of the game, as the EBRD would wish, the Russian government presided over an explosion of corruption and lawlessness. The "New Russians", close to the old party apparatus and still well connected under the new regime, scarcely missed a trick in the rush to get rich. Inequality in the former standard-bearer of Marxism quickly shot up to around US levels – themselves among the highest in the developed world. Between 1990 and 1994 life expectancy for Russian men fell by six years (from 64 to 58) and for Russian women by three years (from 74 to 71), putting adult mortality higher than India's.[15] The rise in deaths was due mainly to heart disease, accidents, suicide, alcohol and drug abuse and murder; the World Bank pointed the finger at economic hardship and declining medical care.

It was a poor recipe for economic stability, but in the early 1990s few were heeding the warning signs. Typical of the starry-eyed euphoria of post-Cold War times was the introduction to a 1996 book on investing in emerging markets: "Now that the influence of communism is gone, the whole world is going to grow more rapidly. There'll be far more international travel, far more investing across international boundaries, far more international trade, less money wasted on armaments, a greater spread of religion and a greater feeling of brotherhood. All these things will speed up the rate of growth, which is already marvellous."[16]

A rare exception was veteran liberal J.K. Galbraith, who wrote in 1994 that the newly independent republics of the former Soviet Union were being driven more towards "the idealized capitalism of free enterprise" than to emulating the established mixed economies of Western Europe and North America. "This was a transition that demanded restraint, careful analysis and, above all, thought. In the place of these, there was action according to metaphor and doctrine," he said. "What has been proposed and what has occurred could scarcely have been a better design for giving both capitalism and democracy a bad name."[17]

Nevertheless, by the early 1990s capitalism was king. The apparent stabilization of Latin America under structural adjustment, the extraordinary success of East Asia, China's discreet ditching of the command economy, and the implosion of European communism wiped the field clear of rival ideologies. "[T]he truth is that the heart has gone out of the opposition to capitalism," wrote Krugman. "For the first time since 1917, we live in a world in which property rights and free markets are viewed as fundamental principles, not grudging expedients; where the unpleasant aspects of a market system – inequality, unemployment, injustice – are accepted as facts of life. As in the Victorian era, capitalism is secure not only because of its successes – which … have been very real – but because nobody has a plausible alternative."[18]

GLOBAL VILLAGE –
THE COMMUNICATIONS REVOLUTION

As free-market capitalism was spreading, the world was shrinking. The explosion of technological change in the second half of the 20th century slashed transport and communication costs, bringing international travel within easy reach of most of the rich world's inhabitants and many in the developing world. Between 1960 and 1990, airline operating costs per mile fell by 60 percent; the price of an international telephone call dropped by 90 percent in the two decades to 1990. By 1997 the number of people tapping into the Internet was more than 50 million, and doubling every year.[19]

The all-embracing shift to economic liberalization forced down trade barriers and fostered a boom in international commerce. World trade in goods and services grew far faster than the world economy itself; between 1988 and 1995, world GDP rose by an average of 3.2 percent a year, while the volume of trade rocketed by an annual 6.7 percent.[20] The process was encouraged by subsequent rounds of multilateral trade liberalization talks through the General Agreement on Tariffs and Trade

(GATT) and its successor body, the World Trade Organization (WTO), and the development of regional common markets such as NAFTA, the European Union, Latin America's Mercosur, and the Association of South East Asian Nations (ASEAN).

Investment was going global at an even faster rate. Developing countries that had closed their doors to foreign direct investment (FDI) in the aftermath of World War Two were suddenly flinging them open again. Faced with high costs at home, and reassured by the now far smaller risk of seeing their foreign businesses confiscated or nationalized by statist governments, North American, European and Japanese corporations began shifting production to poorer countries where they could take advantage of lower wages. Many nations, particularly in East Asia and Eastern Europe, were able to offer an educated and even skilled workforce. What was more, the rapid growth achieved by some of the newly industrializing countries led multinational companies to view developing and transition economies not only as a pool of cheap labour but also as lucrative and expanding consumer markets in their own right. Advances in communications and transport made it increasingly attractive for the corporations to take a more integrated, global view of production and marketing; with the advent of the Internet it became just as easy (and less costly) for US computer firms to employ skilled software developers in India as in Silicon Valley.

> 66 The all-embracing shift to economic liberalization forced down trade barriers and fostered a boom in international commerce 99

By 1995 total world flows of FDI had multiplied nearly sixfold from the early 1980s, to $315 billion.[21] Most of it was still between industrialized nations, but the proportion going to developing countries was also rising sharply, from less than 20 percent in the late 1980s to around 35 percent in the mid-1990s.[22] In 1985, FDI flows to developing economies amounted to $11.3 billion; by 1990 they had reached $24.5 billion; then they really took off, virtually doubling every two or three years to a 1997 peak of $163.4 billion.[23] The biggest investor country by far was the United States, followed some way behind by Britain and Japan, and then Germany and France.

A dozen or so star countries caught the lion's share of the direct investment, among them Mexico, Argentina, Brazil, Malaysia, Indonesia, Thailand, Poland and Hungary. But the undisputed champion was China, which between 1989 and 1995 pulled in a staggering $122 billion in FDI – equivalent to about 30 percent of the country's GDP[24] – contributed partly by the huge and enthusiastic Chinese diaspora scattered from Singapore to San Francisco.

As FDI was rising, official aid to the developing world from governments and multilateral lenders was starting to wane in both relative and absolute terms. Aid fell out of favour under the new free-market doctrine, and even some on the political left were questioning whether it actually worked.[25] The share of official development funding in capital flows to emerging market countries plunged from over half the total in the 1980s to as low as 10 percent in 1996 (*see* Figure 1). Development was being privatized.

"Globalization" became the word of the 1990s. "In its simplest expression," wrote Story, "it describes the availability on the European early morning markets of cut flowers flown in overnight from Colombia or from Kenya, or the fresh salmon available to New Yorkers from suppliers in Chile. At its loftiest, it suggests a programme for action to create common institutions, laws, rights or duties and equal access for all to the markets in what is fast becoming a global village."[26]

Enthusiasts heralded globalization as the start of a brave new world of peace and plenty. Critics attacked it as a steamroller crushing culture and

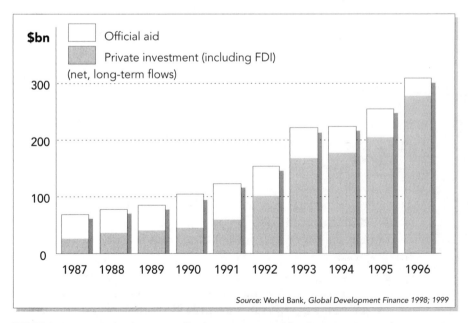

Source: World Bank, *Global Development Finance 1998; 1999*

FIGURE 1 Privatizing development: official vs private capital flows to emerging markets

individuality. In its 1997 *Human Development Report*, the United Nations Development Programme (UNDP) warned that globalization brought both winners and losers, with some countries and individuals more able than others to take advantage of the opportunities it presented. And it pointed out that although the developed world paid lip service to the principle of free global markets, in practice its tenets were applied selectively as rich countries continued to protect their own interests in areas such as agriculture and textiles, while strict immigration controls impeded real labour market flexibility. The word "globalization", it said, was used both descriptively and – in a world dominated by the Washington Consensus – prescriptively:

> The description is the widening and deepening of international flows of trade, finance and information in a single, integrated global market. The prescription is to liberalize national and global markets in the belief that free flows of trade, finance and information will produce the best outcome for growth and human welfare. All is presented with an air of inevitability and overwhelming conviction. Not since the heyday of free trade in the 19th century has economic theory elicited such widespread certainty.[27]

MONEY, MONEY, MONEY – GLOBAL MARKETS EXPLODE

Direct investment was far from the only kind of private capital sluicing into the developing and transitional economies. Those expanding markets also caught the imagination of what Friedman of *The New York Times* called the "Electronic Herd" – "all the faceless stock, bond and currency traders sitting behind computer screens all over the globe, moving their money around with the click of a mouse."[28]

One of the most startling aspects of globalization was the explosion of international, round-the-clock capital markets in the last three decades of the 20th century. The transformation began with the demise of the controlled exchange rate system devised at the Bretton Woods conference to help stabilize international finances. The agreement had fixed most major currencies in a tight range against the dollar, which in turn was pegged to gold at $35 an ounce. But by 1971 the dollar, battered by inflation, a worsening trade balance and heavy budget deficits to finance the Vietnam war, was feeling the strain of anchoring the world monetary system. In August that year President Richard Nixon announced that the United States was unilaterally abandoning the gold standard, a move that effectively wrecked the Bretton Woods agreement. An attempt to restore fixed parities rapidly failed and in 1973 the major Western governments dropped the pegged system, letting their currencies float up and down against each other on the tides of the open market.

Money became a commodity like any other, to be bought, sold and speculated on. The dollar, which had started supplanting sterling as the primary world currency after World War One, became undisputed monarch of the world financial system, and the foreign exchange (or forex) markets became the lynchpin of huge and rapid growth in financial markets across the board. Booming international trade and investment fuelled the need for foreign exchange. Bond markets expanded in the 1960s and 1970s as major Western governments turned increasingly to deficit finance, choosing to borrow on the international capital markets rather than raise taxes. Hundreds of billions of dollars and other major currencies surged into the offshore Euromarket, giving rise not only to the ill-fated syndicated bank loans of the 1970s but to a thriving Eurobond scene tapped by borrower governments and companies alike. The burgeoning Japanese trade surplus swelled foreign exchange reserves and was ploughed back into foreign investment, especially across the rest of Asia, making Japan the world's biggest creditor nation. The privatization of state industries in Britain and other European countries from the 1980s pumped a slew of new share issues into equity markets, and popularized share holding with the general public.

Better technology and communications forced the pace. Trading in the world's major currencies became a 24-hour business without borders, carried on by phone and computer; Tokyo passes the baton to London when it goes to sleep, and London hands over to New York, which keeps things rolling until Tokyo wakes up again. In 1973 the daily turnover on world forex markets was around $15 billion; by the mid-1980s it was approaching $200 billion, and by the late 1990s it was a whopping $1.5 trillion. The financial services industry in the major market centres such as New York, Chicago, London, Frankfurt or Tokyo grew at a cracking pace, reaching its champagne-swilling heyday in the 1980s with the excesses satirized in Tom Wolfe's novel *The Bonfire of the Vanities*, and the Oliver Stone film *Wall Street* (whose anti-hero, Gordon

> 66 Money became a commodity like any other, to be bought, sold and speculated on 99

Gecko, utters the immortal lines: "Greed, for lack of a better word, is good. Greed works. Greed is right").

Exchange rate swings can be violent, even in major currencies. Between the mid-1970s and the mid-1980s the West German mark swung wildly between about 1.70 to the dollar at the top end and 3.45 at the bottom. Dollar/yen – the number of yen that can be bought for one dollar – went from 260 in 1985 to 80 in 1995; in just two months in mid-1998 it toppled from nearly 150 to well below 120. The euro lost almost a quarter of its value against the dollar in the first 16 months of its existence. That volatility spreads through into interest rates, bond and stock markets and the prices of any internationally traded goods. Anyone doing business abroad can be vulnerable to sudden exchange rate shifts.

So financial markets of all kinds became increasingly sophisticated, developing a blizzard of new instruments for hedging against risk or betting on future price movements. From simple "spot" deals, forward contracts grew up agreeing the price of an asset at a future date. New derivatives markets sprang into being with contracts such as futures and options – sometimes fiendishly complicated – which were based on the underlying spot market but allowed greater flexibility. Other derivatives were dreamed up to bet not on individual stocks, bonds or currencies but on interest rates or entire market indices such as New York's Standard & Poor's 500 or Tokyo's Nikkei. "Securitization" spread its tentacles into increasingly unlikely fields, packaging up as tradable assets virtually anything from US student loans to the future musical royalties of David Bowie or James Brown.

The investment herd also includes the corporations investing directly in businesses and factories abroad, but their decisions to shift cash around the world take effect more slowly than the lightning switches of direction made by portfolio investments in stocks, bonds or currencies. Adrenaline fuels the trading room. Dealers in the major banks sit shouting into phones behind mountains of computer screens that glow with a bewilderment of constantly updating prices and news stories, usually from several rival providers. Few read beyond the headline of a story, trading second by second on snap judgements and leaving the bigger picture to the banks' posses of country or sector analysts. Modern technology allows trades worth millions of dollars to be executed in the blink of an eye.

Some markets thrash out deals in the din of "open outcry", where traders yell out their bids and offers. Nick Leeson, the man who broke Barings bank in 1995, conveys the frenzied flavour of the Singapore International Monetary Exchange (SIMEX) in his autobiography:

It was as if you were trundling your trolley around the supermarket, reached for some milk but then you thought you might go for the semi-skimmed. Then, in the split second in which you'd taken your hand off the semi-skimmed and reached back for the full-fat milk, its price had doubled from 30 pence to 60 pence a pint. If you weren't expecting it, or had weak nerves, you might get a bit jumpy. And if that was happening to all the prices up and down the aisles, on every product, you might get into a bit of a fix. You'd be standing there in a trance, watching all the prices flickering up and down and wondering when to buy and when to wait. You'd start rushing from aisle to aisle, shouting and yelling at people to get out of your way if you heard that cornflakes were suddenly showing a good price; then barging your trolley all the way back to the mint sauce if that was rumoured to be a bargain. You'd be a wreck by the time you staggered to the check-out point. And you'd be haunted by the feeling that if only you'd been there earlier or later, you'd have got a much better price.[29]

Bank dealers may buy and sell assets on their employer's account – known as proprietary trading – or on behalf of the bank's customers. These may be individual investors, mutual funds (also known as unit trusts, which bundle their clients' capital together and invest it across a range of assets) or other so-called institutional investors such as pension funds and life assurance companies. Institutional investors can wield serious clout in the markets through the vast sums at their disposal; in 1993 those based in the OECD countries alone managed assets worth a total of $13 trillion.

Some portfolio investors are in for the long haul, but many herd members choose to move their money around on a deliberately short-term basis, jumping from one money-making opportunity to another as market or economic conditions alter. Only a small proportion of daily foreign exchange turnover – probably 10 percent at most – is related to real trade or investment transactions; the rest is speculative froth. (A typical day's forex turnover in the mid-1990s amounted to around 50 times the value of world trade in goods and services.) Speculation oils the wheels of the markets by providing liquidity, enabling investors with a longer-term view of German stocks or a concrete need for Czech crowns to buy and sell with greater ease. But it can also increase volatility and in extreme cases destabilize entire markets.

This skittishness is hugely magnified by the prevalence of leverage, which boils down to placing market bets worth vastly more than the capital you have to play with. One way to do this is by borrowing more money on the back of your existing capital; another is to use the convention of margin payments, by which you do not need to cough up the full price of a particular investment up-front, but only a small proportion of it. Market players often make their money by skimming only slender profits off a high number of deals, and leverage helps them increase their turnover. It feeds the flames of speculation, but it can be an explosive fuel. Galbraith observed that it had played a key role in just about every market boom and bust, including the great Wall Street crash and the leveraged buy-out frenzy that led to Black Monday in 1987. "Imagine a billion dollars stacked on the head of a pin and you have the right idea," wrote Friedman. "As a fund manager, when you win big now, you can win very, very big, and when you lose now, you can also lose very, very big."[30]

The herd instinct is strong and can bring billions of dollars of so-called hot money cascading into the financial assets of a favoured country at the drop of a hat. But equally, it takes only a few spooked herd members to spark an outward stampede. In September 1993, one of Wall Street's most influential stock market strategists, Barton Biggs, announced after a trip to China that he was "maximum bullish" on the Asian giant. Stocks in Hong Kong, the gateway to China, soared 25 percent in a matter of weeks. In November, Biggs said he was not so sure on China after all. Hong Kong shares plunged.

Market "sentiment" is a crucial element in investment decisions, even if that sentiment is subjective, illogical or based on shaky information. And with the gradual lifting of capital controls in the developed countries from the 1970s, and then in the developing economies under the Washington Consensus, there were fewer and fewer fences blocking the exit.

LDCs REVISITED

All this money is constantly looking for the best return, be it from US high-yield corporate "junk bonds" in the 1980s (which eventually lived down to their name) or scorching Internet stocks at the turn of the century. At the start of the 1990s the hot new thing on the financial block was emerging markets, and the herd turned in that direction at a gallop. For one thing, low US interest rates meant the money to be made on US Treasury bonds was not particularly attractive, and Wall Street stocks were in subdued form. At the same time, the bursting of Japan's stock market and real estate bubble had led not only to falling yields in Japan but to deregulation of the Japanese financial system. Japanese investors suddenly had more freedom to invest abroad, and a wave of cash poured offshore, mainly into Asia. Compared to the rather staid major markets, opportunities in the world's smaller, less developed financial outposts looked much more exciting.

For a start, there was simply far more to buy on the emerging market shelves than there had been just a few years previously. The securitization of LDC debt after the 1980s debt crisis, repackaging it into tradable bonds and equities under the Brady Plan and earlier debt swaps, created a whole new class of asset and opened the door to fresh borrowing. From the syndicated loan fever of the 1970s, the trend swung back towards bonds; countries that had been out of favour with the international markets since the debt crisis broke, or even since the defaults of the 1930s, were suddenly issuing sovereign and even corporate paper again.

Economic liberalization encouraged the development of capital markets where none had existed, and kick-started them where they had languished out of official favour. By 1996 more than 60 developing countries had stock markets – twice as many as in 1985. Emerging markets pioneer Mark Mobius recalled the sleepy Indonesian stock exchange before it was revved up by economic reforms: "[J]ust a few individuals could be seen holding a desultory bargaining session for a half hour each day. One gentleman was taking an afternoon nap on his table. Then, after the government liberalized foreign investments in the market, an explosion of activity occurred."[31]

> The hot new thing on the financial block was emerging markets, and the herd turned in that direction at a gallop

Privatization in emerging market countries exploded in the early 1990s, raking in total revenues of around $24 billion a year and creating more equity issues for investors to play with.[32] Between 1993 and 1995 Russia alone privatized more than 125,000 enterprises.[33] "The pace of privatization is enough to make investment bankers drool," wrote financial adviser Mitchell Posner in a 1998 investment manual on emerging markets. "After all, how often do you get a chance to create a blue-chip stock overnight?"[34]

The process was not always above board, even when supposedly fair voucher schemes were created in the transition economies to distribute a share of the spoils to the public. Poland's scheme became mired in scandals over insider trading and other rip-offs. Mobius describes the scene at the Russian stock exchange in 1994:

[A]round 3.00 p.m., give or take an hour or so … a BMW would pull up to the stock exchange building in Moscow to unload a few million bucks worth of cold cash. Brokers would sit at long tables waiting for workers and ordinary citizens who'd been given share vouchers – which could be exchanged for shares in newly privatized Russian companies – to bring them in by the bushel, and sell them for a song. At around 6.00 in the evening the BMW would return to collect the vouchers that the brokers had bought on the cheap from the gullible workers and citizens.[35]

The range of equity investments on offer expanded further with the increasing use of instruments called global or American depository receipts (GDRs and ADRs), which allowed foreign investors to buy stock in emerging market companies without having to stray further than New York or London. (The receipts, denominated in hard currency, are issued by international banks against corresponding bundles of local currency shares held in their vaults in the issuing country.) It was a neat way of getting round local restrictions on foreign share ownership, while sparing investors the risk of exchange rate shifts or having to grapple with deals in a strange country. In 1990, emerging market companies raised just under $3 billion in depository receipts; by 1994 the total for the year had leapt to $18 billion, two-thirds of it from Asia.[36]

What was more, emerging stock markets offered rich pickings and often outperformed the major markets. Between 1989 and 1993 the IFC's main Investable Composite price index (IFCI Composite), covering emerging market stocks as a whole, jumped by an average of 33 percent a year; in the same period the US Standard & Poor's 500 index rose only 12 percent a year, while Japan's Nikkei fell by an annual 6 percent. There were ups and downs, of course, and the overall picture was very patchy. Markets in neighbouring countries could fare very differently from each other, and big gains one year could turn into big losses the next. On an individual company basis, each country had its share of winners and turkeys. Investors had to stay on their toes, and novices or short-termists could get their fingers burned. But the potential gains were outstanding enough in the early 1990s to make the herd sit up and take note. For investors with strong nerves, volatility means opportunity.

There was money to be made on emerging market debt, too. Apart from gambling on price moves, investors can get much higher yields on emerging market bonds than on their major market equivalents for the simple reason that investors lending their money to, say, Brazil or Ukraine, as opposed to the US Treasury, expect to be compensated for the potentially higher risk that they will not see their money again. Emerging market bonds invariably offer yields several percentage points higher than US or European Treasury bonds of a similar maturity – a gap known as the spread. The size of the spread is all to do with perceptions of creditworthiness, reflected in credit ratings from specialist agencies such as Standard & Poor's, Moody's Investors Service and Fitch IBCA.

Rapid economic growth in many developing economies also raised investors' pulses. From 1990 to 1997 the world's advanced industrial economies grew by an average of between 1.2 and 3.1 percent a year, while developing countries as a group consistently notched up growth rates of between 4 and 6.8 percent.[37] The transitional economies were in deep turmoil, but once lumbering Russia, Ukraine and Belarus were stripped out of the equation, Central and Eastern Europe started showing respectable growth from 1994. Only a few years before, the poverty of many developing countries had been accepted as a rationale for not bothering to invest there; emerging market countries accounted for nearly 85 percent of the world's population, but only 20 percent of world GNP. All of a sudden those same statistics were hauled up as arguments for getting in there, demonstrating the huge scope the emerging economies (and their markets) had for catching up with the developed world.

There is no gain without pain, as the cliché goes, and the risks in emerging markets are generally far higher than in developed markets. Problems can come in a variety of guises. Politics tends to loom larger, with the chance that anything from mild unrest to a full-blown coup or war could destabilize the markets. (The Karachi stock market crashed more than 12 percent on the first trading day after Pakistan conducted its first nuclear test in May 1998.) On balance, governments in emerging market countries are still more likely to impose unexpected restrictions on foreign investors (as Malaysia did in September 1998), or change taxes, labour laws or other regulations affecting listed companies. Sudden, sharp currency shifts can erode profits, and markets are often too illiquid to be able to buy or sell with ease, especially if everyone else is trying to get out at the same time.

Transactions are not always transparent to all market players, company accounts are not always audited to international standards, and there may be technical problems with settling deals. Even reliable macroeconomic data can be hard to pin down, particularly as many emerging market countries have a huge informal economy. (Colombia, the world's biggest cocaine producer, took a small but significant step towards more realistic figures when it announced in 1999 it would start including income from illegal drug cultivation in its GDP calculations.) On top of all this, the supervisory and legal framework can be shaky. Foreign investors in several Russian companies found out the hard way just how weak their rights were as minority shareholders. And although there are not necessarily any more sharks in the emerging markets than in the developed world, there is often more chance of them getting a bite as innocent foreigners wade into unfamiliar waters.

Ironically, many investors who turned to the risky emerging markets in the early 1990s were also looking to reduce their overall risk by diversify- ing their investments. The thinking was that emerging markets would not necessarily be affected by world develop- ments to the same extent, or move in the same direction, as major markets; in fact, ana- lysts spotted a low historical correlation between emerging stock markets and Wall Street's Dow Jones Industrial Average. Besides, there seemed no particular reason to think different emerging markets should not move independently of each other; why should trouble in Thailand affect Brazil or Hungary, thou- sands of miles away? And as emerging debt markets took off again there were high hopes that bonds would prove a more resilient investment than the ill-fated bank loans of the 1980s.

> 66 Although there are not necessarily any more sharks in the emerging markets, there is often more chance of them getting a bite 99

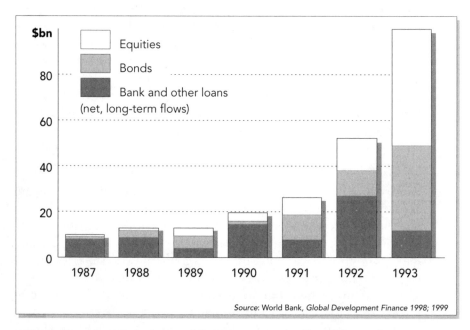

FIGURE 2 The cash stack: foreign portfolio investment in emerging markets

Between 1987 and 1993 annual private portfolio investment in the emerging markets rose almost tenfold to $100 billion; the cash flowing into equities exploded to more than 60 times its 1987 level (*see* Figure 2). Debt was not doing badly, either; according to the New York-based Emerging Market Traders Association (EMTA), trading volume in emerging market debt grew by 170 percent in 1993 alone, to a whisker below $2 trillion.

Specialist emerging market mutual funds were springing up all over the place to channel money into the hot new asset class. In 1984, only a handful of emerging market funds had existed, with a total capitalization of $700 million; 10 years later there were about 1,000 funds, with more than $100 billion under management.[38] At one point in 1994, over half the money invested in US mutual funds was going into emerging market investment vehicles.[39] Emerging market analyst Callum Henderson remembers seeing would-be investors queueing up outside the office of a well-known mutual fund just off Wall Street, eager to get in on the emerging markets act. "This was a classic sign of frenzy, of mass speculation at work," he wrote.[40]

Enthusiasm for certain markets was so great that investors were flinging more cash at them than they could absorb; in early 1995 there were over

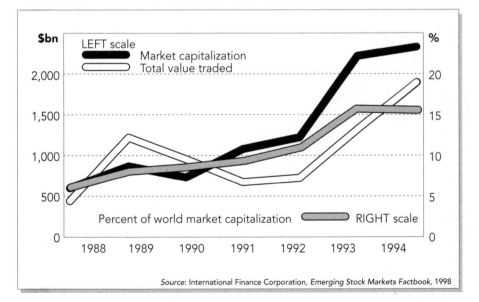

Source: International Finance Corporation, *Emerging Stock Markets Factbook*, 1998

FIGURE 3 The boom: growth in emerging stock markets (including Hong Kong and Singapore)

40 China funds with more than $2.7 billion to invest, yet the entire market value of the Chinese "B" shares open to foreign buyers amounted to only $2.1 billion.[41]

With all this money flooding in, emerging stock markets were growing at extraordinary speed. Emerging stock market capitalization – the total value of all the listed shares at a given moment – nearly quadrupled to more than $2.3 trillion between 1988 and 1994, and its share in world markets shot up from 6 percent to 15 percent (*see* Figure 3).[42] Some individual markets grew even faster, with Indonesia's market capitalization booming from a paltry $250 million to a respectable $47 billion in the same period. By 1993, Hong Kong had the world's sixth biggest stock market capitalization; Mexico's market was roughly the size of Australia's, and the Thai and South Korean bourses were as big as Italy's. More billions of dollars' worth of shares changed hands in Taiwan than in Germany. India had as many listed companies as Japan and Canada combined. The emerging markets were on the march.

NOTES

1   Story, *The Frontiers of Fortune*, pp. 43–44.
2   Robin Broad and John Cavanagh, "The Death of the Washington Consensus?", in *World Policy Journal*, October 1999.
3   Friedman, *The Lexus and the Olive Tree*, p. 86.
4   Story, p. 47.
5   World Bank, *The East Asian Miracle*, pp. 3–4.
6   World Bank figures.
7   Krugman, *The Return of Depression Economics*, p. 24.
8   Edward Paley, "Colleges cash in on ambition", in *South China Morning Post*, September 5, 1993.
9   *The Economist*, November 16, 1991.
10 World Bank, *The East Asian Miracle*, p. 26.
11 World Bank, *The East Asian Miracle*, p. 11.
12 EBRD, *Transition Report 1994*, p. 3.
13 EBRD, *Transition Report 1994*, p. 6.
14 World Bank, *World Development Report, 1996: From Plan to Market*, p. 69.
15 World Bank, *World Development Report, 1996*, p. 128.

16 Introduction by Sir John Templeton in Mobius, *Mobius on Emerging Markets*, p. xix.

17 Galbraith, *The World Economy Since the Wars*, pp. 244–245.

18 Krugman, p. 6.

19 UNDP, *Human Development Report 1997*, p. 83.

20 IMF, *World Economic Outlook*, May 1998, p. 219.

21 UNDP, *Human Development Report 1997*, p. 83.

22 World Bank, *Global Development Finance 1998*, p. 19.

23 IFC, *Emerging Stock Markets Factbook*, 1998, p. 8, and World Bank, *Global Development Finance 1999* (web site version), p. 24.

24 World Bank, *World Development Report 1996*, p. 64.

25 *See*, for example, Graham Hancock's *Lords of Poverty* (London: Mandarin, 1991) or James Morton's *The Poverty of Nations: The aid dilemma at the heart of Africa* (London: I.B. Tauris, 1994).

26 Story, p. 54.

27 UNDP, *Human Development Report 1997*, p. 82.

28 Friedman, p. 90.

29 Leeson, *Rogue Trader*, pp. 135–136.

30 Friedman, p. 103.

31 Mobius, *Mobius on Emerging Markets*, p. 72.

32 World Bank, *Global Development Finance 1998*, p. 109.

33 EBRD, *Transition Report 1998*, p. 15.

34 Posner, *Profiting from Emerging Market Stocks*, p. 102.

35 Mobius, *Passport to Profits*, p. 120.

36 Mobius, *Mobius on Emerging Markets*, p. 230.

37 IMF, *World Economic Outlook*, May 1998, p. 145.

38 IFC, *Investment Funds in Emerging Markets*, p. 1.

39 Soros, *The Crisis of Global Capitalism*, p. xii.

40 Henderson, *Asia Falling*, p. 22.

41 Mobius, *Mobius on Emerging Markets*, p. 220.

42 Figures from IFC, *Emerging Stock Markets Factbook*, 1998, adjusted to include Hong Kong and Singapore.

3

TEQUILA SUNSET

But foreign capital flowing into emerging markets is, by nature, volatile and speculative flight capital. It cannot be otherwise. Financial capital has no national allegiance. It pursues its own interests, not those of the nations it visits – Carlos Fuentes, *A New Time for Mexico*

PROFITS AND PESOS – MEXICO MAKES GOOD

On New Year's Eve, 1993, the sun shone brightly on Mexico. The traffic-choked capital and bustling cities of the north were flushed with a consumer boom. Inflation, which had been in triple figures only a few years before, had been hauled down to single digits. The landmark NAFTA free-trade deal with the United States and Canada was about to take effect after more than two years of careful lobbying and image-polishing, and it looked as though Latin America's second-biggest economy was on the verge of striding into the First World. President Carlos Salinas de Gortari was the darling of the financial markets after pulling the economy around with stern fiscal and monetary reforms that, in next to no time, had banished the 1980s debt debacle to a distant memory. Government finances were showing a slim budget surplus and the country's foreign exchange reserves had been ticking upwards as foreign investors, drawn by the promise of economic and corporate gains under NAFTA, poured more than $33 billion into the country in 1993 alone. The stock market had closed for the New Year holiday on a high after notching up a 12-month rise of 48 percent.

Mexico was not the only country in high fashion on the international financial circuit. Emerging markets around the world were ending their best collective year yet, with the IFCI Composite stock market index shooting up more than 75 percent in dollar terms, compared with a paltry 7.6 percent rise in the US Standard & Poor's 500. Markets in Thailand, Indonesia, Malaysia and the Philippines were all up by well over 100 percent on the year in dollar terms (the measure that most interests foreign investors), while Poland's WIG index rose by an astounding 718 percent – a figure that must surely have prompted questions about how realistic and sustainable the boom really was. Superstitious Hong Kong dealers were jubilant when the territory's Hang Seng index ended 1993 at a record 11,888.39 points – the three eights sounding in Cantonese like the words for growth and prosperity. "In this kind of bull run, all you have to do is throw a dart and you'll make money," one Singapore advertising manager said.

True, a few questions were being asked in some quarters about aspects of Mexico's glittering economic performance. For social campaigners, Salinas' espousal of the Washington Consensus and the advent of NAFTA were stretching existing inequalities even wider. "The country was threatened with an acute case of schizophrenia," wrote Mexican novelist Carlos Fuentes. "A minority centered their lives on the New York Stock Exchange, and a majority on the price of beans. One economy was all gilded wrapping paper, the other all huts and untilled land. The former was the minority's, the latter the majority's."[1]

For some economists, the bugbear was exchange rate policy. The peso was traded on the forex market but the central bank kept the exchange rate within a preset band that allowed for a tiny daily slippage against the dollar, a system known as a crawling peg. If the forces of supply or demand pushed the peso too close to either edge of the band, the bank would intervene to defend those limits by buying or selling the currency. The built-in depreciation was intended to offset Mexican inflation and protect the country's international competitiveness. But some economists were arguing that the peso was still overvalued, hampering exports and wider economic growth while encouraging a flood of consumer imports under newly liberalized trade rules.

By 1993, the current-account deficit had swollen to around 6.5 percent of the country's GDP – a high figure by anyone's standards. And although the country had put on a growth spurt from 1989 of between 2.8 and 4.5 percent a year in real terms, the pace had stalled in 1993 with growth of less than 1 percent. If this was the "Mexican Miracle", as some maintained, where were the Asian-style growth rates? Surely it would be a good idea to devalue the peso, promptly and crisply, to allow export growth to kick in?

66 Mexico was walking a balance-of-payments tightrope, relying entirely on capital from abroad to keep it in the air 99

But Mexican officials firmly dismissed any suggestion of devaluation, putting much of the import surge down to investment in capital goods to develop the country's industry. In any case, they argued, continued huge inflows of foreign investment, logged under the country's capital account, more than covered the shortfall on the current account. Mexico was firmly in the black.

It is easy to understand their reluctance at the time. Devaluation would inevitably push up prices, and the scars of that ran deep in a country that had suffered triple-figure inflation only six years before. It could also endanger the financial credibility Mexico had worked so hard to regain, particularly while sensitive NAFTA negotiations had been going on. Although it did not fully acknowledge it at the time, Mexico was walking a balance-of-payments tightrope, relying entirely on capital from abroad to keep it in the air. And a country banking so heavily on foreign capital flows does not want to upset the apple-cart by doing anything that might unnerve investors – such as cutting the value of the currency they are holding in the shape of shares and domestic bonds.

Besides, these things are emotional. Whether in Mexico in 1994 or Britain in 2000, a currency is often seen as a symbol of national pride and virility; devaluation would be akin to castration.

MEXICO'S BAD YEAR

Then, on January 1, 1994, Mexico's Bad Year began. More than 700 kilometres south of the capital, in the jungle-clad mountains of impoverished Chiapas state, a couple of thousand armed peasants staged a New Year's Day uprising and snatched control of several towns. Most of the rebels were descendants of the ancient Mayans who once held sway over much of Central America, but who now scratched a life of desperate poverty under the yoke of feudalism and racism. Styling themselves the Zapatista National Liberation Army after a Mexican revolutionary hero, they called NAFTA a "death certificate" for Mexico's indigenous people, and demanded land reform and democracy. The army went in hard with air strikes and heavy artillery, and at least 145 people were killed in ten days of intense fighting.

The markets were unnerved, particularly when a cluster of bombs in Mexico City raised fears that the conflict was spreading. Finance officials put in discreet calls to New York investment banks to reassure them the situation was under control, but to little avail – in the first two weeks of the year the stock market dropped 10 percent. The rebels soon retreated to mountain strongholds and a ceasefire was declared. But the incident wiped some of the shine off Mexico's glossy image, underlining the deep disparities between a relatively well-off north and an impoverished south left behind by the economic reforms of Harvard-educated northerner Salinas.

Some foreign investors turned tail; emerging market currency strategist Callum Henderson recounted how one US fund manager jetted down to Chiapas, spent a week tapping the mood on the ground, and then sold off the fund's entire Mexico holding.[2] But most hung on, shrugging off the market slide as a normal correction after the euphoria of late 1993.

In March, the country faced an even bigger crisis of confidence with the murder of the man who, to all intents and purposes, was lined up to be the next president. Luis Donaldo Colosio, the designated candidate of the paradoxically named Institutional Revolutionary Party (PRI) that had ruled Mexico without interruption since 1929, was heir apparent to Salinas in presidential polls set for that August. He was mingling with supporters after a campaign speech at a scrubby park in the seamy frontier town of Tijuana, a stone's throw from the US border, when an assassin shot him twice at close range. Police arrested a young trainee mechanic who worked at a local plastics factory, but his motives were obscure and the killing raised dark questions. The charismatic Colosio had managed to combine deft reformism with popular appeal, and there were suggestions he had fallen foul either of drug lords or corrupt PRI hardliners whose vested interests he threatened to challenge. The ruling party was left with a power vacuum, and Mexico's carefully honed image of stability was shattered.

Salinas appealed on television for unity and calm, and declared the next day a market holiday, ostensibly in mourning for Colosio but also to buy time to try to head off an investor exodus. As the hours ticked away Salinas called together government, business and labour leaders to reaffirm the latest in a regular round of tripartite pacts on wage and price controls, sending a message to the financial world that existing inflation and exchange rate policies were secure. At the same time, he enlisted international help. President Bill Clinton, who now had NAFTA's future to worry about as well, came through with a pledge of US support for the peso and an emergency credit line of $6 billion to help fight off any speculative attack on the currency. Washington's strong political interest in Mexican stability had become clear during the 1980s debt crisis, and US institutions still made up by far the biggest share of foreign investors in Mexico. The icing on the cake in the drive to prove Mexico's sound credentials was news that it would be admitted sooner than expected to the OECD, the prestigious club of the world's rich nations.

> **With elections looming, the Mexican markets were having an increasingly rough ride**

Reporters and television crews crowded into the glass-domed stock exchange when it reopened, ready for the expected rout. They left disappointed; an early slide was quickly reversed, and local financial and political analysts were full of praise for Salinas' handling of the crisis. But the relief was short-lived. The shock at Colosio's murder ran deep and the kidnapping of two prominent businessmen compounded the grave sense of political uncertainty.

With elections looming, the Mexican markets were having an increasingly rough ride. By late April the stock market was down nearly 25 percent from the start of the year. Interest rates on peso-denominated Treasury bills, known as *Cetes*, had soared from 8 to 18 percent in just two months as investors demanded a better return on their risk. Capital was bleeding steadily out of the country and foreign exchange reserves, which opened the year at a healthy $25 billion or more, were already down to around $17 billion – although the full extent of the damage was not yet widely known, such market-sensitive data being published only after a substantial delay.

Mexico's NAFTA partners weighed in again in April, upping the previous US offer of $6 billion to an $8.7 billion US–Canadian system of credit lines designed to bolster investor confidence. Meanwhile, the Mexican government was trying out a new and potentially risky strategy for keeping investors on board. Apart from raising interest rates and buying pesos on the forex market, it started converting a huge amount of public debt from peso *Cetes* to another type of short-term Treasury paper called *Tesobonos*, which were settled in pesos but denominated in dollars – "disguising foreign debt as internal debt", as Fuentes put it.[3] By effectively dollarizing its debt, the government assumed any exchange rate risk in the event of a devaluation – an attractive prospect for nervous investors who fancied staying in Mexico but wanted to hedge their bets on the currency. A growing number ditched *Cetes* and bought *Tesobonos* instead; central bank figures showed that *Tesobonos* accounted for $21 billion out of a total of $71 billion of Mexico's outstanding public debt at the end of April, compared to just over $8 billion in *Tesobonos* at the end of 1993. If Mexico were to devalue after all, the government would have to fork out far more pesos than it was bargaining for to repay these bonds. The seeds of trouble were being sown.

For a while, however, things seemed to be going more smoothly. Colosio's replacement as PRI presidential candidate, Ernesto Zedillo Ponce de Leon, was a bookish, Yale-educated economist, a charmless public speaker but a capable technocrat who seemed to offer both Mexicans and foreign investors the stability they were looking for. The PRI, the world's longest-ruling political party, had routinely resorted to vote-rigging to stay in power, but Salinas promised to clean up the electoral act and admitted foreign monitors for the first time. The government slackened off its monetary policy and went on a spending spree to soften up the voters, laying the foundations for renewed inflation. But voting was peaceful, and although the monitors spotted some cheating, the general view was that Zedillo was the genuine winner in one of Mexico's least fraudulent elections ever.

The president-elect lost no time in reaffirming existing exchange rate policy, and the lack of any nasty election surprises pleased foreign investors. Several banks and mutual funds forecast good times ahead and openly opted for an "overweight" position on Mexico – a vote of confidence meaning that they put a greater proportion of their capital into Mexico than the country's percentage weighting in benchmark indices such as the IFC's.

The cheer was short-lived. On September 29 the PRI's reformist secretary-general, Francisco Ruiz Massieu, was shot dead as he was leaving a Mexico City hotel, raking up fears that the ruling party was being torn apart by feuding. Meanwhile, a steady rise in US interest rates was providing an external lure for money that had previously found a short-term home in Mexico. Pressure was back on the peso. Zedillo was sworn in on December 1, but he was denied any honeymoon period; instead, Chiapas promptly swung back on to the agenda with fresh war talk from the Zapatista rebels. The stock market slithered more than 10 percent in the first half of December, and the peso slumped again to the weak edge of its official intervention band.

The earthquake that rattled Mexico City on December 10 caused little real damage, but anyone given to reading omens would have said it was a little too symbolic for comfort. While Mexican politics lurched from one crisis to another, the country had continued to import far more than it exported, swelling the current-account deficit to a towering $29.7 billion, or around 8 percent of GDP. That would have been manageable, at least in the short term, if the country was still raking in foreign capital, but it wasn't – at least, not at anything like its previous levels. Direct investment had risen during 1994 on the back of NAFTA fever but portfolio investment was sharply down for the year; in fact, what had been a consistent cash inflow into Mexican stocks and bonds since pre-Brady times suddenly turned into a net outflow of $5.5 billion in the fourth quarter of 1994. Total foreign investment for the year was less than two-thirds of the 1993 figure, and other capital flight added to the imbalance.

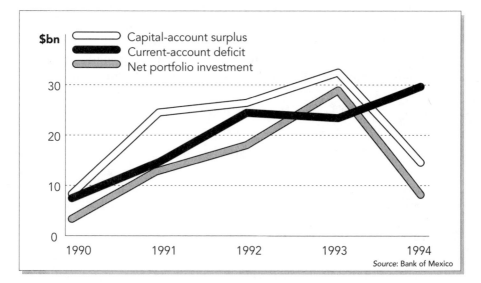

FIGURE 4 Mexico's capital crunch

All of a sudden, the capital-account surplus was falling far short of the amount needed to cover the current-account gap (*see* Figure 4). Of the foreign money that did remain in Mexico, a huge proportion was still invested in stocks and bonds rather than in factories and businesses. Mexico was about to learn the hard way about the dangers of hot money.

CIRCLING SHARKS – SPECULATORS AND "SHORTING"

With investor confidence on the slide, speculators saw their chance to make money by attacking the peso. The curious thing about the global financial markets is that players can gain directly not only from price *rises* but also from price *falls*. Basic logic dictates that if you think a market is heading downwards you will consider selling your assets in that market sooner rather than later, to curb your losses. If you then buy back the same assets at a lower price, you still have those stocks, bonds or whatever, plus a pocketful of change.

But you do not actually have to own the assets to sell them; you can borrow them from somewhere else, or take advantage of accounting delays between agreeing to sell and actually delivering. This is called selling short, or shorting; Mobius defines it neatly as "selling something you don't have at a price you don't want to pay".[4] (The opposite manoeuvre – buying up as much as you can in the expectation of a price rise – is called going long.) Provided you can get hold of the same assets at a lower price by the time you have to give them back to the owner or deliver them to the buyer, you will have made money. Of course, if the price rises rather than falls in the allotted time, you will have lost, and that loss could be huge if the price is sharply up. And if you cannot get hold of the assets that you are committed to delivering, you are in big trouble.

On the other hand, if you go after something hard enough, you can sometimes make it happen. If enough people sell a thing in an open market, its price will fall. And because on a day-to-day level the markets work as much on "sentiment" as on real news, people will often sell because they think a lot of other people are about to sell, and they want to get their blow in first. Others then sell because they see the price turning downwards, and the price drops further still. The movement becomes a self-fulfilling prophecy. By selling short, canny and well-financed speculators can drive down the market and then mop up – just as Hungarian-born investor George Soros did almost single-handedly in

1992 when his Quantum Fund quietly borrowed $15 billion worth of sterling and then sold the pound so hard and so loudly that he forced it out of Europe's Exchange Rate Mechanism (ERM), reaping both fame and about $1 billion in profit at a stroke.

The Big Boys of the speculative world are the secretive hedge funds, such as Quantum, which promise high returns for their investor base of rich individuals and institutions. Contrary to what their name might suggest, they do not exactly "hedge" in the sense of offsetting investment risk; in fact, they usually do more or less the opposite, making as much money as they can from often small and short-term market fluctuations and discrepancies. Subject to less official regulation and monitoring than most other financial operators, they trade aggressively and are typically leveraged to the hilt, a trait that was to become dangerously apparent in 1998 with the LTCM fiasco. As a result, they can wield enormous power in the market on the basis of relatively tiny capital. They are the lords of shorting, the masters of the speculative attack. And their clout is magnified when the big banks that do business with them promptly mimic the hedge funds' positions in their own proprietary trading.

> By selling short, canny and well-financed speculators can drive down the market and then mop up

The potential gains are bigger wherever there is a fixed target to strike against, such as the pound when it was in the ERM, or the Mexican peso in its intervention band. Governments and central banks may choose to defend a floating currency if it shifts too far in either direction for their liking, but they are not obliged to intervene at a particular level. But if a government with a fixed or semi-fixed currency regime gets to the point where it is no longer able, or willing, to prop up its currency, the plunge can be all the more dramatic when it finally lets go.

By mid-December, Mexico had to do something decisive. Speculators had begun to short the peso with a vengeance, and the central bank was having to dig deep into its dollar reserves to keep the currency within the intervention band. Raising interest rates would slow down an already sluggish economy. It was time to bite the bullet and devalue.

Krugman described the theory:

What is supposed to happen when a country's currency is devalued is that speculators say, 'Okay, that's over,' and stop betting on the currency's continued decline. That is the way it worked for Britain and Sweden in 1992. The danger is that speculators will instead view the first devaluation as a sign of more to come, and start speculating all the harder. In order to avoid that, a government is supposed to follow certain rules. First, if you devalue at all, make the devaluation big enough. Otherwise, you will simply set up expectations of more to come. Second, immediately following the devaluation you must give every signal you can that everything is under control, that you are responsible people who understand the importance of treating investors right, and so on. Otherwise the devaluation can crystallize doubts about your economy's soundness and start a panic.[5]

Unfortunately, Mexico's devaluation was a master class in what *not* to do.

A CHAPTER OF ACCIDENTS – MEXICO DEVALUES

On Monday, December 19, the Zapatistas occupied the town of Simojovel and nearby villages in central Chiapas, setting fire to part of the town hall. The Mexican stock market promptly tumbled 4 percent and the peso was straining at the bottom of its trading band. According to Henderson, one US financial house alone bought $200 million against pesos – a huge order in that market at the time. "The tension in dealing rooms around the world became electric, the volume of noise a roar," he wrote.[6]

On December 20, after crisis talks with labour and business leaders, Finance Minister Jaime Serra Puche made the shock announcement that the government was extending the weaker edge of the peso's trading band by 53 centavos, or just over half a peso – an effective devaluation of 13 percent if the currency fell the whole way. It did. By the end of the trading day in Mexico City and New York the peso had plunged from Monday's 3.46 pesos to the dollar to a whisker short of 4.00. (In an unfortunate piece of timing, the OECD picked the same day to forecast a healthy upturn in Mexico's economic growth for 1995.)

But the Chiapas jitters were not going away, and many analysts felt the devaluation was not big enough to make any real dent in the burgeoning current-account deficit. After vowing for months not to devalue, the government and the central bank were now insisting that the devaluation would be a one-off. "The commitment to conserve the new exchange formula is absolute," intoned a central bank spokesman. But few people were listening. "When you repeatedly say you're not going to change the policy, then suddenly do it, people are less willing to believe you," said one financial analyst in Mexico City.

Foreign investors were outraged that some Mexican businesses had been consulted in advance about the devaluation, effectively tipping them off ahead of outsiders. Many were also disgruntled that Serra had chosen to drop his bombshell on national television, rather than alerting them through the usual financial channels. Mexico's markets stumbled through Wednesday, twitching wildly at every rumour. The central bank hurled an estimated $4–6 billion of the country's foreign reserves into the forex market to shore up the toppling peso, and by the end of the day it had just $6 billion left – barely enough to defend the currency from that kind of attack for a day more.

There was no choice left. On Thursday, December 22, Mexico abandoned its intervention band all together and let the peso float. The currency promptly plunged a further 18 percent to around 4.80 per dollar. Mexico's "Par" Brady Bonds, which had been changing hands on Monday at around 63 cents on the dollar and sliding ever since, descended to 54 cents. Everybody was riled, from long-term foreign investors to the Mexican in the street. "We have a major credibility problem," fumed one investment bank analyst. "The Mexican government has botched it." Radio stations were inundated with calls from ordinary Mexicans complaining bitterly about rising prices and credit costs in the middle of the Christmas shopping rush.

Everyone was riled, that is, except the people who had shorted the currency. Put at its most simplistic, a speculator who sold short, say, $1 million worth of pesos on December 19, at a rate of 3.46 pesos to the dollar, would have been able to snap them back up again on December 22 for about $720,000. That would have left him with a cool $280,000 in profit (less any interest or fee payable for borrowing the pesos in the first place) – a 28 percent return in just three days.

After not one but two broken promises from the Mexican authorities, investors were in no mood to hang around. By close of play on the following Monday, December 26, the peso had slid to 5.10 to the dollar. The next day it was at 5.50, down some 37 percent from its pre-devaluation level, and showed no sign of settling. Bonds were still taking a beating, with Par bonds down to just over 52 cents on the dollar. The stock market was see-sawing all over the place, dropping on lack of confidence and then bouncing as braver bargain-hunters stepped in to take advantage of the fact that stocks priced in pesos were suddenly far cheaper if you had dollars. "Everyone is doing the first thing that comes into their heads," one harried Mexican analyst said.

But Mexico's markets were not the only ones hitting the skids. The trouble spread like oil on water, and other Latin American countries were the first in line. By the end of the week Argentina's stock market had lost nearly 9 percent of its value, despite assurances from Economy Minister Domingo Cavallo that the Argentine peso, fixed solidly at one to the US dollar, would not go the way of its distant Mexican cousin. (Cavallo, the architect of the country's radical 1991 currency reform, even made a snap public relations visit to the Buenos Aires stock exchange.) Argentine Brady Bonds plunged by between 5 and 9 cents on the dollar in a few days. Brazilian stocks were down 11.5 percent. Even Chile, usually Latin America's most stable market, was shuddering, despite analysts' insistence that its economy was in much better shape than those of its neighbours.

It was not only Latin America that suffered. Emerging market debt tends to function as a slightly more homogeneous, international type of asset than emerging market stocks, and virtually every debt issue with an "emerging" label came under pressure. "My impression is that no one has remained unscathed," said one banker, singling out Greek and Lebanese issues as the only ones holding steady. Trading in Russian debt had already been edgy because of a military quagmire in the south of the country as Moscow tried to crush a rebellion in the breakaway republic of Chechnya. But the Mexican crisis dealt it another blow. Prices slid again, and in Moscow, trading in dollar-denominated bonds virtually ground to a halt. Even distant South Africa, which had recently returned with a flourish to the international capital markets after years in the apartheid wilderness, felt the pinch as its debut Eurobond traded sharply lower. Any emerging economy that had been planning to borrow on the international markets through a new debt issue saw its hopes dashed; takers would be few and far between.

> 66 The trouble spread like oil on water, and other Latin American countries were the first in line 99

A new phrase was coined to describe the spread of the malaise to emerging market countries that had little or nothing to do with Mexico: the Tequila Effect.

Meanwhile, another black cloud was looming on Mexico's horizon: how was it going to pay out on some $30 billion worth of *Tesobonos* coming due for repayment in 1995 – more than one-third of it in the first three months? The bonds had a maturity of one year at most. If investors agreed to roll their investments over into fresh *Tesobonos*, all well and good. But what if, as seemed likely under the circumstances, they did not? The faintly good news was that because the dollar-denominated bonds were actually settled in pesos, in theory the government would not have to conjure up precious hard currency that it simply did not have. The extremely bad news was that the devaluation had already pushed up the cost of repayment by nearly two-fifths, placing a crippling burden on the government's finances. Any move to print more pesos would stoke inflation. And pressure on the battered peso was intensifying, on the assumption that most *Tesobono* holders would want to move directly into dollars. Mexico needed outside help.

The Mexican government finally kicked into action. Serra resigned (or was sacked) as finance minister, sending a sigh of relief around the unforgiving markets. A few days into 1995 a drastic emergency plan was announced, including price and wage curbs, public spending cuts and sweeping new privatizations, to try to stabilize the markets and drag the country back from a rampant price spiral. Inflation and the current-account deficit would be attacked at the expense of overall economic growth, which was now targeted at 1.5–2 percent in 1995 from an earlier 4 percent. The plan was underpinned by an expanded, $18 billion support fund from Mexico's foreign friends, half of it from the United States, the rest from Canada, Spain and other major industrial nations, plus a small coterie of international banks.

Economists warned the package was highly recessionary, but agreed Zedillo had no choice. For ordinary Mexicans the outlook for 1995 was bleak, offering sky-high borrowing costs and pay rises capped at 7 percent at most, while the government forecast inflation of 19 percent. In a grim address on national television, postponed several times because of wrangling with labour leaders over the small print of the plan, Zedillo appealed for unity and fortitude. "It will demand our utmost determination," he said. "It will mean sacrifices for us all, without exception."

But market sentiment is slippery and often has as much to do with what players expect, or the way things are presented, as with what is actually on the table. Far from stabilizing, the markets fell again – not because investors necessarily thought the plan was a bad one, but because they had wanted to hear more details in Zedillo's much-delayed speech. Some simply thought the president's television performance had been tepid. Some felt the growth and inflation targets in the plan were far too optimistic and undermined the credibility of the plan itself. Besides, the *Tesobono* problem was still unresolved and new fears were springing up that Mexico's banking sector was heading for a crash.

Mexican officials did not know what had hit them. One month they were being borne aloft towards the First World on the shoulders of international capital; the next they were nursing their wounds in the gutter. Thomas Friedman went to interview Zedillo at the presidential palace as the peso was caving in: "We walked in, and there, sitting alone at a table in the corner, was President Zedillo, listening to Tchaikovsky's '1812 Overture' on the office stereo, and looking a lot like Napoleon after Waterloo."[7]

Zedillo's name was mud, with Mexican newspapers railing against his management of the devaluation. Then, suddenly, public opinion did a back-flip. The penny dropped that Zedillo had been forced to devalue the peso just three weeks after taking office, yet the current-account deficit that forced the move had been gaping long before he took office. The finger of blame swung squarely round on Salinas just as he was off on a world tour, lobbying hard to become head of the new WTO. Critics charged that the former president had put his ambition before the good of the country, refusing to face up to a necessary devaluation for fear of damaging his WTO campaign. *Proceso* magazine ran a cover picture of Salinas with the headline "The guilty one".

> 66 Market sentiment is slippery and often has as much to do with what players expect as with what is on the table 99

By leaving the dirty work to Zedillo, Salinas had broken a cardinal rule of Mexican politics. The smooth handover from one PRI president to another had always relied on the convention that the outgoing leader would get any unpopular but necessary policy moves out of the way before stepping down, smoothing the path for the incomer. In return, the former president could expect his interests to be protected under the new leadership.

From there, the Salinas story turned into pure soap opera. In February his brother, Raúl, was arrested and jailed on charges of masterminding the murder of Ruiz Massieu. An opinion poll showed nearly two-thirds of Mexicans believed the former president was also implicated in the killing, and allegations surfaced that he had also covered up Colosio's assassination. Unprecedented public hostility broke out between Salinas and Zedillo, and the United States tersely announced it was reconsidering its support for Salinas' WTO candidacy, forcing him to abandon his dream. The formerly suave Harvard man then embarked on a hunger strike in a bizarre attempt to clear his name. Anxious to cool down a row that was scaring off yet more investors, the government quickly agreed to exonerate him of any misdeeds. But Salinas' reputation was in tatters, and he left Mexico soon afterwards for self-imposed exile. Raúl Salinas went on to face additional charges of running a massive protection racket for drug traffickers; in 1999 he was handed a 50-year jail sentence, later cut to 27½ years.

PASS THE TEQUILA – CRISIS AND BAILOUT

By the end of the first week of January 1995 the peso had lost around 40 percent of its value against the dollar. Officials at the central bank said they were beavering away on a scheme to head off the *Tesobono* crunch by tempting holders to roll over their bonds rather than cashing them in. But it was taking time, and they did not *have* time; investors were dropping *Tesobonos* like hot bricks, buying hardly any new issues despite record interest rates of 20 percent.

Stock markets across Latin America were still plunging, partly because of blanket regional panic and partly because mutual fund managers faced with redemptions by their jittery clients had to raise money somewhere, and were trying to salvage profits in less shaky markets such as Brazil and Chile. January 10 saw the region's most volatile session since the devaluation. "Sales are happening without rhyme or reason," said one trader in Buenos Aires. "Everyone is dumping positions and scurrying for cover." Mexico's blue-chip IPC index was down more than 13 percent since the devaluation, and had only bounced back from an even greater rout because the state development bank, Nacional Financiera, had jumped in to buy stocks and support the market. Other regional *bolsas* had fared even worse; Argentina's Merval index was down more than 27 percent and Brazil's Bovespa had lost nearly 32 percent. The mood across the region was increasingly bitter. "We used to say Mexico was a country south of the United States," said a trader in São Paulo, Brazil's economic powerhouse. "It's now better known as a country north of Guatemala."

By now the tequila fumes had drifted across the Pacific and were making Asia's previously thriving markets totter. Rumours spread that other currencies that were pegged or semi-pegged – the Thai baht, the Hong Kong dollar, the Indonesian rupiah, the Philippine peso – might go the way of Mexico's peso. Asia analysts rushed to pooh-pooh the notion, pointing to the region's glittering growth rates, disciplined fiscal policy, high savings and low debt. "Anybody who compares Mexico with Hong Kong,

Thailand and Indonesia is basically not very well informed," said one Western economist based in Hong Kong, a comment he may have regretted three years later. Still, he had a point to the extent that foreign investors were tarring all emerging markets with the Mexican brush, irrespective of their fundamental economic conditions. As one Argentine economist said: "You can't expect foreign investment funds to differentiate when they're selling if they didn't differentiate when they bought."

The Asian shivers passed, but not before panic selling rocked the baht, rupiah and Singapore dollar and forced Hong Kong's monetary authorities to intervene to maintain the dollar peg. The Philippine forex market got so frenzied that trading had to be suspended for a cooling-off period. Stock markets fell in turn, with the Thai and South Korean indices tumbling 11 percent and Singapore's dropping 12 percent in the first three weeks of the new year.

Even US markets were starting to look edgy. The mighty dollar had already wavered on fears that Mexico would take up the credit lines offered by the United States and Canada, sending billions of dollars flooding into the international currency markets. Now Wall Street stocks were starting to feel the pinch amid concern that US banks would be hurt by Mexican and other emerging market losses. Anxious to stop the rot, the United States made another attempt to calm the markets with news that it was willing to expand the existing $18 billion rescue package. By mid-January President Bill Clinton and US congressional leaders had agreed on a massive support plan for Mexico worth up to $40 billion in government loan guarantees, which would enable Mexico to borrow from commercial banks at much lower interest rates than it could get on its own.

US officials stressed that the package was aimed at restoring investor confidence and averting a flood of short-term debt repayments, rather than actually guaranteeing Mexico's debt. "It's not a blank cheque," one official told journalists. "This is not a grant. It's not foreign aid." Former Treasury Secretary James Baker told a congressional committee that the Mexican crisis was a problem of cash flow rather than solvency, although it was ironic that in trying to distinguish the Tequila Crisis from the 1980s debt crunch, he ended up echoing the bland assurances of the mid-1980s. "Mexico is not bankrupt," he said. "Right now they've got a liquidity problem and they have a problem with confidence."

> 66 Anxious to stop the rot, the United States made another attempt to calm the markets 99

But the plan soon ran into opposition in Congress, which had to approve the bill. Democrats, many of whom had been anti-NAFTA for fear of losing US jobs, wanted to hold Mexico to stringent conditions including improved labour standards and political reforms. Republicans were outraged at any potential cost to US taxpayers. Opinion polls showed the deal was unpopular with the American public. The government warned that failure to help Mexico could weaken the fight against drug trafficking and spark a torrent of illegal immigration. Clinton insisted: "It isn't a bailout for Wall Street. There are a lot of pension plans and ordinary Americans that have their investments tied up there."

By the end of January it looked as though the rescue plan was dead in the water. Market confidence was crumbling further by the day, the peso plunged through 6.00 to the dollar, and the prospect of debt default no longer looked outlandish. Then Clinton pulled off an amazing piece of fancy footwork. Faced with Congress' refusal to pass the $40 billion plan as it stood, he almost immediately announced a fresh package centred on $20 billion from Washington's Exchange Stabilization Fund (ESF), a stock of money kept for forex market intervention. Withdrawals from the ESF did not need congressional approval (although some have argued that congressional leaders on both sides actually urged Clinton to tap the fund, allowing them to duck a difficult vote[8]). The $20 billion would go hand in hand with a $17.8 billion IMF deal – the Fund's biggest financing package ever – and a short-term loan of $10 billion from the Swiss-based Bank for International Settlements (BIS), often described as the central banks' central bank. Mexico would put up crude oil as collateral, and would be expected to meet a number of conditions including further budget cuts and more privatization to balance its books.

The medicine took immediate effect. The peso rebounded from around 6.50 to 5.75 per dollar, and Mexican Par bonds surged back towards pre-devaluation prices. Mexico's *bolsa* bounced up 10 percent – its biggest one-day rise in seven years – and stocks in Brazil, Argentina, Peru and Chile showed dramatic gains. Even Wall Street got a modest lift. Mexican newspaper headlines proclaimed "Viva Clinton!" A few days later it became clear just how close Mexico had been to the brink of disaster when central bank figures showed foreign reserves at the end of January had dwindled to just $3.48 billion.

THE HANGOVER

Of course, it was not quite that simple. A line had been drawn in the sand, but it was not until March that the Mexican markets really began to turn the corner, and months again before they could be said to be recovering. To cement investor confidence, the government was forced to launch an even tougher programme of shock therapy on the orthodox IMF pattern, including sharp spending and job cuts and steep increases in fuel prices and value-added tax. A total of $17 billion sluiced out of Mexico's markets in the 12 months to September 1995.[9] The stock market dropped by more than 75 percent in dollar terms between October 1994 and the end of March 1995, while market-determined *Cetes* interest rates carried on climbing to peak at around 75 percent in April. The peso never really recovered, weathering a further panic in October–November that briefly pushed it beyond 8.00 to the dollar before ending the year at 7.70 – less than half its pre-crisis value (*see* Figure 5).

The fallout for the Mexican population was crippling. Far from growing at 4 percent as the government had originally forecast, the economy shrank by more than 6 percent in 1995 – its worst drop in decades, notwithstanding the 1980s debt crisis, and one of the worst recessions to hit a single country since the 1930s. Inflation came in at nearly 52 per-

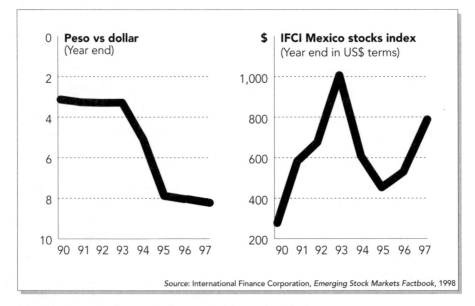

Source: International Finance Corporation, *Emerging Stock Markets Factbook*, 1998

FIGURE 5 Mexican rollercoaster: the peso and the stock market

cent for the year, with prices rocketing not only for imported goods but for basics such as tortillas, the staple food for many people. Commercial lending rates soared above 100 percent at times, forcing some people to sell their cars or other major possessions just to pay off their credit card debts. Tens of thousands of small businesses closed down, and more than a million workers lost their jobs in the first four months of 1995 alone. Crowds thronged pawnbrokers' offices daily to trade in watches, jewellery and other valuables for cash. Mexico City fell hostage to its worst ever crime wave. By 1996 the number of Mexicans living below the poverty line had shot up to nearly 42 million, or 45 percent of the population – far worse even than in the slump of the 1980s.[10] And the effects were lasting; in mid-1999 the World Bank's chief economist, Joseph Stiglitz, said Mexican wages were still not back to where they had been in real terms before the crash.

For most other countries the economic impact of Mexico's troubles was limited. Much of Latin America performed as though there had never been a crisis. Brazil's economy grew by around 4 percent in 1995, Peru's by nearly 7 percent, and Chile's by more than 8 percent. There was one major exception, however: Argentina. On the face of it, it had little in common with Mexico. The two countries had few financial or trade links. Argentina's recent growth had been stellar at between 6 and 9 percent a year, public debt was moderate and mainly long term, and the current-account deficit was only 3.5 percent of GDP in 1994, less than half that of Mexico.

But economists had already been fretting that the Argentine peso was too strong for its own good, and in the panicky Tequila climate the current-account gap was big enough to raise concern over the currency. Cavallo's 1991 reform had revived a little-known monetary system known as the currency board, which made a brief appearance in 1918 in White Russia (on the advice of John Maynard Keynes) and became common in Europe's prewar colonies, but by then was used only in Hong Kong. The mechanism required Argentina to fix its peso (which replaced the shambling austral) at parity with the dollar, and back every peso in circulation with a dollar in its reserves. The country effectively surrendered control of its own monetary policy; interest rates would bob up and down automatically to balance currency demand, and the government lost the right to print any more money unless it was matched by extra dollars. In return Argentina was rewarded with stability, near-zero inflation, and healthy economic growth.

Strictly speaking, Argentina's currency board made the peso highly immune to attack because the country had to have enough dollars in reserve to cover every single peso in circulation. But any big shift from pesos into dollars would automatically mean escalating interest rates and a vice-like squeeze on the country's monetary base, raising the spectre of recession. Doubts set in that the government would have the political will to maintain the dollar peg at its one-to-one rate.

Cavallo held the line, touring the world's major financial centres to try to persuade investors that Argentina was not Mexico. But the Tequila Effect sparked a run on the Argentine banks as nervous savers switched into dollars to be on the safe side. Between mid-December 1994 and the end of February 1995, 7 percent of deposits in the entire banking system were withdrawn; the following month a further 8 percent were taken out.[11] At the same time, at least $5 billion poured out of the country's international reserves as both Argentine and foreign investors turned tail. And because the central bank could not print pesos unless they were backed by dollars, it was unable to act as lender of last resort and pump more cash into the system. Fears of a banking collapse intensified the outward stampede of capital, while the resulting credit squeeze and escalating interest rates slammed the economy into reverse.

> 66 Argentina's currency board made the peso highly immune to attack, but doubts set in that the government would have the political will to maintain the dollar peg at its one-to-one rate 99

So confident had Argentina been before the Tequila Crisis that it had voluntarily given up the last two portions of an earlier IMF loan, saying it could tap the international capital markets at will. Now, like Mexico, it urgently needed outside help. With May elections fast approaching, President Carlos Menem gambled his political future by announcing tax increases and other austerity measures designed to win crucial IMF backing. It paid off. He was rewarded with a support package of $6.7 billion, consisting partly of fresh funds from the IMF, World Bank and Inter-American Development Bank, and partly of a new "Argentine bond" subscribed to by local businesses and foreign banks. The package managed to rebuild some investor confidence, while swift adjustments and reforms in the banking sector headed off a fully fledged banking crash. The price was deep recession, with the economy shrinking by around 2.5 percent in 1995.

ASPIRIN AND AMNESIA – THE INVESTORS RETURN

The first half of 1995 was difficult for emerging market currencies, stocks and bonds across the board, with the IFCI Composite falling by 60 percent between October 1994 and the end of March 1995. The dollar, too, went through a lean period, dropping to historic lows against the yen and the mark. Many analysts said the Tequila Crisis was at least partly to blame as investors worried that the United States would be dragged into providing even more financial support for Mexico.

However, things picked up remarkably quickly and by the end of 1995 the Tequila Crisis was as good as over, at least as far as the markets were concerned. (The Argentine civil servants who rioted over their 40 percent pay cut were probably less convinced.) Far from sulking for years or even decades after getting their fingers burned, as they had after earlier crises, investors soon showed themselves more than willing to lend to Latin America again. Brazil romped back on to the international bond market with two hefty Eurobond issues in May and June 1995, and Argentina got a Eurobond issue away in August. Even Mexico was forgiven with unprecedented speed; by July 1995, demand for the government's new, floating-rate bond was so high that the issue was doubled to $1 billion. In the end the country had to draw on only $12.5 billion of the US support that was offered, and by late 1995 it had started paying that back ahead of schedule out of bond proceeds.

Stock market losses were pared, and by the end of 1995 the IFCI Composite was down by just under 14 percent for the year. Mexico's stock market ended the year some 17 percent up in peso terms, although the devaluation meant it was worth nearly 26 percent less in dollar terms. Some of the biggest market falls had little to do with Mexico; Taiwanese stocks, for example, were ground down by a series of bank scandals. In the secondary debt market, the widely watched EMBI+ index published by investment bank J.P. Morgan, which measures total returns on a wide range of hard-currency Bradies, Eurobonds and other debt instruments, ended 1995 some 27 percent higher. Still, it was a subdued year; bond inflows to emerging markets held steady, but the flow of capital to emerging equities dropped by nearly a third compared with 1994.[12]

Investors were regaining their nerve, and the lure of high growth and high potential returns started to reassert itself. In a survey by *Euromoney* magazine in December 1995, 70 percent of the top mutual funds polled said they would increase their exposure to emerging markets over the coming year, although the amount remained very low as a proportion of their total investment. "Since the Mexican crisis, investors have become more aware of how emerging market economies work, and the fundamentals still look good," it quoted one chief executive officer as saying. Lower share prices in countries hit by the crisis now seemed to offer attractive bargains, especially as the Mexican economy was starting to show signs of export-led growth under its new exchange rate, and Argentina was on the mend. The continued opening of Chinese markets and widespread privatization in Central and Eastern Europe were also attracting more and more attention.

The post-mortems soon began as economists and politicians tried to pick over the lessons of the Mexican meltdown. As early as March 1995, Zedillo pointed out that Mexico was the first emerging market to confront the growing power and speed of the global financial markets, an issue that would lead to far more heated debate a few years later. "It is obvious that the speed at which international financial markets have evolved over the last 25 years has been much faster than the capacity of governments and international organizations to cope," he told *The New York Times* in an interview. "We have a new, global agreement on trade. But we don't have a new financial arrangement. So there's something missing there, and that's very dangerous for the world."[13]

Fuentes elaborated on the same theme, noting that the debt negotiations of the 1980s had been carried out with a finite number of bank syndicates (albeit each composed of many banks); now the creditors were millions of individual bond holders. "Today, to meet with its aggrieved parties, Mexico would have to rent Yankee stadium," he wrote. "We are dealing with management funds that are uncontrollable, volatile, and enamoured of the short term – enemies of productive investment, they are so diversified that whatever happens in Mexico affects the economies of Brazil and Hong Kong. Large corporations are involved, but so, too, are millions of individual investors, banking portfolios, and insurance, mutual, and pension funds. This type of capital easily eludes oversight either by governments or by institutions like the International Monetary Fund and the World Bank."[14]

> **The post-mortems soon began as economists and politicians tried to pick over the lessons of the Mexican meltdown**

The IMF took a different tack, arguing that it was mainly Mexican investors who rushed to sell off peso-denominated stocks, bonds and

other assets in the two weeks *before* the devaluation, whereas most foreigners got in on the act only after December 20. Nevertheless,
Henderson relates that foreign speculators were clearly in play just before
the devaluation, with a sudden rise in trading volumes for previously
illiquid options contracts that could be used to short the currency.[15]

True, local players will often be first to act on fears of a devaluation;
import businesses may rush to buy more dollars than usual, for example,
while exporters hold on to their foreign exchange. Their actions can certainly tip the market off-balance. But the kind of rout suffered by Mexico's
peso does not come about just because local businesses and investors lose
confidence. It is the circling speculators that go in for the kill.

Most of the post-mortems focused on what, if anything, had gone wrong
in Mexico, and how similar crises could be avoided. One criticism – that
the devaluation came as a greater shock because the Mexican authorities
had not been open about their dwindling foreign reserves – was swiftly
remedied: the central bank not only started including its reserves figures
in its weekly accounts but posted the information on an Internet web site.

Many commentators tried to single out characteristics of Mexico's economy that investors should regard as warning signs: a growing current-
account imbalance, an expanding money supply, a large short-term debt
burden, a high reliance on volatile portfolio investment flows. In fact,
some of Asia's shining miracle economies were already showing some of
these features. Thailand, for example, was running a current-account
deficit of nearly 6 percent of GDP in 1994 and had a substantial bulk of
short-term debt. Yet many analysts were still quick to argue that the Mexican crisis would not be repeated in Asia, where financial management was
held to be superior. Latin America's mistake had been to channel capital
inflows into consumption, said the World Bank's chief economist at the
time, Michael Bruno, while Asia turned them to productive investment.

But there was also a widespread feeling that neither the severity nor the
extent of the crisis was entirely justified by economic fundamentals, particularly in Argentina's case. Mexico may have been a crisis waiting to
happen, but did it deserve such a pounding? In a comparative study in
1996, economists Jeffrey Sachs, Aaron Tornell and Andrés Velasco concluded that the countries worst hit by the Tequila Effect had shown
"some degree of previous misbehavior" – specifically, a combination of
an overvalued currency, a weak banking system and low foreign reserves
in relation to the weight of short-term debt commitments. But they went
on: "At the same time … an important element of self-fulfilling panic, or

contagion, is evident in the aftermath of the Mexican crisis. Crises that could have occurred, did not, before the Mexican events. Most visibly, the Argentine banking crisis … almost surely would not have occurred without the provocation of Tequila."[16]

It was only really later that one of the biggest legacies of the Tequila Crisis became apparent: the false sense of security it engendered. Although the sell-off rocked the stock and secondary bond markets, the rescue package ensured that Mexico was able to honour all the debts that were coming due, and most private creditors were spared losses. "This experience may have encouraged excessive optimism about the risks of lending to emerging markets," the World Bank noted later.[17] Krugman said too many commentators at the time blamed the crunch on Mexico's peculiarities alone. "And so, perversely, what might have been seen as a warning instead became, if anything, a source of complacency," he wrote. "The lesson taken, in short, was that Mexico's debacle was of little relevance to the rest of the world."[18] What was more, many saw the resolution of the crisis as proof that the United States and the IMF were well equipped to douse any similar financial fires in the future.

There was another reason why investors flocked back so quickly to the emerging markets: the sheer frenzy of the modern financial industry, the lightning speed of communications and news delivery, and the information overkill that now swamps us all. The world has, quite simply, got faster. "Memory in the financial markets is a very short-term concept," wrote Henderson. "Dealers sitting at their desks, screaming in the phone, are bombarded with a wealth of data and news, the likes of which has never before been experienced by humanity. News items are used and discarded at frightening speed … Those who said Asia was different were also the kind who forgot what Mexico was like before the crisis, when confidence was not high but stratospheric."[19]

A high price would be paid for that forgetfulness.

NOTES

1   Fuentes, *A New Time for Mexico*, p. xiii; p. 122.

2   Henderson, *Asia Falling*, p. 64.

3   Fuentes, p. 164.

4   Mobius, *Passport to Profits*, p. 167.

5   Krugman, *The Return of Depression Economics*, p. 52.

6   Henderson, p. 68.

7   Friedman, *The Lexus and the Olive Tree*, p. 114.

8   *See*, for example, Berkeley's Brad DeLong in his review of Krugman.

9   Bank of Mexico web site, http://www.banxico.org.mx

10 World Bank, *Global Economic Prospects 2000*, p. 52.

11 Sachs, Tornell and Velasco, *Financial Crises in Emerging Markets: the lessons from 1995*, p. 43.

12 World Bank, *Global Development Finance 1999*, p. 24.

13 *The New York Times*, March 13, 1995.

14 Fuentes, p. 137.

15 Henderson, p. 68.

16 Sachs, Tornell and Velasco, p. 28.

17 World Bank, *Global Development Finance 1999*, p. 91.

18 Krugman, p. 57.

19 Henderson, p. 60.

4

ASIAN FLU

Those who cannot remember the past are condemned to repeat it – George Santayana, *The Life of Reason*

LET THE GOOD TIMES ROLL –
EMERGING MARKETS REBOUND

By 1996, the good times were back with a vengeance for emerging markets. The Tequila hangover had worn off and a rampant bull run on Wall Street was generating a slab of wealth that was ripe for reinvestment. Far more money was flooding into emerging markets than ever before; private debt and equity inflows reached $150 billion in 1996 – half as much again as in the pre-Tequila peak year of 1993 – and kept on escalating into 1997.[1] Global forex traders, too, were becoming interested in fresh money-making opportunities in more volatile markets as major Western European currencies began falling into line with each other ahead of economic and monetary union (EMU). "Emerging market investing had become mainstream," wrote Charles Clough, Merrill Lynch's chief investment strategist, in a rueful retrospective. "Asia in particular, was investor paradise, growth was for ever."[2]

Stocks were surging, as long as you picked the right country. Although Wall Street's blue-chip Dow Jones Industrial Average had shot up 26 percent in 1996 – prompting Federal Reserve chairman Alan Greenspan to warn of "irrational exuberance" – several emerging stock markets did even better. Venezuela rocketed 118 percent in dollar terms, Hungary 100 percent, and Poland 72 percent.[3]

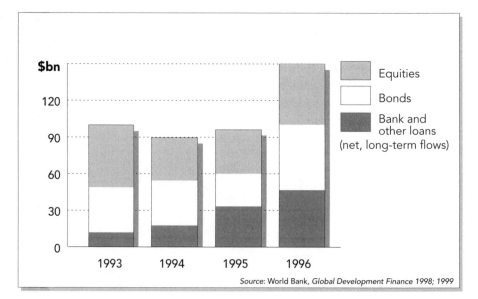

FIGURE 6 More cash: foreign portfolio investment in emerging markets

It seemed everyone, from small sovereign borrowers such as Croatia and Moldova to cities like Buenos Aires and Moscow, was issuing bonds and finding plenty of willing buyers. Even some emerging market companies, a doubly risky prospect for investors, were getting bonds out; corporate debt issuance exploded from $2.1 billion in 1991 to $23 billion in 1996 and $36 billion in 1997.[4] By September 1997 the spread between yields on US Treasury bonds and those offered by Brady Bonds – representing the extra risk priced into emerging market debt – had shrunk to around 350 basis points (3.5 percentage points) compared with a yawning 1,600 basis points in early 1995 at the height of the Tequila Crisis. (A basis point, or one-hundredth of a percentage point, is the market's standard measure for bond yields and interest rates.) Essentially, this meant investors were taking a far more relaxed attitude to emerging market risks. And since the Brady Bond scene is dominated by Latin American issues, it meant the region was well and truly back on the investment map.

In fact, it was offering some of the best bets. The IFC's Investable index for Latin America rose twice as fast as the broad Composite index in 1996. Six months into 1997, the Brazilian stock market was already up 79 percent on the year; Peru was up 40 percent, and Mexico up 33 percent. Brazil, in particular, was riding high, fired up by a bumper privatization programme that was just starting to hit its stride. Latin America's sprawling giant pulled in one-fifth of all emerging market privatization proceeds in 1996;[5] more foreign capital flowed into Brazil in January 1996 alone than in the whole of the previous year.[6]

But the hottest new investment scoop was Russia, a shambling giant that was still struggling to fit into its new capitalist clothes. The re-election in July 1996 of President Boris Yeltsin, who saw off Communist Party challenger Gennady Zyuganov, reassured investors that the country would stick to the free-market path. The impression was cemented by a new funding agreement with the IMF. The rouble was stable after years of decline, annual inflation had been dragged down from triple digits to just over 20 percent, and short-term interest rates were falling. Foreign direct investment remained paltry, but portfolio investors started leaping on to the Russian bandwagon, taking advantage of dirt-cheap assets. Russia's natural resources and economic potential were huge. Besides, the country's strategic importance was so great that surely the West would not *let* it fail. It seemed like a one-way bet, and no one wanted to be left out. "There is now more money that wants to come to Russia than there are places to put it," Andrew Bulgarnie, head of Morgan Stanley's Moscow operation, told *Euromoney* magazine.[7]

In November 1996 Russia tapped the international capital markets for the first time since the 1917 revolution with the biggest ever debut Eurobond issue by a sovereign state: $1 billion. Russian stock prices outperformed the world, shooting up 156 percent in dollar terms,[8] while prices for some dollar-denominated debt exploded by 200 percent. It was more of the same in 1997. Russian stocks were world-beaters again, rising 129 percent in the first half of the year alone; bond issuance multiplied sixfold, pulling in funds for a slew of banks, industrial firms and local authorities. Sibneft (a Siberian oil company) and Nizhny Novgorod (a region east of Moscow) became household names in the bond business. "By summer 1997 investors appeared to be buying Russian securities indiscriminately," the EBRD said in a later report.[9]

> ❝ The hottest new investment scoop was Russia, a shambling giant that was still struggling to fit into its new capitalist clothes ❞

So what if the Russian economy was still shrinking, Yeltsin looked as though he was at death's door, the government could not collect its taxes, and business revolved around graft? Ordinary people were bowed down by unemployment and crime, but the elite "New Russians" were doing just fine, thank you. Moscow's dour, post-communist grey was punctuated by bright advertising signs, sleek cars, and glamorous shopping malls. International banks and businesses were opening Moscow offices as fast as their dollars could carry them, shipping in phalanxes of expatriates and recruiting bright young locals. One investment chief recounted how he won contracts with Siberian gas bosses on the strength of how much vodka he could drink at one sitting.[10] Money was ample and the nightlife was wild. Humorist P.J. O'Rourke describes a visit to the infamous Hungry Duck bar:

A thousand twentysomethings – Americans, Russians, Germans, British, French, Australians, Japanese; the foot-soldier employees of the corporations that have invaded Moscow, the Anne Kleined and Brooks Brothered sentinels who man the mouse pads and keyboards of capitalism's front lines – were having a Thursday night screen saver. Happy youth was pressed breast to pec in one raving mass while fifty people danced on the bar top and giggling waitresses passed out free vodka shots from some booze company promoting a new brand. Ties were yanked off. Blouses were unbuttoned. Beer spills were whipped to foam by flapping loafer tassels. Arms waved in the air. Legs waved in the air. Whole bodies fluttered in the smoky space above the crowd. And on the sound system, through speakers so big they would have done Stalin proud and played at volume enough to wake the old shit in his grave, Coolio sang 'Gangsta's Paradise'.[11]

In Asia, the boom spirit was still thriving. Skyscrapers were *de rigueur* across the region, and Kuala Lumpur snatched the claim to the world's tallest buildings as the gleaming, 88-storey Petronas Twin Towers neared completion. China's free-market bonanza was turning cities such as Shanghai and Guangzhou, not to mention brand new economic centres like Shenzhen, into giant construction sites. More than 600 new cars were hitting the choking streets of the Thai capital every day,[12] and the real estate market was exploding. Bangkok, which only 25 years before had been a graceful town of canals, temples and palaces, had become a jungle of cranes, flyovers and concrete skeletons climbing into the smoggy sky. "The new business elite of Bangkok was born, mobile phone in hand, dapperly dressed, driving a Mercedes, and eating at only the finest establishments," wrote Henderson.[13]

South Korean and Taiwanese companies were stretching their limbs, setting up car or computer factories as far away as Britain and Poland to be nearer to their major markets. Hong Kong's imminent handover from British to Chinese rule at the end of June 1997 put no dampener on the territory's stock market, where "red-chip" shares in mainland Chinese companies were selling furiously, nor on stratospheric property prices: tiny flats in unfashionable areas were selling for $500,000. The glittering designer shops along Hong Kong's Chater Road and Singapore's Orchard Road were doing brisk trade. Stephen Fay describes the scene in Singapore's pristine financial district: "Standing in Raffles Place, at the heart of the financial centre, you are penned in by soaring towers of shiny steel, of grey and bronze marble, and of bleached concrete, rising between fifty and sixty storeys. These skyscrapers, which would dwarf anything in London, would not look out of place in New York or Chicago."[14]

THE ASIAN MIRACLE TARNISHES

But underneath the bonnet, something in the Asian engine was starting to misfire.

Most East Asian currencies were tied directly or indirectly to the dollar, which had been bumping along the ground ever since it collapsed against the yen in the mid-1980s. As a direct result, the Tiger economies were handed the gift of international competitiveness on a plate, embarking on an export boom to the huge North American and European markets at the expense of more highly priced Japanese goods. But in 1995 the dollar suddenly staged a comeback when determined forex intervention by the Fed wrong-footed the market and reversed the greenback's decline. A Japanese interest rate cut set the seal on the turnaround. From lows of less than 80 yen in April, the dollar surged to more than 100 yen by the end of the year and finished 1996 around 116 yen – some 45 percent stronger than its lowest point. Other Asian currencies ascended with it.

Japanese exporters were suddenly back in the game, but they were not the only competitors in the neighbourhood. China was honing its international edge through structural reforms and an effective devaluation of the yuan in 1994 that made its exports cheaper at a stroke. What was more, the dollar had also rebounded against the mark and other major European currencies. Through no action of their own, most Asian countries suddenly lost competitiveness against Japan and China in major world markets. They might have hoped to sell more to the Japanese, whose buying power was suddenly enhanced. But Japan was used to running a fat trade surplus with the rest of the world, and its protectionist habits – a bone of bitter contention with the United States – meant its domestic market was too closed to take up the slack in Asian production.

Few people were really paying attention; they were too busy raving about the Asian Miracle, and in any case export growth in the main emerging Asian economies was bouncing along at exuberant levels, averaging well over 20 percent in 1995. But to make matters worse, a global glut of computer chips – to which Taiwanese and South Korean production had enthusiastically contributed – slashed export prices. And storming growth had pushed up Asian wages, without a commensurate rise in productivity. Tiger workforces were becoming more expensive, and foreign companies were moving on to poorer pastures in China, Vietnam or Bangladesh.

Suddenly, in 1996, the Tigers' exports sprinted into a brick wall. South Korea's export growth plunged from 32 percent the previous year to just over 4 percent, and Malaysia's from 26 percent to 9 percent. Thailand was worst hit, showing barely a whimper of export growth compared to a confident 25 percent in 1995; in fact, its traditional footwear and clothing exports fell sharply. Inevitably this had a knock-on effect on current-account balances, which were already being squeezed by rapid import growth in a region that had been used to years of healthy trade surpluses. Governments urged their citizens to tighten their belts but did little on fiscal or monetary policy to rein in demand. South Korea's current-account deficit ballooned from 1 percent of GDP in 1991–95 to 5 percent in 1996. Thailand's was steadier, but that was cold comfort considering the gap was already vast, at around 8 percent of GDP.

That was not all. East Asians were still saving a higher proportion of their incomes than anywhere else in the world, but they were investing even more. Domestic savings averaged more than 30 percent of GDP in Thailand, South Korea and Malaysia in the mid-1990s, but investment rates were topping 40 percent of GDP. That might sound like good news, but there were a couple of problems.

Obviously, the extra capital had to be borrowed from abroad. One Tiger economy after another had opened up and deregulated its financial sector with the encouragement of the Washington establishment, and since international interest rates were lower than domestic rates, it was not only possible but very worthwhile for Asian firms to take out offshore loans. What's more, enterprising Asian banks and "finance companies" (which ran on political connections and could often circumvent local bank lending regulations) were able to borrow hard currency, exchange it for local currency and lend the money on domestically at higher rates. South Korean banks even lent across the region.

> 66 Suddenly, in 1996, the Tigers' exports sprinted into a brick wall 99

Government guarantees for the loans were implicit, given the close links between state and business, and the big Japanese and other international banks were falling over each other to lend. "It was so easy to have money," Thai politician and businessman Narongchai Akrasanee told journalist Robert Garran. "Every time I wanted to borrow money, I would have all these investment bankers offering much more than I could absorb. So I ended up with indigestion."[15] (Sound familiar?)

By 1997 the private sector accounted for well over half of Thai and Indonesian foreign debt, and a staggering 90 percent of South Korea's external obligations.[16] The borrowers were opening up an immense risk for themselves if exchange rates shifted, particularly as the off-shore loans were usually short term and would need to be rolled over regularly. But because many Asian currencies in the slipstream of the dollar had been so stable for so long, they came to take exchange rate stability for granted. Few insured against their currency risk by hedging (taking opposite currency positions in the financial markets that would cancel out the effect of a shift). Besides, borrowers as well as lenders were assuming the government would see them right if anything went wrong.

Even worse, the quality of the investment itself was no longer all it should have been. At first, capital had flowed into industry, often to the point of building huge excess capacity. But as the boom continued, much of it was poured willy-nilly into the speculative real estate and stock market bubbles that swelled across the region. Across the Tiger economies, banks and finance companies were lending hand over fist to get-rich-quick developers and white-elephant projects such as golf courses and country clubs. By 1996 nearly 15 percent of property in Bangkok and Jakarta was lying empty, yet new office and apartment blocks were still being thrown up.[17] Inflows of capital from abroad not only fuelled the speculative frenzy in their own right but also fanned the flames by encouraging an explosion of domestic credit. Slack financial regulation and cronyism made matters worse.

So much for the conventional wisdom that Asian financial management was somehow superior to that of other regions. By mid-1997 Thai banks already had on their books an estimated $15 billion in bad debts owed by property developers.[18] The bubble had to burst, just as Japan's had at the start of the decade.

THAILAND TRIPS

It was no coincidence that two of the worst performing emerging stock markets in 1996 were South Korea's, which lost 39 percent in dollar terms, and Thailand's, which plunged 41 percent to approach four-year lows. The Thai nosedive had begun with nerves over political instability. A crescendo of bribery and corruption scandals had brought down the government of Prime minister Banharn Silpa-archa in September 1996; but the ensuing elections, riddled with vote-rigging and violence, had done little to reassure the markets that the Thai economy was in either capable or honest hands under new premier Chavalit Yongchaiyudh. The Thai baht weathered several speculative attacks in 1996 as devaluation rumours started to circulate. But the government insisted it would keep the exchange rate system unchanged, allowing the currency to move by up to two satang (that is, by two one-hundredths of a baht) on either side of a daily mid-point, which was fixed by the Bank of Thailand against a currency basket dominated by the dollar.

By early 1997 a rash of major corporate defaults was rattling South Korea's financial system, Thai stocks were crumbling further as the property bubble burst, and other South-East Asian markets were following Bangkok south. Some far-sighted observers worried aloud about the direction Thailand was taking. "Thailand is exhibiting many of the features that characterized the run-up to Mexico's troubles – a large current-account deficit, high levels of short-term debt and an overvalued currency," *Euromoney* journalist Brian Caplen wrote in September 1996. "And the Thai government seems to be taking no short-term measures to solve the problems."

But most of the research reports churned out by international banks and think-tanks glossed over the potential problems in favour of optimistic conclusions; even those that were nervous on Thailand did not antici-pate the full consequences if the house of cards did tumble. "Another stellar year of growth nonetheless," predicted the London-based Econo-mist Intelligence Unit in its Thailand forecast for 1997.[19] Morgan Stanley's Barton Biggs wrote in January 1997: "Thailand is not Mexico in late 1994 ... On the numbers, Thailand qualifies for the EMU and looks healthier than Germany."[20] The major credit rating agencies were main-taining a sunny view, with investment-grade ratings implying a fair degree of security on Thai, Malaysian, South Korean and even Indone-sian sovereign debt.

Complacency was prevalent: most foreigners went along with the cliché that Asians were prudent and hardworking, and Asians were not inclined to disagree. The budgets of most East Asian countries were modestly in surplus, and governments had borrowed little abroad; the looming mountain of private sector foreign borrowing was rarely addressed. "It was a classic case of elementary economic fundamentals," wrote Henderson. "[B]ut if economic history teaches us two things it is that (1) markets never learn from their mistakes (partly because the twenty-eight-year-old who gets fired for making the mistake is replaced by a twenty-two-year-old with no experience and more importantly no history) and (2) in the passionate throes of economic excess, fundamentals are forgotten entirely."[21]

Nevertheless, out on the fringes of the herd some speculators had started to scent blood. The baht came under increasing pressure in early 1997 as a bond default by a major property developer, and the collapse of Thailand's biggest finance company, began to reveal the colossal extent of highly leveraged exposure to the now crumbing real estate sector. Confidence took another knock in February when credit rating agency Moody's said it was considering downgrading Thailand's foreign currency debt, an announcement that sparked a panicky 4.5 percent tumble on the Bangkok stock exchange. For ten years the baht had remained rock-steady at between 24.5 and 25.5 to the dollar; now it slipped through 26.

❝ Even those that were nervous on Thailand did not anticipate the full consequences if the house of cards did tumble ❞

The Bank of Thailand was determined to fend off the attacks, not least because of the dire consequences of a devaluation for all the banks and companies that had borrowed abroad, many of them with persuasive personal connections to Thai ministers and top officials. It had two major weapons at its disposal: sizeable foreign reserves, which amounted to nearly $39 billion at the end of 1996, and the ability to force up local money market interest rates. The latter could make life very uncomfortable for speculators trying to borrow baht in order to sell the currency short.

The next big assault came in mid-May. Persistent devaluation rumours had persuaded some of the big Thai companies to hedge their exposure to the baht by buying dollars several months further ahead than they usually would for business purposes. Hedge funds and other speculators saw a chink in the baht's armour and pounced. They were joined by frightened Thai corporates, and their combined selling pressure in both spot and forward contracts drove the currency down from 26 to the dollar to as low as 26.60 in a single day.

But the Bank of Thailand struck back quickly, delivering a knockout one-two to the market's chin. Not only did it intervene strongly to sell dollars for baht, but it got its friends to do the same. Suddenly the Singapore Monetary Authority was also buying baht; so, traders suggested, were the Hong Kong Monetary Authority (HKMA) and Malaysia's central Bank Negara. (In fact, the other authorities were using Thailand's foreign reserves to intervene, but traders could not immediately be sure of that and the united Asian front sent out a powerful message not to mess with the baht.)

Then the Thai central bank effectively imposed capital controls by ordering domestic banks not to lend to offshore parties. This left foreign speculators with short baht positions high and dry, unable to find Thai currency to square their market positions. "With suddenly no liquidity to borrow offshore and the need to instantly cover positions to avoid massive losses, many panicked," wrote Henderson, who as an Asian currency analyst had a ringside seat for the turmoil. "Some screamed into their phones, into the broker boxes for anyone who would lend them baht in any form; some swore and threw their chairs across the dealing room; others just looked dazed at their screens."[22] The only place they could get hold of baht was through the money market from the central bank, which hammered them with punitive interest rates equivalent to 1,000 percent or more on an annual basis.

The baht quickly bounced back as battered speculators limped off to lick their wounds. According to Henderson, some bank's proprietary trading desks were suddenly some $50–60 million poorer, while hedge funds lost an estimated $450 million. Word had it that Soros had been badly burned; the financier said there had been "some exaggerated rumours".

The baht was not the only emerging market currency to have a rough time that month. Over in Europe, the Czech crown also received a kicking. The Czech Republic had been held up as a shining example of a relatively smooth transition from communism, but growth had started to falter and the current-account gap was soaring. Besides, emerging market players were feeling jittery about the strengthening yen and the prospect of rising Japanese interest rates, as many had borrowed cheaply in yen to fund their trading activities. After propping up the crown with intervention for a couple of weeks to keep it within its official trading band, the Czechs caved in and let the currency float freely. It promptly weakened about 10 percent.

The Bank of Thailand had won the battle, but it had not won the war. It had spent around $4 billion of the country's foreign reserves in May alone to defend the baht in the spot forex market, and the country's underlying economic problems had not changed. In fact, the situation was even worse than it looked, as the fall in foreign reserves understated the size of the intervention. In August it emerged that the central bank had also run up a vast forward-market position, committing it to deliver more than $23 billion at a later date – a huge chunk of what was left in the country's coffers.

When the speculators charged again, the Bank of Thailand finally gave way. On June 30, Prime Minister Chavalit assured the nation in a televised address that there would be no devaluation. Two days later, instead of announcing the daily pegged baht rate, the central bank said it would no longer defend the peg and would move to a managed float. The Thai currency dropped like a stone and ended the day as low as 29 to the dollar in offshore trading, an effective devaluation of 15–20 percent.

The plunge spelt disaster for banks and companies that had borrowed in hard currency and were already plagued by debt problems. But the Thai stock market, relieved to have the devaluation business out of the way, rallied sharply on the news. In the heat of the moment, many analysts played down the significance of the float. "This should remain a local or at best a regional story," said one senior bank economist. "There may be some spin-offs in Indonesia, Malaysia and possibly the Philippines, as these countries have lost significant competitiveness, but this is not another Mexico."

> **The market had proved it could beat an Asian central bank into submission. Now it was eager to pick another fight**

In fact, it turned out to be far bigger than Mexico – it was the catalyst for an emerging markets panic that would last nearly two years and drag down a trail of other currencies in its wake. But the economist could be forgiven for arguing that, in principle at least, it should not have had the catastrophic effect it did.

THE DOMINOES START TO TOPPLE

The market had proved it could beat an Asian central bank into submission. Now it was eager to pick another fight, and its beady eye fixed on Thailand's South-East Asian neighbours. After all, in Mobius' words: "What global currency traders spend a great deal of time doing is probing for weaknesses in a nation's defences."[23]

Taken in isolation, nothing had changed overnight in the economies of Malaysia, Indonesia or the Philippines between July 1 and July 2. But they were in direct competition with Thailand in world export markets, and the weaker baht had suddenly given Thai goods a strong edge. The fact that the Thais had abandoned their currency peg, after vowing so strongly to defend it, called into question the will of other countries to maintain similar exchange rate regimes. Jittery market conditions meant foreign lenders became more wary of rolling over short-term loans to private sector borrowers, whether the firms and banks were in good shape or not. For people doing real business in the region, these were warning signals; the worry was that they could get caught out on the wrong side of another snap devaluation, or find their loans abruptly called in. For currency speculators, they were meat and drink.

Within a week the rupiah was starting to slide, and the Philippine and Malaysian central banks were having to intervene aggressively to defend the peso and the ringgit. On July 11 the Philippines crumbled after spending an estimated $2 billion – nearly one-fifth of its reserves – on intervention in less than two weeks. In principle the peso already floated freely, but in practice the central bank kept a firm hand on exchange rates; now it announced it would let the currency move in a wider range against the dollar. The peso immediately sank more than 11 percent, adding to the regional malaise.

On the same Friday, the Indonesian central bank said it was widening the intervention band that kept the rupiah steady against a dollar-dominated basket of currencies. Henceforth it would allow a daily fluctuation of up to 12 percent, from the previous 8 percent. It was playing the same game that Mexico had initially tried, hoping to relieve some of the pressure rather than opening the floodgates. But within days the rupiah was challenging its new limits.

The following Monday, Bank Negara threw in the towel. Although it made no official announcement, it stopped intervening to support the ringgit at its pegged level, which had also been tied to a currency basket composed predominantly of dollars. Let off the leash, the currency dropped to its weakest for almost three years. Although the central bank would continue to step into the market from time to time, the peg had effectively been set aside.

Soon the Singapore dollar, usually a bulwark of stability, was being battered. But the currency peg of the affluent city-state had always been more flexible than those of its neighbours, and instead of fighting, the Singapore dollar rolled with the punches. On July 24, all five major South-East Asian currencies crashed through psychological barriers to new lows against the dollar. By now, general confidence in the region was in pieces; the nature of the selling had gone beyond a speculative play into full-blown fear. At an ASEAN meeting, Malaysian Prime Minister Mahathir Mohamad launched into a bitter public attack on "rogue speculators", accusing them of being "anarchists wanting to destroy weak countries … to force us all to submit to the dictatorship of international manipulators". It was a theme he would return to at length.

So far the Hong Kong dollar, pegged rigidly to the dollar under a currency board system, had appeared unaffected by the turmoil to the south. But the territory later revealed that it spent $1 billion on intervention during a single two-hour period on an unspecified day in July. The sharks were starting to test wider waters.

Indonesia managed to hold on to its expanded band for longer than Mexico, but after a month the pressure was too much to bear. On August 14 the band was abolished and the rupiah immediately plunged to 2,755 to the dollar – nearly 12 percent weaker than it had been before the Thai devaluation. Indonesian companies that had believed the official, no-devaluation message were aghast and scrambled desperately for dollars to help them pay their foreign debts, driving the rupiah lower still. By the end of the month it was pushing 3,000 to the dollar.

Stock markets were continuing to fall across South-East Asia as confidence evaporated and sinking currencies undermined the attractiveness of shares. On August 28, Malaysia took up the cudgels against speculators by imposing restrictions on selling stocks short. It was a disastrous step; long-term investors who might have held on to their shares read the move as a harbinger of further market and capital controls, and sold off while they could. Besides, who was to say on the spot whether someone was selling short, or just selling up?

> **❝ In less than two months, four currency pegs had snapped like twigs and a fifth had been badly buffeted ❞**

The stock market suffered one of its largest drops in history; the restrictions were hastily lifted the next day. It seemed whatever Asian governments did, they were destined to be trampled by the herd.

In less than two months, four currency pegs had snapped like twigs and a fifth had been badly buffeted. Mexico had its pre-Tequila earthquake; now the Asian crisis had its own baleful metaphor – a choking smog from uncontrolled forest fires that smothered the whole of South-East Asia. The fires were in Indonesia; had they blazed in Thailand, the symbolism would have been perfect.

ENTER THE IMF

Meanwhile, Thailand had been struggling with its pride. It requested "technical assistance" from the IMF on the day it devalued, and a team from Washington had been dispatched to Bangkok. The question was, would Thailand ask for money to shore up its diminished reserves? The IMF had already offered the Philippines almost $1.1 billion in financial support under fast-track regulations drawn up after the Tequila Crisis. Finally, in early August, Thailand unveiled an IMF-backed austerity plan and a complete revamp of its financial sector. It was the cue for the Fund to stitch together the biggest bailout package since the Mexican rescue: $17.2 billion, contributed not only by the IMF and other multilateral lenders but also by a cluster of regional countries. These included not only the big boys on the block – Japan and Australia – but smaller contributors including Malaysia, South Korea and Indonesia, whose generosity was tinged with a natural desperation to stop the rot spreading further. The notable absentee was the United States, white knight of the Mexican crisis, which was embroiled in congressional rows over increasing its own contribution to IMF coffers.

The annual IMF/World Bank meeting in Hong Kong that September was a lively, if not entirely harmonious, gathering. Originally conceived as a celebration of the Asian Miracle, underscored by the host's continued prosperity under Chinese rule, it turned into a sometimes bad-tempered talking shop for the crisis sweeping the region. The West slapped down Asian proposals for a regional emergency fund of up to $100 billion, saying any bailout that did not demand tough policy reforms would pour money down the drain. East–West battle lines were drawn: Asian leaders wanted some way of taming international capital, while the IMF and the major Western countries blamed Asian policies and weak financial systems. Both were at least partly right, but recriminations drowned out any common ground.

The biggest attraction was a very public sparring match between Soros and Mahathir, who the previous month had called the financier a "moron" and accused him personally of orchestrating the attack on the ringgit. In a speech on the sidelines of the conference, the outspoken Malaysian prime minister launched into a denunciation of all currency trading. "Currency traders have become rich – very, very rich – through making other people poor," he raged. "They are billionaires who really do not need any more money. Currency trading is unnecessary, unproductive and totally immoral. It should be stopped. It should be made illegal." In a further twist, he told a Hong Kong newspaper that foreign exchange activity in Malaysia would be limited to what was needed to finance the country's trade.

Soros struck back, drawing loud applause and shouts of approval from his besuited audience when he called Mahathir "a menace to his own country", and said the proposal to ban currency trading was "so inappropriate that it does not deserve serious consideration". Meanwhile, it was left to Mahathir's deputy premier and finance minister, Anwar Ibrahim, to try to soothe the markets with what he diplomatically called a "clarification": Malaysia was not considering any change in its forex trading rules. But the damage was done. On the next trading day, September 22, the Malaysian currency slumped to 3.12 against the dollar – its weakest since 1971, and down 19 percent since the end of June.

If Mahathir hoped his fighting talk would ward off attacks on the ringgit, he was sadly mistaken. A month later he aroused diplomatic ire with remarks implying Jews were behind Malaysia's economic woes, reminding a 10,000-strong rally in the firmly Moslem east Malaysian state of Terengganu that Soros was Jewish. "And, incidentally, we are Moslems and the Jews are not happy to see Moslems progress," Malaysia's Bernama news agency quoted him as saying. Every new outburst fuelled fresh ringgit selling by speculators, companies and long-term investors alike. Friedman of *The New York Times* recounted how Anwar told him he and some colleagues had finally gone to Mahathir with a currency chart and tried to persuade him to pipe down, saying something like: "Look, you said this about Soros on Monday, and the Malaysian ringgit fell to here. You said this about the Jews on Tuesday, and the ringgit fell to here. You said this about global investors on Wednesday, and the ringgit fell to here. SHUT UP!"[24]

Perhaps inevitably, Anwar, who had been in line eventually to succeed Mahathir, was to fall dramatically from favour. A year later he was brusquely sacked after a mysterious book called *Fifty Reasons Why Anwar Cannot Become Prime Minister* made the rounds in Malaysia. Soon afterwards he was arrested and charged with sodomizing his former driver, an illegal act in Malaysia and one he roundly denied, saying he had been framed by allies of Mahathir while trying to expose government corruption. The court case was continuing in early 2000.

In fact, Mahathir's fulminations were a little disingenuous, to say the least. Malaysia itself has a colourful history of market acrobatics. In the 1970s it launched a series of spectacular stock market raids to capture prime British tin and plantation companies that it turned into Malaysian-run conglomerates. In the early 1980s it tried, unsuccessfully, to corner the world tin market. And until the early 1990s Bank Negara had a fearsome reputation as an aggressive currency speculator, using the country's foreign reserves as gambling chips and ignoring warnings from the Federal Reserve and the Bank of England that it was causing market instability. It was such a powerful player that London traders had a nickname for it: "The Beast from the East." That all came to a sticky end in 1992 when it lost around $3.5 billion betting the wrong way on sterling during the ERM crisis – the very crisis that made Soros' name.

Mahathir swore Malaysia would never go cap in hand to the IMF, selling its sovereignty over economic policy in return for cash. In fact, after much rhetoric and a budget that failed to rein in big spending projects, the country knuckled down in December 1997 to a home-grown emergency plan masterminded by Anwar. The plan cancelled grandiose government investment plans, slashed spending and ruled out any bailout for struggling financial institutions. It was widely seen as an "IMF plan without the IMF".

> 66 Bank Negara was such a powerful player that London traders had a nickname for it: "The Beast from the East" 99

Indonesia also unveiled a reform package in September 1997, including a bold ten-point austerity plan and a cut in market interest rates, easing monetary policy to foster economic confidence. It had some success in stabilizing the rupiah, but in the general climate of panic the currency could not hold, and in early October the government asked for IMF help. The subsequent $42.3 billion package, announced at the end of that month, dwarfed Thailand's bailout. Within days, Indonesia had started to fulfil IMF conditions by shutting down 16 sick banks, and its first $3 billion was disbursed. The relationship with the Fund would not always be so smooth.

THE PANIC SPREADS NORTH – AND WEST

In the three months after Thailand's devaluation the baht had lost nearly 29 percent of its value, the rupiah 26 percent, the peso 23 percent and the ringgit 22 percent. That was bad enough, but in October the crisis shifted into a distinct second phase that would make those falls look modest. "Contagion" was getting into full swing; not only were speculators turning north in search of fresh targets, but less aggressive investors were starting to panic in earnest. Many who had piled into emerging markets at the height of the boom lacked the knowledge to discriminate between the fundamentals of creaking Thailand and, say, Hong Kong, which was widely regarded as one of the region's strongest economies. Others did know the difference but decided it was safer to go with the herd. And the more small investors pulled out of Asian or emerging market mutual funds, the more the fund managers were forced to sell. Those self-fulfilling prophecies were back on the rampage.

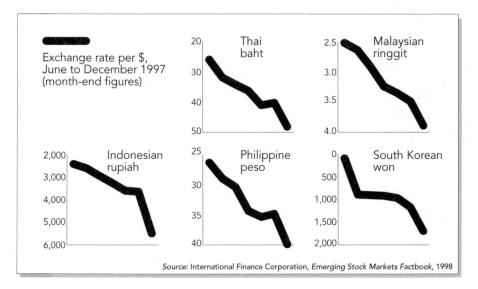

FIGURE 7 Asia's currency collapse, 1997

The Hong Kong and Taiwan dollars and the South Korean won had taken some knocks, but nothing like the drubbing their southern cousins had suffered. Suddenly the real pressure was on. After months of dogged intervention to hold its currency above 28.50 to the greenback, Taiwan's central bank abruptly abandoned its defence on October 17. The country had low debt, a current-account surplus and massive foreign reserves of around $90 billion, but it feared losing competitiveness and its stock market was being pounded. The next trading day the Taiwan dollar fell through the powerful psychological barrier of 30 to the US currency for the first time in ten years.

Taiwan's unexpected move was traumatic for Hong Kong, raising nagging questions about the territory's commitment to its rigid currency peg. Sensing weakness, the market charged the seemingly unassailable currency board system, similar to Argentina's, which held the Hong Kong dollar in a straitjacket around 7.80 to the US dollar. The HKMA did not give an inch, drawing on its foreign reserves of more than $88 billion and squeezing overnight interest rates as high as 300 percent (from a more normal 6 percent) to hammer short-sellers. (It had far more leeway than Argentina two years before, as the territory's reserves did not just match local cash in circulation but covered it several times over.)

The sharks retreated, but it was the Hong Kong stock exchange that emerged bleeding from the scrap. The logic – inasmuch as there was any amid the panic – was that the high interest rates and a strong currency relative to its regional neighbours would hurt local companies. Stock prices stumbled badly on October 20, and kept on falling. On October 23 they dropped off a cliff, with the blue-chip Hang Seng index plunging more than 1,200 points or 10 percent – its biggest ever one-day fall in point terms. In just four days, it had lost nearly a quarter of its value.

It was a crushing blow in one of the world's most rabidly market-hungry societies, where just about everyone from taxi drivers to secretaries takes a punt on the stock exchange. Anxious small investors massed outside bank windows, their eyes glued to monitors charting the crash. "It's carnage out there today," said James Osborn, ING Barings' head of sales in Hong Kong. "This fall is far more damaging than we've seen in the '87 crash, Tiananmen Square or the Gulf War crisis. I mean, this is really hurting domestic investors." A modest recovery the next day, provoked largely by local firms buying their own stocks back on the cheap, still left the index down by 18 percent on the week, and a massive 33 percent off the record high it had celebrated only two months before.

Now the crisis ceased to be just a regional affair. Hong Kong's sophisticated, liquid and well established markets straddled the border between the emerging and the developed worlds, and the shock waves from the Hang Seng's crash radiated out across the globe. Singapore's share index was sliced back to its lowest for nearly five years. The ripples rocked emerging currencies and stock markets from Poland to South Africa.

Latin American stocks suffered one of their biggest knocks of the year, with Brazil reeling to an 8 percent loss. Argentina's peso–dollar peg came back under scrutiny and tiny Estonia suddenly found itself in an unwelcome spotlight as speculators lunged at its kroon currency, which also happened to be run on currency board lines.

Major markets were also bruised, with the worst hammering aimed at companies and banks doing business in Asia. On October 23, Wall Street closed more than 2 percent lower, while British, Japanese, French and Dutch stocks lost more than 3 percent; Frankfurt dropped 4.7 percent and New Zealand more than 5 percent.

It was Hong Kong's worst financial crisis in decades, and the first real test for Hong Kong's new leader, Tung Chee-hwa. Tung, who was in London, stood firmly and vocally behind the currency peg; back home, Finance Secretary Donald Tsang was pumping out the same message. "The first priority is to defend the exchange rate. This is our top priority," he told reporters. Beaming at the auspicious significance of the twin eights in the territory's $88 billion stash of reserves, he said he would not hesitate to spend whatever was needed to hold the peg. In Beijing, China's central bank indicated it stood ready to help if needed; to tamper with the peg would wreck confidence in the new Special Administrative Region just months after China had taken over the reins. Pressure eased and Hong Kong had won its first real currency battle, but there was no ceasefire in sight. There was also a real price to be paid for the victory: although short-term market interest rates quickly fell back to less vertiginous levels, a sharp rise in bank lending rates would drag down growth in the coming months.

> **Asia panic had become a catalyst for a much wider pruning of stock market values**

There was worse to come. On October 27 – almost exactly ten years after the Black Monday crash of 1987 – Wall Street suffered its biggest single-day point loss in history. Asia panic had become a catalyst for a much wider, long-awaited pruning of bullish stock market values. The Dow ended down more than 550 points, or 7.2 percent – not as grave in percentage terms as Black Monday's 23 percent demolition, but enough to turn stomachs. Dealing was halted twice as plunging prices steamrollered through stock exchange "circuit breakers" designed to slow big sell-offs, and the exchange was forced to close half an hour early.

The Wall Street rout sent markets round the world running for cover. Canadian stocks saw their biggest ever one-day points fall and ended more than 6 percent lower. There was even worse carnage in Latin America;

stocks in Brazil, Mexico and Argentina suffered their biggest single-day losses in years, with Brazil's main index crashing 15 percent and the others down more than 12 percent. Mexico's peso, which had been rock-solid for months, slithered more than 6 percent to a record low against the dollar. "This is a river of blood," one frantic Mexican currency trader said.

The panic continued when Asia woke up. Japan's benchmark Nikkei index shed more than 4 percent – a relatively modest loss under the circumstances – but the main Australian and New Zealand indices slumped by more than a tenth of their value in early trade. By the time the Dow was due to reopen, most Western European bourses were down 7 or 8 percent.

Emerging market assets were being dumped across the board as investors veered away from anything that smelt remotely of risk, piling into the safest bets they could think of: US Treasury bonds, the Swiss franc, gold. The selling frenzy that had been triggered in Hong Kong boomeranged back to kick the Hang Seng down nearly 14 percent on the day. An enterprising wine shop near the stock exchange invited punters to drown their sorrows, offering discounts equal to the day's percentage fall. Other East Asian markets shed 6–8 percent and even India, which often shelters from world market storms behind a barrier of capital controls, ended nearly 8 percent lower. Everywhere you looked, stocks were in meltdown. Hungary lost more than 16 percent, Estonia 12 percent, South Africa 11 percent, Poland 10 percent. Moscow halted trading for several hours, but leading shares still ended the day 20 percent cheaper.

Then Wall Street reopened after a night's sleep, and frenzied selling turned to frenzied buying. This was the market rollercoaster at its most dizzying and bizarre. A record 1.2 billion shares changed hands on October 28 and the Dow posted what was then its biggest ever single-day point gain – up 337 points, or 4.7 percent. "It turns out that on October 28 the American economy was still there," O'Rourke wrote. "None of America's factories or malls had been abducted by space aliens. American workers hadn't forgotten how to flip burgers during the night."[25] Positive data on the US budget deficit, wages and company profits soothed nerves and after some lingering uncertainty the major markets pulled themselves together, although they remained edgy and vulnerable to Asian frights. The Dow ended 1997 up nearly 23 percent – the first time the benchmark index had lodged gains of more than 20 percent for three years running.

The damage across emerging markets was less easily repaired. Brazil's stock market managed to end the year in positive territory, but its currency, the real, took a beating, forcing the central bank to spend $8 billion on intervention and almost double interest rates to 42 percent to keep it within its prescribed limits against the dollar. (The currency operated on a crawling peg system similar to Mexico's before the 1995 devaluation, but with two bands: a broad "maxi-band" for the year as a whole, and a much tighter "mini-band" for day-to-day trading.) The real had won respect and gratitude in Brazil for quelling a seemingly endless nightmare of hyperinflation – a feature previously so ingrained in Brazilian life that an official system of indexation existed to ensure wages rose in tandem with prices – and the country was not going to let the currency go in a hurry. But there was a heavy price to be paid in terms of growth, and Brazil's troubles revived fears of a Latin American recession. Stocks and bonds toppled again across the region. Attempting to restore market confidence, the Brazilian government promised $18 billion in tax increases and spending cuts to prune its swelling budget deficit. It did the trick in the short term, but most of the steps were not implemented – unfinished business that would come back to haunt the country.

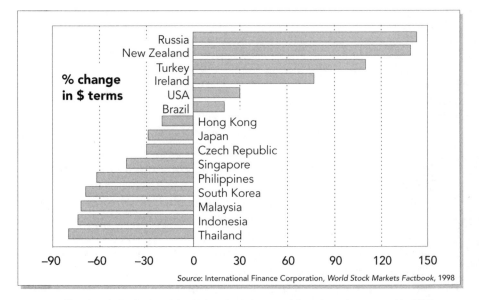

Source: International Finance Corporation, *World Stock Markets Factbook*, 1998

FIGURE 8 The Good, the Bad and the Ugly, take 1: how world stock markets scored in 1997

Russia, too, was left with a throbbing hangover. Its markets might have been the height of financial fashion, but the Asian turmoil compounded lurking local worries. There was still a lot wrong with the economy, and Russian politics was far from restful, especially with Yeltsin lurching from one illness to another. To cap it all, in October the IMF halted payments on its $10 billion, three-year loan because of concern over the country's dismal record on tax collection.

The central bank had to sell dollars and crank up its basic interest rate to 28 percent to defend the rouble, which was also pegged to the green-back. But foreign investors still dumped billions of dollars worth of Russian bonds, driving yields on the country's Treasury bills as high as 45 percent by early December from 17–18 percent in mid-October. (A bond's yield is the total income it offers, taking into account not only the interest rate but the potential capital gain on the gap between a dis-counted market price and the bond's face value. Since the interest rate on a bond is usually fixed, the yield rises as the market price falls.) Russian shares took a further beating, though they still managed to end the year 143 percent higher in dollar terms, carrying off the honours as the world's best performing stock market for the second year running. The government even started talks with Western banks for an emergency injection of finance, but by the end of the year fresh expressions of sup-port from the IMF and the World Bank helped to calm nerves and the central bank sounded an optimistic all-clear on Russia's market health.

HEADS BEGIN TO ROLL

Meanwhile, the Asian crisis had claimed its first big political scalp. On November 4 Chavalit, who had been under pressure for months to resign as Thailand's economic pain dragged on, announced he was quitting as head of the coalition government. Far from panicking at the prospect of political instability, the Thai markets celebrated the departure of a prem-ier they disliked heartily; the baht surged more than 5 percent in one day, and stocks jumped nearly 7 percent. Within a week the widely respected Democrat Party leader, Chuan Leekpai, had taken over at the head of a new, eight-party coalition. Chuan not only had a rare reputa-tion for honesty but built an economic team around him that the markets trusted. A month later the government took the first real step on the long path of financial reform, closing down 56 of 58 finance compa-nies whose operations had been suspended under the IMF deal.

But the Asian meltdown was far from done. The biggest prize for speculators, China's yuan (also called the renminbi), was too solid for a head-on attack, protected not only by vast foreign reserves and a huge trade surplus but by capital controls that made it hard to get at. There was another plump target: South Korea, then the world's eleventh largest economy and bigger than Thailand, Indonesia and Malaysia put together. Here again, foreign speculators had a problem: Seoul's markets offered few mechanisms for shorting the won. But with panic spreading, local businesses were also betting the currency would tumble, and getting out of it wherever they could.

Although it had escaped the worst excesses of property speculation and was starting to trim its current-account gap, South Korea had the biggest debt problem in the region. Cronyism was rife, controls on lending were lax, and companies commonly borrowed as much as four or even five times their capital. As a result, the banks and the giant *chaebol* conglomerates that dominated the economy were up to their necks in hard-currency debt, most of it short term. By mid-1997 South Korea's short-term borrowing alone amounted to three times the country's entire foreign reserves, a ratio twice as high as its nearest rival, Indonesia, and nearly six times as high as Malaysia.[26]

> 66 South Korea had the biggest debt problem in the region. Cronyism was rife, controls on lending were lax, and companies commonly borrowed four or even five times their capital 99

It was an accident waiting to happen. South Koreans had been talking about economic crisis as early as January, when leading steelmaker Hanbo, the flagship of the country's fourteenth largest *chaebol*, collapsed under a mountain of debt. The default uncovered a tangled web of corruption stretching to President Kim Young-sam's inner circle, with the opposition clamouring to know how a fundamentally shaky company had been able to borrow about 20 times its net worth. The collapse sparked a chain reaction of corporate failures just as Kim, the country's first elected civilian leader, was struggling to push through financial and labour reforms. The corporate chickens were coming home to roost; the protracted collapse of the Kia Group, the country's eighth largest conglomerate, sent fresh jitters through South Korean markets well before the Hong Kong stock market massacre, and it was partly pressure on the won that contributed to Taiwan's devaluation. By the end of October the banking system was on the brink of collapse, and the won was really hitting the skids.

The won was not pegged in quite the same way as its neighbours, and had managed to avoid the kind of overvaluation that had undermined the baht or the ringgit. It was allowed to fluctuate by up to 2.25 percent on either side of a basic rate set daily by the central bank, but since this rate was based on the previous day's foreign exchange transactions, the limit was not so much an anchor as a brake on sudden movements. The won's slide was far too sharp for the central bank's liking, but despite determined intervention, the currency continually nudged at its lower limits and piled through 950 to the dollar. From there, traders targeted the magical 1,000 barrier. The central bank tried desperately to resist, with officials insisting the won would "never, never, never" breach 1,000. But the market paid no attention, selling the South Korean currency relentlessly and openly speculating that Seoul would have to seek IMF help. On November 10 the won closed at 999; a week later the central bank cracked and announced it would no longer hold the line. (It later emerged that the country's foreign reserves, which stood at $31 billion in early October, had fallen below $10 billion.)

The won immediately plunged the full extent of its daily limit, ending at just under 1,009, but the market scented further falls to come. On November 19 the won's permitted daily shift was increased from 2.25 to 10 percent, leaving it in a virtual free float or, more accurately, free fall. By the end of November, the currency was beyond 1,150 to the dollar and by the end of the year it was pushing 1,700; in three months it had lost 46 percent of its value.

In late November the South Korean government reluctantly bowed to the inevitable and said it was discussing details of a bailout package with the IMF, originally for some $20 billion. At the same time, it approached foreign banks for a deal to roll over a large chunk of short-term debt. The IMF-backed package, when it was announced in early December after a bout of confusion and crossed wires between Seoul and Washington, was much bigger: $58.2 billion, including $21 billion from the IMF over three years, $10 billion from the World Bank, and $4 billion from the Asian Development Bank. Other countries would pitch in more than $20 billion. It was the biggest ever international rescue package, outstripping the $50 billion pledged to Mexico in 1995 (and, unlike Mexico, South Korea very quickly drew on most of the cash). Reluctantly, US, European and Japanese banks – the latter mired in their own acute bad-debt problems – agreed to give South Korean banks more time to pay.

The markets were relieved, but many South Koreans reacted to the IMF deal with deep anger and humiliation. A country that prided itself on self-reliance had been forced not only to ask for outside help but also to swallow tough conditions in return. As well as drastic budget cuts and higher taxes, the terms of the rescue included closing insolvent financial institutions and reforming the way the *chaebol* did business – in other words, a radical overhaul of the country's entire business and financial system. Local newspapers called the bailout a "national shame", and one militant trade union promised all-out strikes if companies pushed for layoffs.

It was not a recipe for political popularity, and the government had the huge misfortune to be facing elections for a new president on December 18. For most of the year the election campaign had seemed to turn a strangely blind eye to the financial crisis engulfing the country, but the IMF bailout was too big to ignore; so unpopular was it that none of the three major candidates was prepared to endorse it outright at the hustings. The race was nail-bitingly close, but main opposition leader Kim Dae-jung pipped ruling party candidate Lee Hoi-chang to the post. For the first time ever, South Korean voters had rejected the governing party, and there was no doubt that anger at the economic crisis had played its part. "We accept the result as a scolding by the people," Lee's spokesman said. But Kim, a veteran socialist and pro-democracy campaigner, was inheriting a poison chalice; after campaigning on a platform to renegotiate the IMF package and cut unemployment and taxes, he now had little option but to pledge full support for the deal, and the pain that went with it.

> 66 Emerging market countries that had planned to launch international bonds were forced to think again 99

The crisis was feeding off itself, as each twist of bad news in one country stirred up fresh waves that tossed other markets about like corks on the ocean. In 1997 as a whole the rupiah lost 57 percent of its value against the dollar, the won 50 percent, the baht 47 percent. An estimated $7 billion was sucked out of Asian stock markets during the year.[27] The IFCI Asia index plunged 53 percent between June and December, and the Composite dropped 25 percent. Emerging market countries that had planned to launch international bonds were forced to think again, as the soaring premiums that nervous investors were now demanding over US Treasuries drove the cost of borrowing sky-high. The new fear of risk was reflected in escalating spreads over comparable US bonds, which at one point blew out to average nearly 700 basis points compared with a record low of 330 only weeks previously.

"We have to accept that in this world there is no equality," an uncharacteristically subdued Mahathir told a regional summit in December. "We are not in a position to do anything. We are just the victims."

And just as political events could unhinge the markets, the financial and economic turmoil was feeding back into political upheaval. Two governments had fallen; several more heads would roll before the dust settled.

NOTES

1   World Bank, *Global Development Finance 1999*, p. 24.

2   Merrill Lynch, *1998 – The year ahead: A portfolio manager's review*, December 2, 1997.

3   According to IFC Investable price indices.

4   World Bank, *Global Development Finance 1998*, p. 15.

5   World Bank, *Global Development Finance 1998*, p. 103.

6   Mobius, *Mobius on Emerging Markets*, p. 91.

7   *Euromoney*, January 1997.

8   IFC Global index; Russia was not included in the Investable indices until 1998.

9   EBRD, *Transition Report 1998*, p. 13.

10 *Observer*, September 6, 1998.

11 O'Rourke, *Eat the Rich*, p. 130.

12 *Euromoney*, August 1996.

13 Henderson, *Asia Falling*, p. 85.

14 Fay, *The Collapse of Barings*, p. 82.

15 Garran, *Tiger Tamed: The end of the Asian Miracle*, p. 94.

16 World Bank, *Global Development Finance 1999*, p. 84.

17 World Bank, *Global Development Finance 1998*, p. 33.

18 Garran, p. 95.

19 *The Economist, The World in 1997*, p. 88.

20 Quoted in *Euromoney*, December 1997.

21 Henderson, p. 97.

22 Henderson, p. 105.

23 Mobius, *Passport to Profits*, p. 175.

24 Friedman, *The Lexus and the Olive Tree*, p. 115.

25 O'Rourke, p. 29.

26 World Bank, *Global Development Finance 1998*, p. 35.

27 World Bank, *Global Development Finance 1998*, p. 13.

5

DOMINOES

It is not my interest to pay the principal, nor my principle to pay the interest –
Attributed to Richard Brinsley Sheridan

INDONESIA EXPLODES

1998 started as it meant to go on for Indonesia – badly. The sprawling
archipelago was the poorest of the Tiger economies, and it was caught
more painfully than any of its neighbours between the rock of IMF
policy demands and the hard place of worsening poverty. Fuel and food
prices were rocketing, half the country's businesses were bankrupt or
close to it, and unemployment was on the rise. It was becoming increasingly clear that what had started as a financial problem would have a
devastating impact on everyday life.

Unused to challenges to his authoritarian rule over more than three
decades in power, President Suharto had fluctuated between implementing IMF conditions and repudiating them. Sure enough, when the
1998/99 budget was unveiled on January 6 it seemed to stand little
chance of keeping the IMF happy, projecting rosy economic growth,
moderate inflation, and a one-third rise in both revenue and expendi-
ture. The figures bore little relation to reality, and market rumours
sprang up that Indonesia might declare a debt moratorium. The rupiah

had already slithered to around 7,000 to the dollar; in three days it dropped beyond 10,000. Frightened Indonesians besieged shops and markets to stockpile food.

The IMF wanted a stiff chat, and its top brass, including Managing Director Michel Camdessus, flew to Jakarta. The two sides quickly signed an agreement to strengthen economic reforms, but the gesture did little to restore market confidence. On January 22 the rupiah collapsed to 17,000 to the dollar before central bank intervention forced it back past 12,000. Perhaps worse, the deal did nothing to reconcile Indonesians to the Fund's strict policy dictates. The signing ceremony was a public relations disaster, with Camdessus photographed standing cross-armed and stony-faced looking down on Suharto – an image of national humiliation.

> Almost every day saw another demonstration or riot, from the simmering capital to the far-flung tourist island of Lombok

Indonesia's private debt problem, amounting to an estimated $74 billion, was soon to claim its first foreign victim. On January 12, Hong Kong's Peregrine Investment Holdings, one of Asia's largest independent investment banks, collapsed under a mountain of bad loans to Indonesian borrowers, triggering sharp stock market falls not only in Hong Kong but in China and Singapore, too. "Clearly Indonesia did disappoint everyone," Peregrine co-founder Philip Tose told reporters with classic understatement, his voice choked with emotion.

By now the crisis was starting to threaten the political status quo. Suharto's iron hand had presided over dramatic economic growth, but it had also kept a stranglehold on political opponents and on minority ethnic groups who resented Jakarta's domination over a vast and diverse nation of 200 million people. Indonesia's highest legislative body, the People's Consultative Assembly (MPR), was due to vote in an indirect presidential election in March, and the 76-year-old leader was showing no sign of bowing out, despite his increasingly poor health. What's more, he had no clear political successor.

Anger against falling living standards joined broader political discontent and exploded into increasingly violent street protest. Almost every day saw another demonstration or riot, from the simmering capital to the far-flung tourist island of Lombok. Mobs looted shops, gutted buildings and torched cars. Chinese shopkeepers were singled out for special attack as frustration found a racist outlet against a community that, despite its small size, dominated Indonesian business. Mass arrests became increasingly common, and in mid-February at least three people were killed in the turmoil; police warned they would shoot rioters on sight.

On March 10, to a crescendo of furious student rallies, the 1,000-member MPR handed the president a seventh five-year term. His new cabinet was scarcely a model of anti-cronyism; Suharto surrounded himself with loyal allies including his daughter, Siti Hardiyanti Rukmana, and Mohamad "Bob" Hasan, an old golfing friend and a tycoon with a finger in many pies.

While Suharto was seeing to the business of getting himself re-elected, another policy row erupted. In response to a suggestion by Steve Hanke of John Hopkins University, the government considered adopting a currency board system to try to douse inflation and stabilize the rupiah's wild swings. The IMF and the United States (whose currency would probably end up as the anchor for such a system) stamped on the notion, saying it was premature until the government tackled deep-seated problems in banking and corporate debt; the IMF threatened to halt its bailout if Indonesia went ahead. But Suharto, clutching at economic straws, clung to the currency board plan and sacked central bank chief Soedradjad Djiwandono for opposing it. The dismissal outraged international lenders even more. Suharto insisted – with some justification – that the IMF prescriptions had not worked. But the ultimate power lay in the purse-strings; the IMF said its board would not discuss Indonesia before April, effectively delaying a $3 billion bailout payment that had been expected by mid-March. Within two weeks Indonesia had backed down, saying it was dropping the currency board idea for the time being.

Relations with the United States and the IMF remained prickly, but Suharto had little choice but to fall more into step with the Fund's policies. The country set a more realistic budget and froze the minimum wage at 1997 levels, a move that, with inflation expected to reach 50 percent in 1998, promised to slash the real income of Indonesia's urban poor. But by now the IMF was also coming in for some international flak over the severity of its approach, and Indonesia was able to wrest some minor concessions, such as phasing out food subsidies gradually rather than halting them at a stroke. The government also got more serious about banking reform, suspending the licences of seven banks and placing seven others under official supervision – quite a breakthrough considering relatives and friends of the president were known to control large stakes in several of them.

On the street, fury against Suharto was reaching boiling point. When the army killed six student protesters in Jakarta in mid-May, it was the trigger for the worst explosion of violence and mayhem Indonesia had seen in more than three decades. The urban poor threw their weight behind the students, but the protest turned into a four-day orgy of looting and destruction in which more than 500 people were killed, many of them burned to death in blazing shops. Panicky foreigners rushed to leave the country; the Chinese fled their homes and businesses. International bailout funds were put on hold, financial markets shuddered to a halt, and the banking system was barely functioning. Suharto was abroad, attending a summit of the G15 developing countries in Cairo, where he studiously avoided journalists' attentions. The atmosphere at the conference was like a deathwatch: would the frail-looking Indonesian leader go home? If he did, would he still be president?

He did, and he was – but only just. Thousands of people gathered in and around Indonesia's parliament complex, demanding his immediate resignation. Clapping, singing students kept up a steady chant of "Down with Suharto" and "Long live reforms". They were joined by doctors and nurses, lawyers and sailors, bureaucrats and retired army officers, all shouting that it was time for the president to go. This time, troops did not stop them. Suharto went on television to sketch out an outline for his departure from office, but he gave no time frame. It was not enough, and on May 21 he was back in front of the cameras at the presidential palace. "I have decided to resign today," he said, adding with a catch in his voice: "I wish to say thank you and beg forgiveness from the people."

The crisis had claimed its third scalp, and it was a major one. Vice President Jusuf Habibie, a Suharto protégé widely disliked in financial and diplomatic circles, took over running the country but came under immediate pressure to call elections rather than see out the rest of Suharto's five-year term. Nor did the change at the helm steer the Indonesian markets away from the rocks, despite a deal in early June between foreign banks and Indonesian companies to reschedule the massive corporate debt. Indonesia's descent into turmoil intensified capital flight and swept away any pretence of an IMF programme; it was only after the country signed yet another IMF agreement – its fourth, in late June – that calm gradually started to return. The rupiah spiked below 15,000 to the dollar, but the worst was over, for the markets, at least. The economy was a different matter: the much revised IMF deal now expected GDP to plunge by 10 percent in 1998, and in the end even that figure proved optimistic.

THE LAND OF THE FALLING YEN –
JAPAN'S TROUBLES DEEPEN

Beyond Indonesia, early 1998 had been a period of recuperation for emerging markets. Thailand and South Korea had been working quietly on the terms of their IMF bailouts, with Seoul wrapping up a deal with foreign banks to swap $24 billion of short-term debt for new loans with more manageable maturities of up to three years. The markets rewarded them with a New Year boost; in January, the Bangkok stock market bounced 33 percent and Seoul 48 percent. February brought stock market rallies in Malaysia, the Philippines and Taiwan. The IFCI Asia index rose an encouraging 25 percent in February alone, and the overall Composite emerging market index crept up 10 percent. Regional currencies enjoyed a bout of relative calm, and by March all except the rupiah were showing a clear upturn against the dollar. It seemed the storm might have blown over.

No such luck. By mid-April things were starting to go wrong again, largely as a result of another external influence: trouble in Japan. The world's second biggest economy had been wrestling throughout the 1990s with its own deep crisis; by 1997 just about the only thing that was going right for Japan was its export sector, lifted by the weaker yen. But the country's exposure to the rest of Asia was huge; not only did 45 percent of Japanese exports go to the region, but Japanese manufacturers had farmed out production to neighbouring countries and Japanese banks had lent heavily to fuel the Tiger boom.

66 The Asian meltdown was a sickening blow to the region's economic giant and mentor 99

The Asian meltdown was a sickening blow to the region's economic giant and mentor. Suddenly all Japan's new-found export competitiveness was evaporating as its neighbours' currencies were devalued. At the same time, Japanese banks that were barely alive underneath an estimated 100 trillion yen ($730 billion) of home-grown bad loans were hit by a fresh bad-debt avalanche from abroad. Exact figures were hard to pin down, but Henderson estimated Japanese banks' loan exposure to the rest of the region at around $150 billion – about three times bigger than the exposure of US banks to Asia.[1] A couple of financial institutions went bust in late 1997, despite rescue attempts by Japan's powerful Finance Ministry, but the failure in late November of the country's fourth biggest brokerage, the venerable, 100-year-old Yamaichi Securities, stirred up a hornet's nest. It was Japan's biggest ever corporate failure, and the news drove the yen to a five-year low against the dollar.

Despite superficial similarities, Japan's economy was very different from those of its smaller neighbours; it was a net creditor rather than a debtor, ran a current-account surplus, and had more than $200 billion in foreign reserves – four times the reserves of the United States. But the country was in dire straits nevertheless, plunging into its first recession in more than two decades. The government hurriedly pumped public money into the top 19 banks to boost their capital base – a move critics said was out of step with a planned "Big Bang" to reform Japan's market practices and make them "free, fair and global" by 2001 – and rushed out sketchy details of a $120 billion economic stimulus package, but the mood remained one of pervasive gloom. "All the (economic indicator) numbers coming out these days are very bad," Bank of Japan Governor Masaru Hayami told a parliamentary panel at the beginning of April 1998. The chairman of electronics giant Sony, Norio Ohga, warned that the Japanese economy was on the verge of collapse.

Yet while Japan's recovery prospects were being ravaged by the Asian crisis, the rest of the world was still looking to Japan to pull the region out of trouble. "We are worried whether the Japanese economy has the strength to make an Asian recovery possible," President Clinton told Japanese Prime Minister Ryutaro Hashimoto as he arrived in Vancouver for the annual summit of the Asia Pacific Economic Co-operation group (APEC).

By May the yen was at well over 130 to the dollar and tumbling fast. The whiff of panic spread to other Asian markets, which were starting to worry about recession elsewhere in the region as austerity measures and high domestic interest rates ate away at growth. South Korean shares plunged more than 12 percent in two days on fears of recession and strikes by the country's increasingly restive trades unions. Then Hong Kong stocks dropped more than 5 percent in a day after Chief Executive Tung Chee-hwa warned of possible recession. Soon afterwards, Hong Kong, Indonesia and Malaysia confirmed their economies had shrunk in the first quarter of the year. "What's the only safe investment in Asia?" went the grim joke in Western dealing rooms. "Cash and canned food."

Federal Reserve Chairman Alan Greenspan warned that the impact of the Asian crisis was just starting to make itself felt in the US economy. "There was and is … a small but not negligible probability that the upset in East Asia could have unexpectedly large negative effects on Japan, Latin America, and Eastern and Central Europe that, in turn, could have repercussions elsewhere, including the United States," he told a congressional committee. Some analysts feared this was an understatement.

In the midst of all this came a political wild card: nuclear tests by India and a tit-for-tat response by arch-rival Pakistan. Fears of a nuclear arms race in Asia sent investors skittering for the safe-haven dollar, while the flight out of the yen was intensified by news that Japan's unemployment rate had hit 4.1 percent in April – its highest since the end of World War Two. On May 29 the dollar rocketed to a seven-year high of 139 yen; just over a week later it broke 140. Asian stocks and currencies were tumbling again like ninepins.

In mid-June niggling worries about the possibility of a Chinese devaluation came to the fore when China's central bank warned that the weak yen was having a severe impact on Beijing's foreign trade. The warning resonated strongly round the region; not only were Chinese exports already equal to about 70 percent of exports from the five worst hit Asian countries put together,[2] but a cheaper yuan would almost certainly take Hong Kong's dollar peg down with it. Asian stocks and currencies plunged even further at the spectre of a round of cut-throat competitive devaluations like the one which swept the major industrial countries during the 1930s.

But the message coming from Washington – specifically, from Treasury Secretary Robert Rubin – was that the weak yen reflected the weak Japanese economy, and the major industrial powers would make no joint effort to bolster the currency. When Japan's first-quarter GDP figures showed an annualized 5.3 percent fall, the yen dived towards 145 to the dollar. Finally, it seemed things had gone too far; the Fed took the rare step of joining with the Bank of Japan to sell dollars, wrong-footing the market and driving the yen back as far as 134. A few days later top G7 finance officials met in Tokyo and pledged to co-operate as appropriate in the forex markets.

The respite for the yen was temporary; within two months it would be back around 145 to the dollar. Relief for the government was even briefer: on July 12, Japanese voters turned out in force to deal the ruling Liberal Democratic Party a stunning defeat in elections to the Upper House. It was a stinging rebuke for failing to cure the country's economic ills. "My hopes were so high when Hashimoto came into office," one housewife said. "But he did not listen to the people and that cost him the election." The prime minister had been given his marching orders, and he quit the next day. Scalp number four.

LOCKING HORNS – SOUTH KOREAN JOBS
AND HONG KONG STOCKS

Things were also heating up in South Korea, where the new government, at the IMF's behest, was starting to get tough on closing down banks and restructuring the *chaebol*. President Kim Dae-jung found himself in a daunting position, at loggerheads with both the defensive conglomerates and the unions that had helped elect him. In mid-July, tens of thousands of workers downed tools to protest against the planned wage and job cuts that went hand in hand with the corporate upheaval. They returned to work, but within days thousands of angry Hyundai motor workers were pitching tents in the grounds of their factory in the south-eastern city of Ulsan, protesting against the company's plans to lay off 1,500 people – the first mass job losses in a country where lifetime employment had long been seen as an inalienable right. The occupation led to a series of strikes and plant shutdowns that would drag on for well over a month. With thousands of riot police surrounding the barricaded factory and the smell of potential violence in the air, in late August management and unions locked horns directly in four days of almost non-stop talks. They emerged exhausted, but with a deal: the unions accepted for the first time that there would be some layoffs, but the management slashed the number of job losses back to less than 300.

It looked very much like a victory for the workers, and the markets were not impressed. Previous South Korean governments had shown little compunction in breaking up strikes and demonstrations with brute force, and financial analysts suggested the socialist Kim might have set a damaging precedent with his softly-softly approach. They need not have worried. In early September riot police stormed plant owned by Mando Machinery, the country's largest auto-parts producer, to break up a strike over planned layoffs.

A clash of a different kind was brewing over in Hong Kong, as jitters about a Chinese devaluation focused attention once more on the territory's fixed currency peg. In early August the hedge funds pounced again – but not only against the Hong Kong dollar; they adopted a double-barrelled strategy in which they sold short both the currency and the stock market at the same time. In principle, they could not lose. If the peg snapped, they would make money on the tumbling currency; if it held, the high interest rates needed to defend it would drive stock prices down. A bout of determined selling on both fronts forced the HKMA to intervene heavily in the currency market, and drove the Hang Seng index down to its lowest for more than five years.

By August 14 the HKMA had had enough. Bending its own strict free-market principles, it slammed into the stock market for the first time, using Hong Kong's foreign reserves to squeeze out speculators by buying up blue-chip shares and futures contracts based on the Hang Seng. The index soared 8.5 percent in one day.

Officials were at pains to stress that their stock market defence (in which they bought up about 10 percent of the market over the course of a couple of weeks) did not mean they were abandoning their hands-off stance. "We do not tolerate attempts by speculators to manipulate our interest rates by engineering extreme conditions in the money market so that they can benefit from the short positions they have built up in Hang Seng futures," a grim-faced Tsang told reporters. "I must emphasize that our long-standing policy of non-intervention in the stock and futures markets remains unchanged. We only contemplate intervention in very exceptional circumstances."

The ploy drew cautious support in the local media and fierce condemnation in investment circles. Yet a few months later a survey by *Euromoney* found the indignation had largely evaporated, with more than half the investors and businesses polled saying the government had been right to intervene. "I am still a market fundamentalist, but I also believe there are times that markets can fail – in extreme circumstances," Tsang told the magazine.[3] For the first time, an Asian government had fought back and won.

GRAFT AND GECKOS – RUSSIA'S SEAMY UNDERBELLY

Russia too was still struggling to retain the confidence of domestic and foreign investors alike. It was not just a question of falling stock market values. The way the economy had been allowed to evolve since the fall of communism, and the way the government found funds to run the country, had made Russia acutely vulnerable to an investor exodus.

The collapse of the old Soviet system had not exactly allowed a new broom to sweep through Russian politics and business. On the contrary, the lower house of parliament, the State Duma, was dominated by an unreconstructed Communist Party. Most of the country's desperately inefficient industry was not only still managed by Soviet-era appar-atchiks but in many cases was now controlled by them, and they were not keen to let outside investors on to their patch. Standards of account-ing and corporate governance were shambolic, and foreigners who invested in Russian companies were often taken to the cleaners by unscrupulous managements with little regard for the rights of minority shareholders. A survey in 1997 by international business consultancy Control Risks Group named Russia as the world's most corrupt country (followed closely by Nigeria, Ukraine and three other former Soviet republics). In another study, more than three-quarters of Moscow shop-keepers questioned said they needed to pay off private protection rackets to keep their businesses open.[4]

Just about the only new and thriving aspect of the Russian economy was also one of its most dubious: a plethora of commercial banks, many of which were operating on very shaky finances. In 1997 the central bank considered only one-third of the country's 1,847 licensed banks to be "basically sound".[5] But the strongest grew at an astonishing rate, mainly by exploiting distortions and weak-nesses in the financial system. Then they tightened their grip on Russia's economic fabric by capturing fat stakes in major companies through inside contacts and an infamous 1995 "loans for shares" scheme, in which they effec-tively snapped up state holdings in strategic industries at dirt-cheap prices, in auctions that were far from transparent. Seven top bankers – dubbed the "grey cardinals" or *semibankirshchina* ("rule of the seven bankers", a pun on the name given to the seven noblemen who briefly ruled Russia in the 17th century) – built a corporate oligarchy whose "financial-industrial groups" had a stranglehold on up to 50 percent of the Russian economy.[6]

> The whole country was struggling under a dead weight of vested interests, cronyism and graft

The whole country was struggling under a dead weight of vested inter-ests, cronyism and graft. And although President Yeltsin made attempts to put bright young reformists in key government positions, they were hamstrung at virtually every turn by the old guard – not least because the oligarchs had bankrolled Yeltsin in the 1996 presidential election and were not shy about calling in political favours in return.

One of the few clear achievements of Yeltsin's rule had been to kill hyperinflation and stabilize the rouble, which had dissolved into Monopoly money after the demise of the Soviet Union. In 1995 the Russian currency was tied to the dollar under a sliding corridor system similar to Mexico's old crawling peg. Battered by the Asian whirlwind and wary of the dangers of overvaluation, the central bank adjusted the system from the start of 1998; it set a considerably wider corridor allow-ing the rouble to move 15 percent above or below a so-called pivot rate of 6.2 roubles to the dollar until the end of 2000 (in effect, between 5.27 and 7.13 to the greenback), although the currency was managed day to day in a narrower mini-band. At the same time, it redenominated the rouble by knocking three zeros off the old rate, making calculations easier and helping to restore an air of respectability. Some Russians were even starting to place a very tentative trust in the rouble, although many continued to keep their savings in cash dollars under the mattress.

Generally speaking, though, confidence and optimism were in short supply. Russians were increasingly disillusioned with so-called market reforms, and increasingly mistrustful of the government. Far from expanding in the post-communist era, the economy shrank by an average of 8 percent a year between 1991 and 1996, and showed only a flicker of growth – less than 1 percent – in 1997. Law and order were a pipe dream and the Russian tax system was still a shambles despite the best efforts of the reformists, with small business tied up in fiscal red tape while big business dodged payment. (The EBRD called the system "onerous and arbitrarily applied ... causing massive tax evasion and avoidance".[7]) Unable to raise adequate revenue, which was covering only about half of state spending, by 1998 the government faced a yawning budget deficit of around 7 percent of GDP.[8] The Russian state was failing even to pay its own workers and pensioners on time, or in full.

To try to make good the shortfall, the government began to borrow more and more money through the domestic bond market, issuing a blizzard of short-term bills known as GKOs (dubbed "Geckos" by some foreign investors, recalling Hollywood's *Wall Street* anti-hero) and longer-dated, less popular OFZ bonds. At the start of 1996, the face value of outstanding GKOs and OFZs amounted to 3.4 percent of Russia's GDP; by the end of the year it was 8.2 percent – more than all the rouble deposits in the banking system put together.[9] To attract buyers it had to offer high returns; GKO yields spiked above 200 percent around the time of the 1996 election and were still providing an annual 20–30 percent or more in the first half of 1997, compared to around 5 percent on short-term US Treasury bills. "Since 1996 the Russian government has been in a race between its need to collect more taxes and a rising interest bill on its growing debt," wrote the IMF's first deputy managing director, Stanley Fischer.[10]

Foreigners were initially barred from the GKO market, but were so desperate to get in that they often pursued legally dubious schemes involving Russian intermediaries. "Unfortunately very few of these schemes obey the letter of the law and even those that are cleverly structured contravene its spirit," *Euromoney* noted at the time.[11] As soon as the barriers were eased, foreign investors rushed in wholesale, soothed by government assurances that the fixed exchange rate system and the stable rouble were there to stay. By the end of 1997 they had snapped up one-third of all GKOs and OFZs.[12] They were not alone in their enthusiasm; rather than providing credit for businesses and individuals, the big Russian banks poured their deposits into government paper and sat back to rake in the returns. Like generations of investors before them, all were lulled by the conviction that a government armed with the power to raise taxes and print money would never default on its domestic debt. Meanwhile, the government was having to issue more and more debt in order to roll over about $1 billion of GKOs maturing every week.[13]

As well as dabbling in GKOs, foreign banks, led overwhelmingly by the Germans, had also been lending large sums to Russian banks, businesses and public-sector bodies. Many of these loans were short term, and much of the money was coming up for repayment; BIS figures showed more than $38 billion falling due to banks in the major industrial countries between mid-1997 and mid-1998. As early as January 1998 some analysts had warned that these repayments might be in danger: "The clock is ticking," wrote Philip Poole and Mark Stenner at ING Barings.[14]

WOUNDED BEAR – MOSCOW STRUGGLES

Now that the emerging market euphoria had been replaced by panic and gloom, the mood of foreign investors was hostage to every fit and start of the struggling reform process. In the spring of 1998 the markets were unnerved by a lengthy political standoff, when Yeltsin sacked long-serving Prime Minister Viktor Chernomyrdin and his entire cabinet, and then went through a month of brinkmanship (and three nail-biting votes) before the Duma finally approved his nominated successor, virtually unknown energy minister Sergei Kiriyenko.

No sooner was that drama over than Tokobank, which had pulled in a lot of foreign credits, was placed under temporary administration because of liquidity problems and bad management. Then parliament forced through a law limiting foreign ownership in the stock market's most liquid security, electricity giant Unified Energy Systems. In the Arctic north, coal miners angry over unpaid wages blocked a major railway line, and the protest soon spread to miners elsewhere. Then there was the wider backdrop of turmoil in Asia.

The stock market was tumbling and the rouble was under mounting pressure, forcing the central bank to sell dollars and raise key interest rates in the hope of shielding the currency. The story was the same in the Treasury bill market, where the government was finding it increasingly difficult to attract buyers for its new GKO issues, and having to tempt them with higher returns. At the same time, local banks with a shortfall of roubles turned their backs on dizzying overnight borrowing rates of 55–60 percent and instead offloaded government paper to make up the difference. Yields started to escalate, bursting through limits outlined by the central bank to hit 18-month highs of more than 50 percent on May 25. But dealers in Moscow said capital was still flowing out of the market despite the astronomical returns. "The fact that interest in investment is scarce even at such high yields is alarming," one Western trader said.

> 66 Yeltsin said the crisis was so acute that it was stirring "social and political dangers" 99

The next day Yeltsin signed an austerity package aimed at stabilizing the budget and cutting government spending, but it did nothing to stop the mounting panic. Not a single bidder put in for a 75 percent stake in Rosneft, the last big oil firm still in state hands. A new GKO issue on May 27 saw the average yield hit 61 percent, while the main Moscow share index plunged 11 percent. Desperate times called for desperate measures; the central bank tripled key interest rates to a staggering 150 percent. Yeltsin declared Russia had sufficient reserves to avoid a market crash. Influential tycoons pledged support for the president. Nerves steadied slightly and rates were soon pruned to a still-high 60 percent, but the relief was short-lived. In June, the IMF again delayed funding to Russia – an expected $670 million instalment of its existing $9.2 billion loan – citing problems with fiscal reforms.

An increasingly anxious Russia promptly asked for an extra $10–15 billion credit package from the IMF and other lenders and wheeled out an anti-crisis plan consisting mainly of tax laws. Sounding a warning both for foreign lenders and the recalcitrant Duma, Yeltsin said the crisis was so acute that it was stirring "social and political dangers", and hinted at stiff action if the lower house failed to pass the legislation smoothly. The $670 million IMF tranche was released, but the markets continued to tumble and the rouble was on its last legs.

By now Russia was also grappling with a serious external problem: world oil prices, which had been shaky for months, were approaching their lowest levels in ten years, and prices for other commodities were also depressed. Russia, the world's third largest crude producer and biggest source of natural gas, relied on oil and gas for around half its export earnings, and on metals for a further 15 percent or so. What was more, taxes on the companies doing the exporting accounted for a serious chunk of government revenue. (Gas company Gazprom was the state's main cash cow, generating a staggering quarter of all Russia's tax receipts.) The lower the oil prices, the lower the revenue.

By mid-July it was plain that something more dramatic was needed to help Russia out of the pit it was descending into. "[T]he international community faced a hard choice: whether to help Russia try to prevent devaluation," Fischer wrote later. "The adverse effects of a devaluation were clear and the reformist Kiriyenko government was making progress on taxes and in other areas. So the decision was made to help, recognizing that this was a calculated risk."[15] The IMF rapidly pieced together yet another bailout package, this time for $22.6 billion (made up of some $17 billion in new money, plus previously agreed loans), on condition that the Russians implement major tax reforms. The deal comprised just over $11 billion from the IMF's own coffers (which by now had started to dwindle), $1.5 billion from the World Bank, and nearly $10 billion from major industrial countries. At the same time, a debt restructuring scheme was drawn up whereby GKO holders could roll their rouble paper into longer-term dollar Eurobonds, taking the immediate pressure off government funds.

But the Duma threw a large spanner in the works, pulling to pieces the crisis plan presented by Yeltsin and Kiriyenko; the measures that were left would provide only a third of the revenues the frustrated prime minister had targeted. Yeltsin retaliated by vetoing the Duma's reduction in tax cuts and using his presidential powers of decree to hike land taxes four-fold. Fresh picketing by Siberian miners did not help the increasingly bleak mood, and rather than take up the Eurobond offer, most GKO holders chose to sell up and get out when their Treasury bills matured.

By August, devaluation talk was at fever pitch and the Russian markets were in meltdown. The more Russian shares and GKOs were sold off, the higher the demand for dollars. And the more people dived for the US currency, the more likely devaluation became. The rouble was staggering on its feet, and the central bank was haemorrhaging dollars – mostly lifted straight from the bailout funds – to try to prop it up. By the middle of the month Russia had blown the whole first tranche of its IMF rescue package, $4.8 billion, on defending the rouble.[16] GKO yields had soared above 100 percent, and the interbank currency market was virtually paralysed by liquidity shortages and plain fear. The government was running out of roubles to pay its domestic debt, and faced a stark choice: default on the GKOs, or set the printing presses rolling at the mint and risk plunging the country back into hyperinflation.

In a letter to London's *Financial Times*, published on August 13, Soros entered the fray by advising the Russian government to take the plunge: devalue by 15–25 percent, he said, and introduce a currency board pegging the rouble to the dollar or the euro. Russia's response was cool; after all, a currency board mechanism effectively deprives a country of sovereignty over its own monetary policy. But the name "Soros" was still enough to make investors prick up their ears, and stocks immediately plunged to their lowest in more than two years; GKO yields soared above 150 percent.

Yeltsin, on holiday in Novgorod, declared on Friday 14: "There will be no devaluation – that's firm and definite." (His brief media appearance was not a model of confidence building; reporters noted that he sometimes looked confused and had brief trouble recognizing a top aide.) But dollars had become scarce on the streets as ordinary Russians scrambled to turn their rouble savings into a currency they knew would hold its value. Some major banks were having trouble meeting payments to each other, and the rouble had sunk to 6.37 to the dollar – still within the broad corridor but outside the daily mini-band. The central bank had burned through about $9 billion in less than two months trying to prop up the rouble, and foreign reserves had dwindled to $15 billion.

The writing was on the wall. "We saw the result of the trading day and then we had the information about the behaviour of Moscow residents – the people were in lines and they wanted to buy dollars at any price," the then central bank chief, Sergei Dubinin, told Reuters journalist Peter Henderson a year later. "That was the start of the real devaluation, uncontrolled by any market measures."

RUSSIA'S DOUBLE WHAMMY

"Like anyone living beyond his means, Russia had simply dug itself into a financial hole," wrote Rose Brady, former Moscow bureau chief for *Business Week* magazine. "In August 1998, the walls of that hole came crashing in."[17] On Monday, August 17, Russia abandoned the mini-band

and shifted the target corridor downwards to between 6.0 and 9.5 to the dollar. Yet again, a country facing a full-blown run on its currency was trying to tinker with a fixed exchange rate mechanism that in itself was providing a target for attack. The government denied the change amounted to devaluation. "It is a new approach to currency policy," Kiriyenko insisted.

The market begged to differ. The central bank fixed Monday's official exchange rate at 6.43 roubles to the dollar but spot market rates quickly plunged beyond 7.0. Street rates at banks and foreign exchange booths went even further, ranging from 7.50 to 9.50 per dollar – a drop of 15–30 percent from the previous Friday. Many street outlets were fast running out of dollars to feed the frenzied demand, and some were not prepared to part with hard currency at any price. "We can get into semantics but this is a devaluation any way you slice it," said Richard Deitz, head of bond trading at MFK Renaissance, one of Moscow's bright new investment houses.

> Many street outlets were fast running out of dollars to feed the frenzied demand, and some were not prepared to part with hard currency at any price

The central bank hiked its overnight credit rate from 150 to 250 percent in a vain attempt to stem the tide. Russians unable to change their spare roubles into hard currency dashed to buy food or consumer goods before shop prices escalated. It was a luxury not everybody enjoyed. "Many people haven't been paid in months, so what to do with their roubles is not even a question," said one government worker in the far eastern city of Magadan.

But Russia did not stop at currency somersaults. At the same time it dropped an even bigger bombshell: a 90-day moratorium on some foreign debt servicing (which, in a rather unclear statement, appeared to refer to commercial bank loans) and a freeze on some $40 billion worth of GKOs and OFZs, which were to be restructured into new, longer-term debt instruments. It was reneging on the original terms of the bonds and imposing a unilateral solution. It amounted to default, no matter how much the Russians insisted otherwise.

Investors howled with rage and disbelief, although considering Russia's deservedly lawless reputation, perhaps they should not have been so surprised. "[I]t is hard to credit that sophisticated investors who had earned an average of 50 percent a year on GKOs since 1994 really believed these investments were safe," remarked the IMF's Fischer.[18] Details of the Russian restructuring proposal were sketchy and emerged at snail's pace, keeping the market on tenterhooks. Tempers ran even higher when word got out that domestic investors might get a better deal than foreigners. Eventually, over the course of several months, Russia's final terms were revealed: investors would get 10 percent of their holding in cash roubles and the rest in a mixture of rouble bonds with a three- to five-year maturity. It became clear that foreign investors could hope to recoup only 5–15 percent of the bonds' face value, depending on how well the domestic debt market fared; they would not even necessarily be able to get their money out of Russia, as they would have to compete at auction to exchange their roubles for limited dollars. There was talk that they would be able to swap the bonds for other assets, such as shares or corporate bonds, but again details were scarce.

"The way in which Russia handled the situation was very shocking to a lot of people," said Merrill Lynch economist Andrew Kenningham. "It wasn't just that they found themselves in a hole and they simply couldn't pay. It was extraordinary the way they just didn't consult, didn't apologize, just didn't seem to care. They basically told the financial markets to get lost."

It was the start of a long, increasingly poisonous and ultimately unsuccessful battle for an improved deal, a process complicated by the fact that GKOs and OFZs had been bought not only by the big banks but by thousands of fund managers and individual investors, all of whom had an axe to grind. The struggle ended up pitting small investors against banks, banks against each other, and everyone against the Russians, all in an atmosphere thick with accusations of arrogance and betrayal. One anecdote told of Russia's first deputy finance minister, Mikhail Kasyanov, running his finger down a list of ten bank proposals, saying: "No, no, no, no, no, no, no, no, no, no. But I like the font you are using."[19]

The group of 19 international banks charged with representing foreign creditors came close to collapse after three of their number – Chase Manhattan, Crédit Lyonnais and Deutsche Bank (which was chairing the committee) – broke ranks and accepted Moscow's controversial terms. Crédit Suisse First Boston (CSFB), which had perhaps the most to lose, tried to press ahead with an alternative proposal. Appeals and threats alike fell on deaf ears and in April 1999 Moscow finally declared the saga closed, saying nearly 90 percent of foreign debt holders had agreed to accept the Russian deal. (CSFB and several other banks begged to differ, refusing to put their bonds up for restructuring. And even months later, those who accepted were still in the dark about such crucial details as what exactly they could buy with their swapped bonds.)

For the Russian banking system, the implications of the devaluation and default were devastating. The banks were hit from all sides. The GKOs and OFZs that they had shovelled on to their books had been slashed in value, and could no longer be sold off quickly to raise cash when needed. The rouble's plunge left many banks with crippling forex market positions. At the same time, savers were rushing to pull out their cash; before long many banks simply ran out of money and locked their doors, leaving droves of disconsolate customers outside in the autumn rain. "I'll never put my money in a bank again," said one middle-aged Muscovite, who was forced to withdraw his dollar savings in small daily batches of roubles, at an artificially low exchange rate. The banks did not even trust each other with what little money they did have, bringing the whole payments system to the verge of collapse and leaving companies unable to settle bills or get paid themselves.

A NUCLEAR POWER ADRIFT

While markets and Russians were still reeling, the emerging market maelstrom shook up another political career. Yeltsin fell back on what was becoming his stock response to bad news and policy failures: on August 23 he sacked the government, calling Chernomyrdin back on stage to replace Kiriyenko. But the Duma would not play ball, first delaying the debate to confirm Chernomyrdin and then voting overwhelmingly against him. Yeltsin promptly renominated him for a second vote. The IMF put its bailout funds on hold and warned Russia not to retreat back to a Soviet-style command economy. In the midst of financial meltdown, Russia found itself without a functioning government and hostage to yet another political squabble.

Confusion ruled, but one thing was sure: the Russian markets were on the skids. By the end of August Russia's stock market had lost 59 percent of its value in dollar terms in just one month, and 84 percent since the start of the year. Currency trading soon seized up almost completely as official central bank rates, fixed at the daily trading sessions of the Moscow Interbank Currency Exchange (MICEX), remained radically out of kilter with rates on the electronic interbank market (known as SELT) or on the streets. The supply of cash dollars was drying up from St Petersburg to Vladivostok. "The quoted rates are irrelevant," said Paul McNamara, an emerging markets economist at Julius Bär Investments in London. "If you turn up with roubles looking for a large quantity of marks or dollars, you won't be able to change them."

Increasingly unable to defend the gulf between its official currency fix, which was still below 8.0 to the dollar, and actual, traded exchange rates, in late August the central bank suspended MICEX currency trading.

Rates on the SELT continued to slide, stooping as low as 12 or 13 to the dollar, and a week later government officials admitted they had abandoned their by now meaningless new target band. The old fixing system was quietly dropped in favour of a new official rate that reflected trades on the SELT, but the collapse continued.

By September 4 even the official fix put the rouble a whisker short of 17 to the dollar, a devaluation of 62 percent in three weeks. Worse, liquidity was so thin that even relatively small trades could knock the exchange rate sideways. There was talk that Russian banks temporarily ramped up the rouble to a more favourable rate before they were due to deliver on forward contracts, and then let it drop again. The Russian currency lost all semblance of stability and began to yo-yo wildly.

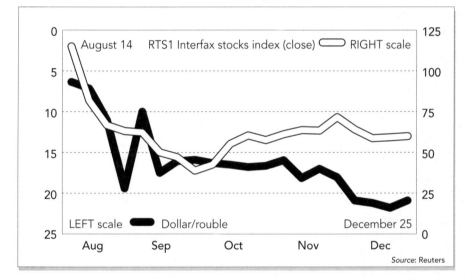

FIGURE 9 Russia's market meltdown, 1998

On September 7, after endless wrangling between the president and parliament, the Duma again rejected Chernomyrdin in a second vote. This was brinkmanship of the first order. Communist deputies were holding out for a policy swerve towards old remedies: printing money, curbing prices, controlling capital flows. Yeltsin dug in his heels. Western leaders warned that Russia could expect no support if it veered away from market reforms. The country with the world's second biggest nuclear arsenal was adrift, politically and economically, and to hear some opposition politicians, it seemed outraged Russians were ripe for revolution. In fact, the country's stoical citizens were taking it all more calmly than their leaders had any right to expect, and most neutral commentators dismissed the warnings of unrest as political opportunism. But as the stalemate dragged on, some could not help becoming a little more uneasy.

Finally, three days later, Yeltsin blinked. Instead of putting Chernomyrdin up for a third vote, he nominated Foreign Minister Yevgeny Primakov, a former Soviet spy chief, as a compromise candidate. Primakov won a swift thumbs-up from the Duma and quickly signalled a more conservative approach to economic reforms. He was joined by moderate Communist Yuri Maslyukov, a former Soviet planning chief, as first deputy prime minister for the economy. The West was nervous,

> 66 The country with the world's second biggest nuclear arsenal was adrift, politically and economically 99

although many Russia-watchers suggested the well respected Primakov was the only figure who could unite Communists and reformists behind a common crisis strategy. Even more worrying to the West, from an economic point of view, was the reappointment of Viktor Gerashchenko as central bank chief. Gerashchenko, who had presided over an earlier rouble crash and hyperinflation in 1994, was once dubbed "the world's worst central banker" by Harvard's Jeffrey Sachs. His immediate policy: print more roubles.

Still the political turmoil was not over. With Yeltsin badly undermined by the crisis and tucked away at his country residence outside Moscow, Primakov struggled to construct a cabinet with members who could do business together. Communists and liberals alike declined to join the government; by the end of September the cabinet was still not quite complete and economic plans remained unclear. "Primakov was groping for a policy that would restore Russia's banking system and bolster its industry while paying pensions and wages due Russians and debts due foreigners," Brady wrote. "It seemed an impossible task."[20]

EMERGING MARKET MELTDOWN

The Asian crisis had leapt across to Europe like a brush fire, and soon started to roast any country that had real or perceived links with Russia, be it through trade, geographical proximity, similar economic indicators, or merely by association as another emerging market. In fact, many Central European countries had long since toned down their trade links with Moscow in the post-Cold War era, and their transition from communism had been considerably smoother and more honest. But that did not stop them getting hammered.

With Europe now in the front line, nervous eyes shot across the Atlantic to Latin America, where Brazil's currency peg still looked like a juicy target for speculators. And there was no chance that still-shaky Asia would get off the hook. Investors were not necessarily feeling at their most rational, and sold off any emerging market that moved.

Stocks went into freefall across the board. Of the 33 exchanges covered in the IFC's emerging market indices, only three – Pakistan, Jordan and Morocco, all secluded financial spots at the best of times – did *not* fall in August 1998. In one month the IFC's Asia index dropped 19 percent, emerging Europe, the Middle East and Africa (classified together as "EMEA") plunged 28 percent, and Latin America collapsed nearly 34 percent. The downward spiral in hard-currency emerging market debt was equally indiscriminate; analysts said the mood was even grimmer than during the Tequila Crisis. "This one is much worse than 1995 and there is more of this to go," said debt strategist David McWilliams of Banque Nationale de Paris. Within a week of Russia's bombshell, average yield spreads over US Treasuries had leapt to nearly 1,100 basis points (a huge 11 percentage points), doubling from their early August level of around 650 basis points. In September they hit just over 1,700 basis points, still below their peak of around 1,950 at the height of the Mexican crisis, but a body blow nevertheless for emerging market borrowers.

Some of the countries that were worst hit had scarcely anything to do with Russia and were reasonably healthy in their own right, but were sold off just because they were easy to sell. The first two currencies to suffer rouble fallout were the Mexican peso and the Czech crown – simply because they were the most freely traded in the emerging market sphere, and acted as lightning conductors for the general mood. (The peso hit record lows, falling around 10 percent during August to within a whisker of 10 to the dollar.) South Africa's long-established bond and equity markets were also a victim of their own liquidity, with Johannesburg's main share index shedding 30 percent of its value in August. "South Africa's falling because it can," said John Clemmow, head of Africa research at Investec Securities in London. "If you're an emerging market fund manager, you're looking at some pretty ugly numbers right now. One of the only ways you can claw back losses is to short South Africa."

Others were more obvious targets. Ukraine, which lived in the shadow of Moscow's market whims, had a slow record on economic reform and depended on its giant neighbour for nearly half its foreign trade. Central bank governor Viktor Yushchenko had staked his reputation on keeping the relatively new hryvnia currency stable, but struggling to hold it within its trading band of 1.80–2.25 to the dollar had drained foreign reserves down to just $800 million – the market equivalent of small change. On September 4 the central bank gave in with what amounted to a sharp devaluation, uprooting the trading band and replanting it at 2.50–3.50 to the dollar. Predictably, the hryvnia was soon knocking up against 3.50, but for once the attempt to adjust rather than scrap a currency peg was not an immediate disaster, and a new 1999 band of 3.40–4.60 managed to accommodate further selling pressure without a major bust-up. That might have been that, if the economy had not been in such a mess in other ways. But with suspicion growing that Ukraine might default on its external debts, in August 1999 the currency finally slunk out of its corridor, and the central bank quietly let it go.

In contrast, Slovakia went for the big-bang approach. Burdened with a large budget deficit and a current-account chasm equalling 11 percent of GDP, the country was under heavy currency attack. On October 1, 1998, it threw in the towel, abandoning its trading band and floating the crown. Astonishingly, after a brief downward spike, the currency bobbed back again; it was only in early 1999 that it began a long, slow slide.

SLAMMING THE DOOR – MALAYSIA IMPOSES CAPITAL CONTROLS

After toeing the free-market line through more than a year of crisis, Malaysia's blood was up. Thumbing its nose at world finance and its accepted wisdom, on September 1, 1998, the country imposed a range of foreign exchange and capital controls to try to stem the outward tide. Offshore ringgit trading was effectively outlawed, and while foreigners were still free to buy Malaysian stocks, they would have to keep the proceeds of any share sales in the country for a full year. The following day the government announced that the ringgit would be fixed indefinitely at 3.80 to the dollar. "We believe in the free market, but we are not going to allow you to touch the ringgit," Mahathir said. Mahathir's fingerprints were all over the new policy, and the simultaneous sacking of Finance Minister Anwar, architect of Malaysia's IMF-lookalike crisis programme, underlined the snub to outside capital.

The investment community cried foul. Financial sages declared Malaysia had ruled itself out of any outside support and any possible Asian recovery. The United States said it was concerned. The IMF said any restrictions on capital movement were not conducive to building investor confidence. The IFC removed Malaysia from its "investable" stock indices. "[M]any foreigners are likely to wish the Malaysian market good riddance after serving their year in lock-up," *The Economist* predicted.[21] But some analysts, including a few bank economists, said the ploy might just work.

> 66 After toeing the free-market line through more than a year of crisis, Malaysia's blood was up 99

Round in Latin America, Brazil was taking another violent mauling. The general doom-laden mood was intensified by worries about the country's growing current-account gap, ballooning budget deficit (now around 7 percent of GDP) and a large amount of domestic short-term debt falling due. Latin America analysts pointed out that Brazil's debt situation, although superficially similar to Russia's, was actually very different; most of its short-term paper was held by local pension funds and insurance companies, which were more likely to roll over the debt than skittish foreigners and shady banks. Few investors were listening, and the real's trading band system looked increasingly vulnerable. But President Fernando Henrique Cardoso would not budge on an inflation-busting system that he had designed when he was finance minister.

São Paulo's benchmark Bovespa share index plummeted nearly 40 percent in August, and carried on downwards. Hundreds of millions of dollars were flooding each day out of the country's forex markets, forcing the central bank to pump in an estimated $15 billion of its foreign reserves over the first two weeks of September to support the currency. The exodus reached a crescendo on September 10 when the forex markets lost $2 billion in a single day and panicked the Bovespa into a 16 percent plunge, its biggest one-day drop for nearly 11 years. The government had already cranked interest rates back up from 19 percent to 30 percent just a few days before; now it hiked them again to 50 percent. Brazil still had foreign reserves of about $50 billion, but the experience of Thailand, South Korea and Russia had shown the pointlessness of running them into the ground, only to devalue anyway. The government needed to win back the market's confidence, but with presidential elections looming on October 4, public spending cuts could prove a vote-loser. On the other hand, opinion polls showed Brazilians trusted Cardoso as a steady hand in difficult times; to let the currency go before the polls could be political suicide.

The government announced $5 billion in emergency spending cuts and said it was talking to the IMF. Cardoso was staking his career on the real.

GLOBAL PANIC

Brazil's stock market rout sparked tumbles in other world markets from Argentina to Japan. And so it continued – the merry-go-round kept turning, drawing in emerging and major markets alike. After brushing off the wobble of October 1997, the major Western stock markets had gone on to scale new heights, but the euphoria obscured an uncomfortable fact: stock prices were now looking even more overblown than they had the previous autumn. Price/earnings ratios of over 20 were common, implying it would take at least 20 years for projected company dividends to add up to the price paid for the share. It was all looking more bubble-like by the week, and some investors were already starting to hold their breath, fearing any suggestion of bad news could prove to be the pin-prick. After peaking more or less together in mid-July, major North American and European stock markets had started easing back, unnerved by the deteriorating situation to the east.

Russia's devaluation and default was the new catalyst for deeper-seated panic. In a practical sense, Western exposure to Russia through bond purchases and bank lending was big (particularly in Germany), but not necessarily crippling. Western economies were in reasonable shape, by and large, and scarcely dependent for their well-being on a country with a GDP only about four-fifths the size of Spain's. But as in Asia, the breadth and complexity of many fund investments meant markets that could not have had less to do with Russia – from stock index derivatives to bonds bundling up US student loans – were sold off to cover Russian losses. And on a purely gut level, Russia's wider significance was immense. The realization that the decaying nuclear power had not, after all, been "too big to fail" was a grave shock to the financial world, raising the spectre of political destabilization.

> " The realization that the decaying nuclear power had not been "too big to fail" was a grave shock to the financial world "

There was an immediate frantic scurry into traditional safe havens. On August 18 the dollar raced to a five-week high against the mark, while yields on the US 30-year Treasury bond (the ultra-solid "long bond") shrank to a record low of 5.51 percent from 5.65 percent only two trading days earlier. On August 31 the Duma's first rejection of Chernomyrdin tipped the Dow into its second-largest point loss in history, shedding 512 points, or more than 6 percent. Once again it bounced smartly the next day in record trading volume, climbing more than 188 points, or 3.8 percent, to stage its second-biggest point comeback ever.

But this time the US rebound was not enough to turn the tide. The Dow steadied, but other major bourses were tumbling into an accelerated slide. By mid-September London stocks were down 17 percent and Frankfurt 23 percent from their July peaks, and still falling. Madrid, with its strong business links to Latin America, was down 30 percent. The enfeebled Tokyo market was scraping 12-year lows. Yields on the US long bond were approaching a historic 5 percent low as investors rushed for cover.

Things would get even worse before they got better.

NOTES

1   Henderson, *Asia Falling*, p. 171.

2   World Bank, *Global Development Finance 1998*, p. 47.

3   *Euromoney*, July 1999.

4   Andrei Shleifer, "Will Russia Grow?", in *The Economist*'s *The World in 1997*, p. 122.

5   EBRD, *Transition Report 1997*, p. 196.

6   Story, *The Frontiers of Fortune*, p. 118.

7   EBRD, *Transition Report 1998*, p. 187.

8   World Bank, *Global Development Finance 1999*, p. 92.

9   EBRD, *Transition Report 1998*, p. 13.

10 "Reforming World Finance: Lessons from a crisis", in *The Economist*, October 3, 1998.

11 *Euromoney*, August 1996.

12 EBRD, *Transition Report 1998*, p. 13.

13 World Bank, *Global Development Finance 1999*, p. 92.

14 ING Barings Fixed Income Research, *Emerging Markets Weekly Report*, January 30, 1998, p. 29.

15 *The Economist*, October 3, 1998.

16 EBRD, *Transition Report 1998*, p. 14.

17 Brady, *Kapitalizm: Russia's Struggle to Free its Economy*, p. 246.

18 *The Economist*, October 3, 1998.

19 *Euromoney*, March 1999.

20 Brady, p. 246.

21 *The Economist*, September 12, 1998.

6

EMERGENCY TREATMENT

No man is an Island, entire of itself – John Donne, *Devotions upon Emergent Occasions*

BACK TO THE '30s? – FEARS OF A WORLD SLUMP

By September 1998 there was a mounting sense of fear that the entire world might be heading for a serious recession, or even worse: a full-blown depression, 1930s-style.

Russia and most of Asia were already on their knees. Japan's economy had contracted for the third quarter in a row in April–June, the first time it had registered such a long losing streak since the country started counting its GDP that way in 1955. Government forecasts suggested South Korea's economy would shrink by 4 percent in 1998, Thailand's by 7 percent, and Indonesia's by more than 10 percent, while the IMF was predicting a 6 percent contraction in Russia. Other emerging economies, forced to keep their interest rates at astronomical levels to defend their currencies and try to restore market confidence, were being sucked backwards into the vortex; the high cost of borrowing was not only crippling investment and hamstringing growth but cranking up governments' domestic debt costs at a time when the markets and the IMF were demanding smaller budget deficits.

Job cuts, wage curbs and inflation were taking their toll. Lower import demand in one country translated into lower exports from another, spreading the pinch to other industries in distant lands. Rock-bottom commodity prices, initially driven down by the Asian crisis, were squeezing many of the world's poorest countries, including some that had never dreamt of issuing a Eurobond or getting entangled in the vagaries of foreign portfolio investment.

Growth was slowing in the West and asset prices were collapsing around the globe, with hundreds of billions of dollars wiped off the value of listed companies. (HSBC Securities' strategist Sharon Coombs put the combined stock market loss in just two months at a minimum of $4.3 trillion[1] – more than Japan's annual GDP.) Wounded Asian banks were already less willing to lend, and there were fears of a more widespread credit crunch as Western banks counted the cost of their emerging market losses.

Since the early 1970s Western policymakers had been preoccupied with inflation, but now deflation was starting to emerge as the new bogey. Japan, caught in a classic "liquidity trap", was already providing an object lesson in the dangers of falling rather than rising prices. Who wants to buy today if the same goods will be cheaper tomorrow? To put it simplistically, if nobody buys anything, the economy shrivels up. Companies go bust, and with jobs disappearing, people are even less likely to splash out on anything but essential purchases. The Bank of Japan had long ago pruned interest rates about as far as they could go without literally paying people to borrow – its leading short-term interest rate was a tiny 0.5 percent – but consumption was still dead in the water. The country was stuck in a vicious circle of falling demand and falling prices. And despite its still very positive growth figures, China was showing every sign of falling into the same trap, with interest rate cuts failing to stop prices falling consistently over the previous 12 months.

> 66 The prosperity of the so-called Goldilocks economy had allowed the United States to act as a global shock-absorber 99

The United States, pillar of the world economy and home of the gravity-defying Dow, was throwing up a few worrying pointers of its own. The prosperity of the so-called Goldilocks economy – not too hot, not too cold – had allowed the country to act as a global shock-absorber, running a substantial current-account deficit which helped to prop up exports from the crisis-torn regions. But that did not mean Washington was not concerned about its export prospects, which had already taken a knock in Asian markets. Industrial production was slipping, and if Latin America (which sucked up around a fifth of US exports) went the same way as Asia and Russia, US factories would feel an even greater chill. Farmers were in trouble too, and analysts were slashing their US growth estimates. A sharp fall in the wholesale price index in August raised eyebrows, suggesting the economy could indeed be cooling off to the point where deflation, rather than inflation, became an issue. If the taut Dow bubble were to burst with a bang, who knows what impact it could have on the world's biggest economy.

Little wonder, then, that the IMF revised its forecast for world economic growth in 1998 sharply downwards to 2 percent – less than half the 4.1 percent growth seen in 1997, and cut from an earlier prediction of 3.1 percent – and said even that could be overly optimistic. This was a global crisis by anyone's standards, yet there seemed little sign that the major industrial countries were going to do anything very concrete about it. "In the short term, there is now a crying need for globally co-ordinated interest rate cuts," Harvard's Jeffrey Sachs wrote in *The Economist*,[2] but US and European officials were pouring cold water on such suggestions. In early September Greenspan signalled a subtle shift in the Federal Reserve's hawkish view on inflation, warning that the United States could not hope to escape the international turmoil. "It is just not credible that the United States can remain an oasis of prosperity unaffected by a world that is experiencing greatly increased stress," he said. But his follow-up remark that the skittish market environment "counsels caution" seemed designed to dampen expectations of an immediate rate cut.

President Clinton could perhaps be forgiven for having his mind on other things: the threat that he would be impeached over the sex-and-perjury scandal following his affair with White House intern Monica Lewinsky. Conservative German Chancellor Helmut Kohl was also understandably preoccupied: after four terms in office, it looked as though he was about to lose general elections on September 27. Most other European leaders seemed too mesmerized by the imminent birth of the euro to look much beyond the borders of the European Union. "With international financial markets in turmoil and the risk of a global slump mounting, where is the world's economic leadership?" asked *The Los Angeles Times*. "Mostly out of sight."[3]

Soros, consummate insider in the capital game, sounded a grim warning. "The global capitalist system which has been responsible for the remarkable prosperity of this country in the last decade is coming apart at the seams," he told a US congressional committee in mid-September. "The current decline in the US stock market is only a symptom, and a belated symptom at that, of the more profound problems that are afflicting the world economy. Some Asian stock markets have suffered worse declines than the Wall Street crash of 1929 and in addition their currencies have fallen to a fraction of what their value was when they were tied to the US dollar … Russia has undergone a total financial meltdown. It is a scary spectacle and it will have incalculable human and political consequences. The contagion has now also spread to Latin America. It would be regrettable if we remained complacent just because most of the trouble is occurring beyond our borders."[4]

Gradually the penny was dropping that something really did have to be done if the world economy was not to career over the edge of a cliff, and the pace of high-level contacts between G7 countries started to pick up. The G7 member in by far the deepest trouble – but with least leeway to lower rates – was the first to act. On September 9 the Bank of Japan cut interest rates for the first time in three years, shaving a further 25 basis points off its main short-term rate to leave it at a wafer-thin 0.25 percent.

A few days later Clinton sounded what would become a recurring refrain: "This is the biggest financial challenge facing the world in a half century," he told the Council on Foreign Relations in New York. Sketching out a range of immediate moves needed to pull the world economy back from the brink, Clinton's speech gave a heavy hint that rate cuts might be in the offing after all. "For most of the last 30 years, the United States and the rest of the world have been preoccupied by inflation, for reasons that all of you here know all too well," he said. "But clearly, the balance of risks has now shifted with a full quarter of the world's population living in countries with declining economic growth or negative economic growth. Therefore, I believe the industrial world's chief priority today plainly is to spur growth."

It was clearly no coincidence that a statement the same day from G7 finance ministers and central bank heads used the same phrase: the "balance of risks" in the world economy had shifted. Yet individually, the central bank chiefs – Greenspan, Britain's Eddie George, Germany's Hans Tietmeyer – were still distancing themselves from any whiff of co-ordinated rate cuts. Germany, Europe's biggest economy, was pointing out that its key interest rate was already at a historic low of 3.3 percent – more than 200 basis points lower than the main US rate. If there were to be cuts, they would have to come from somewhere else.

FALL OF A HEDGE FUND – THE LTCM DILEMMA

But there was another bombshell to come. Since early September the major markets had been unnerved by rumours that hedge funds had made big losses in the Russian crash and might even be on the verge of defaulting on highly leveraged market positions. Specifically, there was anxious talk that the "Rolls-Royce of hedge funds", Long-Term Capital Management, was in deep trouble. Based not on jostling Wall Street but in the calm of suburban Connecticut, LTCM was set up in 1994 by John Meriwether, formerly a star bond trader at Salomon Brothers in the swashbuckling heyday of the 1980s. Meriwether hired a crack team of "rocket scientists" – top mathematicians, physicists and computer experts including two Nobel prize-winning economists – who built highly sophisticated computer models to search out areas where different assets (mainly bonds) might be over- or underpriced in relation to one another. LTCM might go long in, say, Danish mortgage-backed securities on the calculation that they were cheap compared to their historical levels, and therefore their price should rise. At the same time, it would hedge its position by shorting other securities it felt were overpriced – particularly the secure and highly liquid US long bond. On top of that, it would hedge again with a plethora of complex derivatives.

It was supposed to be a foolproof, risk-free money machine, generating wads of cash by skimming off sometimes tiny profits on a very high number of transactions. Its select band of clients, including the major investment banks, paid handsome fees for its services, but they also raked in handsome profits; in 1995 and 1996 LTCM provided returns of 40 percent, and even in the more difficult climate of 1997 it earned its clients nearly 20 percent on their money.[5] Like any hedge fund, it leveraged up its investors' original capital by borrowing, and then leveraged its market positions even further by making small margin payments against the full value of the securities.

By September 1998 LTCM was indeed in trouble, although its mistake was not to bet the wrong way on emerging markets as such; in fact, around 80 percent of its investment was in G7 government bonds.[6] But the crisis that originated in emerging markets did lead directly to LTCM's downfall. The hedge fund's brainy models worked on the assumption that prices for various securities would move in different directions from one another under typical market conditions. What they were not prepared for was the risk of unprecedented events – the spread of the Asian crisis and Russia's financial collapse – and the way they could stand "normal" market patterns on their head. In the panic of August and September 1998 just about every market worldwide was dropping; the only thing that was rising was US Treasuries, which was exactly what LTCM had tipped to fall. The notion that LTCM's risks offset each other was suddenly blown out of the water; everything was moving against it, and not by inches but by miles.

Since the banks that had done business with LTCM had also often mimicked its trusted strategies in their proprietary trading, everyone was trying to get out of the same market positions at once. Prices slumped even further and liquidity evaporated, making it hard to sell anything. LTCM was caught in a vice of mounting "margin calls", the requirement to top up margin payments as the assets they covered fell in value. During August alone the fund's underlying capital was nearly halved from $4.1 billion to $2.3 billion. Meriwether wrote to his clients asking for more money, but no one obliged. In the following three weeks LTCM's equity crashed to $600 million. The Rolls-Royce of hedge funds had lost 85 percent of its capital in less than two months, and was on the verge of going under.

LTCM's balance sheet at the end of August showed it had leveraged its basic capital by around 30 times into more than $125 billion in assets – money which nervous creditors now wanted back. But the potential to destabilize the markets went much further than that. LTCM had built a house of cards in various derivatives markets, including some very far away from its traditional bonds expertise, multiplying its assets into gross positions that nominally totalled more than $1.4 trillion[7] – about the size of Britain's annual GDP. These contracts were "off-balance-sheet" – that is, they did not have to be booked in LTCM's main accounts. What was more, they were intricately linked, so that default on one could trigger default on all of them. If LTCM collapsed, all its positions would have to be unwound in what Greenspan would later refer to as a "fire sale" – a massive simultaneous sell-off that would reinforce the landslide already in motion and shake the global markets to their boots.

> **If LTCM collapsed, all its positions would have to be unwound in a massive sell-off that would reinforce the landslide**

On September 22 the chairman of the regional New York Federal Reserve Bank, Bill McDonough, flew to New York for an emergency meeting after telling a London audience he saw the situation as "by some considerable margin ... the most dangerous since the Second World War".[8] He joined a cluster of frightened bankers assembled behind the New York Fed's forbidding, Italianate exterior. The banks had been trying for some time to find a solution to the looming LTCM disaster, but it was only when the Fed banged heads together (and an alternative offer to buy the hedge fund had fallen through) that they came up with a bailout plan – an extra $3.6 billion in capital, stumped up by 14 mainly Wall Street investment houses. Russia may not have been considered too big to fail, but LTCM was.

The deal drew a great deal of flak, with Wall Street standing accused of crony capitalism and "looking after its own" in saving Meriwether's otherwise bankrupt fund from collapse. The Federal Reserve also came in for close questioning on its role in the rescue, although (contrary to many people's assumption) no public money had gone into it; McDonough wryly told a congressional banking committee the US tax-payers' contribution stretched only to buying sandwiches for the bankers' meeting. Greenspan, testifying to the same committee, defended the move in blunt language. "Had the failure of LTCM triggered the seizing up of markets, substantial damage could have been inflicted on many market participants, including some not directly involved with the firm, and could have potentially impaired the economies of many nations, including our own," he said.

In Asia, a region struggling to negotiate debt write-downs from many of the same banks that bailed out LTCM, the response was cynical. "There's no denying the system works in favour of the advantaged," said one Western researcher based in Hong Kong. "At the end of the day, the big boys get to say what the rules are."

THE DOLLAR LURCHES

Although the rescue no doubt warded off even greater chaos, the markets were unnerved that things could have got so bad at LTCM in the first place, and fretted about whether any more of the secretive hedge funds could be ready to spring similar surprises. Banking shares were badly hit around the world, knocking down stock markets still further, especially when individual banks started releasing details of their multimillion-dollar exposure to the hedge fund. Swiss bank UBS announced it would take a $700 million "charge" in its accounts (effectively set aside as a loss) as a result of its investment in LTCM. More eyebrows were raised when it emerged that the Italian Exchange Office (UIC), an agency of Italy's central bank, had invested $250 million of the country's foreign reserves in LTCM. "As far as we knew, it was not a hedge fund, it was a long-term investment fund," UIC's hapless director, Pierantonio Ciampicali, admitted to Reuters' Clelia Oziel before being yanked away by central bank chief Antonio Fazio.

LTCM seemed to snap central bankers out of their trance. Finally, on September 29, the Fed trimmed its main rate by 25 basis points to 5.25 percent. Canada followed suit, by the same margin. But the reaction in the markets was disappointment. They had been expecting a bigger cut; one Canadian-based banking publication described it as "no more than a squashed bug on the windscreen of the world's runaway deflationary train".[9] The slide continued, and in some markets even intensified. The Dow was barely off its lows of late August, and on October 1 trading on the Lisbon stock exchange had to be halted for two hours after a panicky 15 percent plunge.

On the political front things were picking up steam, with mounting calls from various G7 and other national leaders for reforms to the world financial system. Clinton proposed that the G7 and the IMF create a new funding mechanism to provide countries under threat of contagion with the extra financial muscle they needed to ward off the crisis *before* they were on their knees – prevention, rather than cure. (Critics suggested the United States was ill-placed to urge any further IMF spending when its refusal to top up the financial pot, as a hostile Congress blocked $18 billion in US contributions, meant the Fund was already close to running out of cash.)

The annual IMF and World Bank meeting, held this time in Washington, provided an ideal chance for the world's economic movers and shakers to put their heads together. The mood was grim and the agenda set squarely on global financial reforms. Japanese Finance Minister Kiichi Miyazawa took advantage of the platform to launch a $30 billion aid initiative to promote economic stability in the Asian countries worst hit by the crisis. The rationale of what became known as the Miyazawa Plan was that by pumping cash into countries such as Thailand or South Korea, they would not only be able to mend their own houses but buy more Japanese goods, helping to pull the region's sick economic giant out of recession.

> **The dollar, that bastion of supposed safety in an unruly financial world, took a stomach-churning dive against the yen**

It was a welcome step from a country that the West still saw as pivotal to Asia's recovery. But at the same time, Japan was causing infuriation with its snail's-pace progress on its own banking mess. Government and opposition were locked in a seemingly interminable battle over whether, and how, public money could be used to shore up teetering institutions such as Long-Term Credit Bank of Japan, a pillar of the country's post-war reconstruction brought low by bad loans. "[The Miyazawa Plan] is worthy and generous, no doubt, but effective measures to fix the country's banks would be worth ten such schemes," *The Economist* said in an editorial.[10]

Then something very unnerving happened in the forex markets. The dollar, that bastion of supposed safety in an unruly financial world, took a stomach-churning dive against the yen. In four days, from October 5 to October 8, it plunged 18 percent against the Japanese currency, from Monday's high of 136 yen to less than 112 at its lowest point on Thursday. The greenback had already eased back from August highs of over 145 against the yen, partly on expectations of a slowing US economy and interest rate cuts. But this collapse, and a simultaneous crash of the mark against the yen, left the markets in shock.

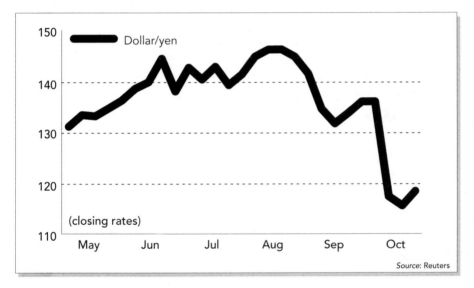

FIGURE 10 Dollar/yen yo-yo, 1998

It happened to coincide with tentative progress in Tokyo on plans to recapitalize sick banks, which briefly cheered the Japanese stock market, but few people put the seismic exchange rate shift down to such a tenuous cause. The main reason, traders said, was hedge fund activity – only this time they were not in ebullient, attacking form, but on the run. Borrowing cheaply in yen had been a classic way for hedge funds to leverage up their investment in other, higher-yielding assets. Now they were losing money, unwinding those positions, and having to buy yen to repay the loans. Many people feared there was a lot more unwinding to come, particularly if LTCM's new beneficiaries decided to sell off some or even all of its portfolio. As the yen started to shoot up, more people baled out of the US and German currencies. They panicked; the slide grew steeper. "Dollar/yen should not be at these levels," said economist Tony Norfield at ABN Amro. "It's all getting out of hand. There is potential for a market breakdown."

Other markets were reeling too, sending yields on the safe-haven US long bond crashing through the magic 5 percent barrier to around 4.8 percent. The sudden chaos was a clear sign that investors all over the world were punch-drunk and desperate to cut down their risks at all costs. Reliable, high-liquidity investments were the order of the day and some weird market distortions were springing up, reflecting a pervasive fear of being trapped in a falling asset. It was natural enough for yields on emerging market debt or low-grade US junk bonds to shoot up in times of uncertainty. But yields on 29-year US Treasury bonds also ballooned significantly higher than on the 30-year long bond – not because 12 months would make a jot of difference to whether they were repaid, but because they traded in a smaller, less liquid market and might therefore be harder to pull out of.[11]

The terror afflicted banks just as much as small investors, and if banks became too risk-averse, a broad credit crunch could not be far behind. Hinting at further rate cuts, Greenspan said US banks were looking more reluctant to lend – even to healthy businesses – than he had seen in 50 years of watching the economy. "It is pretty obvious that the outlook for 1999 for the US economy has deteriorated sharply," he told an audience of economists.

STRONG MEDICINE – PRUNING GLOBAL INTEREST RATES

As the dollar was dropping, an avalanche of another kind was starting to move. On October 6, Spain cut its main interest rate by half a percentage point to 3.75 percent, taking it nearer to the low "core" euro zone rates of countries such as Germany and France. On October 8, Britain and Denmark trimmed rates by 25 basis points. The next day it was the turn of Portugal (50 basis points) and Ireland (a hefty 125 basis points). The momentum carried into the following week, with a Greek cut of 25 basis points.

Then the Fed sprang a big surprise: without waiting for the next meeting of its policy-setting Federal Open Market Committee (FOMC), Greenspan weighed in on October 15 with a further 25-basis-point cut (and again, Canada followed suit). The move, which took US rates to their lowest for four years, galvanized global markets: the Dow closed 4 percent up, its highest for nearly two months, while Canadian stocks posted their second biggest one-day gain ever. "It's telling you they don't give a toss about inflation any more – let's go out and save the world," said one trader.

There were other encouraging signs. The dollar's plunge against the yen may have depressed Japanese exporters and scared the life out of major market players, but it was greeted with delight in South Korea and other East Asian countries competing with Japan to sell their goods abroad. There were signs – admittedly faint and fragile – that Asia might be starting a tentative recovery on the back of financial sector reforms, falling local interest rates, and sharply improved current-account balances. Cardoso escaped joining the list of discarded politicians, coasting home in Brazil's presidential election, and the IMF made encouraging noises about the chances of a Fund-led rescue package for the country.

66 Intentionally or unintentionally, a rescue plan for the entire world financial system was gradually coalescing 99

In addition, two protracted but crucial sagas came to a head. On October 15, after hard-hitting persuasion from Greenspan and Rubin, the US Congress at last okayed Washington's long-blocked $18 billion contribution to the IMF, albeit with strings attached on reforming the Fund. ("We risked having a fireman deprived of his water supply," a relieved Camdessus said.) The next day, in a sometimes stormy session, Japan's parliament finally passed hard-fought measures providing more than $500 billion in public funds to support the rickety financial sector.

Intentionally or unintentionally, a rescue plan for the entire world financial system was gradually coalescing. On October 26, Italy joined the interest rate bonanza, slashing its discount rate by a full percentage point to 4 percent. Then Brazil came out with details of a swingeing austerity programme, setting the stage for an IMF deal. G7 finance ministers and central bank governors endorsed a plan to shore up the international financial framework, including $90 billion in extra funds for the IMF to create an economic safety net for struggling countries. In mid-November Brazil's IMF-led international aid package was announced, worth more than $41 billion. Japan chimed in with its biggest ever economic stimulus package, aiming to prime the pump of domestic demand with around $150 billion in new public spending and $50 billion in tax cuts.

But pressure for further interest rate reductions was still running high, and on November 17 the OECD warned that the world economy could screech to a halt if major nations were not prepared to make credit even cheaper. The report was released on the same day that the Fed's FOMC was due to meet, and it acted right on cue, trimming US rates by a further 25 basis points. Canada once more echoed the move. US and world markets were euphoric.

There was one more dose of emergency medicine to come. Germany's new centre-left government and other European politicians had been lobbying hard for interest rate cuts to avoid a domestic slowdown, but the region's independent central bankers had stuck to their monetary guns and rejected the demands. Then, on December 3, in absolute secrecy and without a hitch, the fledgling European Central Bank (ECB) orchestrated simultaneous rate cuts in all 11 countries that were preparing to adopt the euro. The operation stunned world markets and won warm applause from Washington. The ECB had not yet even taken official control of the euro zone – EMU went into effect the following month with the introduction of the euro – but the smoothness of the operation earned the new institution its spurs and hammered home the message that global growth, rather than inflation, was the new priority.

The drugs worked. By the end of the year the twisted US bond markets had been ironed out, with long bond yields returning above 5 percent as investors felt brave enough to start putting their money somewhere else. The Dow had rebounded to within a hair of its July peak, and most other major stock markets had narrowed the gap dramatically. Nearly all ended 1998 sharply higher than 1997. One of the most closely watched developed stock market indicators, the Morgan Stanley Capital International (MSCI) World index, rose nearly 23 percent over the year as a whole. Italy and Belgium showed gains of more than 50 percent on the year in dollar terms, and Finland was up by more than 80 percent.

By trimming rates by three-quarters of a percentage point in less than two months, the Fed had led the global money doctors. "Meriwether almost destroyed the international financial system. Alan Greenspan saved it," John Taylor, chairman of FX Concepts in New York, told Reuters in a poll that voted the US central banker "financial newsmaker of the year". Yet as Krugman related, success had been far from a foregone conclusion, and even Fed officials were not quite sure how they pulled it off. "At the height of the crisis it seemed entirely possible that cutting interest rates would be entirely ineffectual – after all, if nobody can borrow, what difference does it make what the price would be if they could," he wrote. "And if everyone had believed that the world was coming to an end, their panic might – as in so many other countries – have ended up being a self-fulfilling prophecy. In retrospect Greenspan seemed to have been like a general who rides out in front of his demoralized army, waves his sword and shouts encouragement, and somehow turns the tide of battle: well done, but not something you would want to count on working next time."[12]

Emerging markets also breathed far easier once global calm was restored, although most were still too sick to do much other than lie quietly in bed. The IFCI Composite emerging stock market index dropped 24 percent in 1998 as a whole, while Latin America shed 38 percent. Russia, the world's best performing stock market for two years running, lost nearly 88 percent of its value in dollar terms and slumped in disgrace to bottom place in the IFC's ranking of 87 major and emerging markets.[13]

But there were bright spots, from perhaps an unexpected quarter. Building quietly, from an admittedly low starting point, South Korea crept back up to steal the title of the world's best performer with a startling

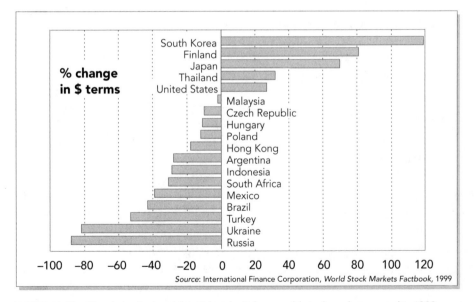

Source: International Finance Corporation, *World Stock Markets Factbook*, 1999

FIGURE 11 The Good, the Bad and the Ugly, take 2: how world stock markets scored in 1998

119 percent rise. And the Thai market grew by 32 percent, coming in ahead of German or US stocks. First or almost first into the crisis, it seemed they could be the first out.

BRAZIL CLINGS ON – BUT LOSES IN THE END

Brazil shared in the global sigh of relief. It had the fears and expectations not only of Latin America but of the world riding on its shoulders. There had always been the risk that if Latin America were infected with the same flu that had ravaged Asia and Russia, the US economy could expect to catch a bad cold at the very least. But in the current climate it could turn out to be a chill that the Fed would be unable to cure.

Cardoso's austerity plan, put together under the stern eye of the IMF and the United States, combined high interest rates with budget cuts and tax hikes designed to save a massive $84 billion over three years. Its severity showed how desperate both Brazil and the IMF were to shore up market confidence. "The program for Brazil was peculiarly extreme; it was almost like a caricature of the policies that had been introduced in Asia the preceding year," Krugman wrote.[14]

Brazil's notoriously fractious Congress put up heavy resistance to a package that, on the ground, was bound to speed the country's slide into recession. But in early November the lower house finally approved a bill to shake up the unwieldy social security system, a long-delayed piece of legislation that had been written into the austerity plan. It was enough to unlock international funding, although a host of other belt-tightening measures were still to be approved. Brazil was swiftly rewarded with the $41 billion IMF-led support package, including contributions from the World Bank, the Inter-American Development Bank, and leading industrial nations. Its importance lay less in the cash itself than in the positive message it sent to the markets. "It's all a matter of confidence," said Peter West, chief economist at BBV Securities. "It's a matter of making the package big enough that you don't have to use it."

The government still faced an uphill struggle in getting the other emergency measures through Congress; setbacks in December, when legislators threw out a key pension reform and delayed another crucial vote, threatened to leave state coffers some $5.6 billion short of the target agreed with the IMF. But Cardoso was more or less holding the line, and few doubted that the next tranche of the rescue package would be shelled out without a hitch. Brazil entered 1999 with a sense that the worst of the market panic was over – as long as there were no nasty surprises on the road to continued fiscal reform.

It was too good to be true. Virtually out of the blue, on January 6 the governor of Minas Gerais state, former Brazilian president Itamar Franco, declared a 90-day moratorium on the state's debt payments to the federal government. The amount of money in question was limited, but the move was a direct snub to Cardoso and drove a coach and horses through the government's austerity drive. Market players were immediately back on the defensive – or in some cases, on a speculative offensive – selling off the real and forcing the central bank to cut through about $1 billion a day in foreign reserves.

Panic was back with a vengeance, and after sticking fast to the real throughout the Asian and Russian crises, Brazil could not hold on any longer. Yet again, it tried to do what other crisis-hit countries had failed to do: pull off a limited devaluation. On Wednesday, January 13 the central bank said it was abandoning the mini trading band used to control the currency's gradual depreciation under the crawling peg system, but would keep the broader maxi-band intact, although its edges were tweaked slightly lower and would be readjusted every three days. This meant the real, which was around 1.21 to the dollar the previous day, would in theory be allowed to trade as low as 1.32 before hitting the edge of the new band. It immediately did so – a drop of 8 percent. Markets around the world shuddered and central bank president Gustavo Franco resigned. An estimated $2.5 billion poured out of Brazil's currency markets on Wednesday and Thursday alone – an exodus harking back to the days of the Russian devaluation – and by Friday, January 15 the real was starting to creep outside its designated corridor.

> Brazil entered 1999 with a sense that the worst of the market panic was over

The gamble of tinkering with Brazil's inflation-busting currency system had failed to stabilize the markets, and the central bank had nowhere else to turn. On Friday it stopped intervening in the markets, ditched the maxi-band completely, and let the real float freely. The result took many people (including currency analysts) by surprise: knee-jerk selling rapidly drove the currency as low as 1.58 to the dollar, but it quickly stabilized around 1.40–1.45, a total fall of less than 17 percent from Tuesday's pre-devaluation level. Now that the target bands were gone, there seemed to be nothing more to shoot at, and the overriding emotion in the markets was relief that Brazil was not pouring more reserves down the drain. The Bovespa share index rocketed an ecstatic 33 percent – its second biggest one-day rise ever – on the assumption that the country could afford to cut its crippling interest rates now that it was no longer defending the currency. Markets around the world had a fresh spring in their step.

Unfortunately for Brazil, that was not quite the end of the matter. Granted, the euphoria was overdone; the government still had a hard row to hoe in pushing forward its catalogue of fiscal reforms. But when Finance Minister Pedro Malan flew to Washington for weekend meetings with IMF and US officials, he was told interest rates should be raised, not lowered. The following Monday the central bank boosted its prime overnight lending rate for banks to 41 percent from 29 percent, casting a pall of gloom over the economy. Not only did higher domestic rates squeeze borrower companies, but they automatically increased the cost to the government of servicing its domestic debts, putting still more pressure on state finances and the budget deficit. By the end of the month the real had sunk below the psychological two-per-dollar barrier for the first time ever, and was trading around 2.10 – more than 40 percent below its pre-devaluation level. Interest rates were still rising, but the higher they went, the less impact the hikes seemed to have on the market mood. Fresh tremors rippled through emerging markers – weaker than before, but still unnerving. Asian stock markets slid by up to 8 percent, and the Polish zloty lost nearly 5 percent of its value against the euro.

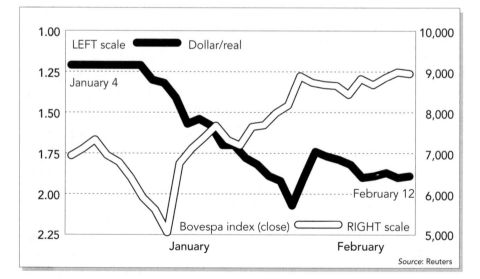

FIGURE 12   Real trouble: Brazil's big dipper, 1999

KEEPING UP WITH THE SLIDE An exchange house employee in Mexico City updates its rates in March 1995 as the peso plunges against the dollar.

ASIAN GLITZ The world's tallest buildings, the 452-metre Petronas Twin Towers, dominate the high-rise skyline of central Kuala Lumpur.

MARKET ANGUISH Floor traders at the Hong Kong Stock Exchange watch in disbelief in late 1997 as the Asian crisis drives stocks relentlessly lower.

DOWN WITH THE IMF Workers in South Korea's financial sector protest in December 1997 against a record $58 billion IMF-led rescue package, which involved tough austerity measures.

SUHARTO OUT! Looters rampage through Jakarta in May 1998 in Indonesia's worst riots for more than three decades, forcing veteran President Suharto to resign.

BANKING ON NOTHING Anxious Muscovites try to withdraw their savings in September 1998 as Russia's banking system crumbles.

THE BUCKS STOP HERE Malaysian Prime Minister Mahathir Mohamad, who imposed capital controls in September 1998 to try to stop "hot money" flooding out of the country's reeling markets.

PANIC IN SÃO PAULO Brazilian stock market dealers scream their trades on January 13, 1999, as prices collapse after the real was devalued 9 percent – a short-lived adjustment before the markets forced the government to adopt a free float.

Something more had to be done to soothe market nerves, and Brazil had a secret weapon up its sleeve. On February 2 investors were stunned, and delighted, to learn the name of the new central bank president: Arminio Fraga, a former aide to Soros who knew what made the markets tick. The poacher was turning gamekeeper. Market players knew Fraga and respected him; they were happy to have one of their own at the helm, and the real immediately rebounded sharply to around 1.75. Fraga's appointment was not enough in itself to turn Brazil's prospects around but it was a big help; the markets were further soothed when the country made more headway on reforms and agreed fresh budget targets with the IMF (replacing the now meaningless figures set before the devaluation). By mid-March, the worst was over.

THE END OF THE AFFAIR

The tidal wave that engulfed much of Asia and Russia, and flooded a host of other economies as it raged across the globe, had finally broken on the beaches of Brazil. The powerful wash was still capable of drowning the odd victim; Ecuador was forced in February to scrap its exchange rate bands and float – or rather sink – its sucre currency. But the struggling country, already lashed by low prices for its oil exports and storm damage from El Niño, was at this point barely capable of swimming.

66 The tidal wave that engulfed much of Asia and Russia had finally broken on the beaches of Brazil 99

Latin America's more robust economies held the line, with Argentina battening down the hatches and suggesting it could go as far as adopting the dollar as its national currency rather than become the next devaluation victim. The dramatic regional meltdown that many had predicted did not materialize, and by the end of the first quarter of 1999 the picture for emerging markets – and for the global economy as a whole – was looking a great deal safer than it had six months previously. In fact, Argentina and Mexico were even able to launch large global bond issues within spitting distance of the Brazilian devaluation, in sharp contrast to the shutdown in new bonds that followed the Asian and Russian disasters. Times had changed.

There were good, practical reasons why Brazil's devaluation caused far less dramatic fallout than earlier currency collapses from Thailand to Russia. First, the markets were relieved that Brazil had not bled its foreign reserves dry in a futile defence of the real, and still had a fairly healthy $40 billion in its purse, even without the IMF support package. Second, Brazil's financial system was far more solid than the rickety banks of Asia or Russia, and held fast through the shock of the devaluation. Third, Brazil's fight against devaluation was so protracted that by the time it finally surrendered, the move was expected and had been priced in. "This was an event which had been greatly discounted in advance – not only discounted, but the market forced it to happen," said James Graham-Maw of British-based fund managers Foreign & Colonial. "The float was the only way in which the market's concerns could be addressed on a sustainable basis, hence the very rapid U-turn in sentiment."

More importantly on a broader level, the world had changed dramatically since Thailand first unleashed the storm in July 1997. The markets were beginning to run out of juicy currency targets; most of the major pegs had already been smashed, although jitters about the Argentine and Hong Kong currency boards and the Big One – China's yuan – would continue to reverberate. (Even that spectre began to diminish as investors regained their nerve, realizing that despite its deflation problems China still had a solid trade surplus and towering foreign reserves of more than $150 billion at the end of 1999. In any case, many analysts started suggesting a change in the yuan exchange rate might no longer be such a big deal after all; if it did happen, it was likely to be carried out at Beijing's leisure and without the hullabaloo of a forced devaluation.) And although speculation in itself was far from dead, Russia's crash had shaken out most of the highly leveraged market positions that had forced hedge funds and other speculative investors to sell off assets in one part of the world to cover losses in another.

Besides, by now there was precious little hot money left in emerging markets anywhere, and if it wasn't there, it couldn't leave. World Bank figures show net long-term inflows from the international capital markets almost halved in 1998 to $72 billion, from $136 billion in 1997.[15] (In fact, the real picture was even bleaker, as those figures do not reflect several important factors including short-term flows.) "Global contagion is much more muted as a force than was the case in either 1997 or 1998," analysts at Chase Securities wrote in a market review in mid-1999. "This reflects the fact that banks' appetite for emerging market exposure was dramatically reduced through the last two years … We see little evidence that this appetite has returned."[16]

AFTERSHOCKS – THE RACE TO SOVEREIGN DEFAULT

A field of investment as diverse and geographically scattered as emerging markets was bound to be buffeted by more panics, from the Kosovo crisis to devaluation in Colombia. The difference was that no one suggested these setbacks would wreak the same global or even regional havoc. In April 1999 Camdessus told reporters the world economic climate was "distinctly better". In May senior World Bank official Eliana Cardoso said conditions in emerging markets had improved so much that no country was standing out as the next potential victim for attack. By June, the Federal Reserve felt able to turn its attention once more to domestic inflation risks, tweaking its main interest rate back up by 25 basis points; when it did so again in August it set a symbolic full stop on the global crisis, saying: "With financial markets functioning more normally ... the degree of monetary ease required to address the global financial market turmoil of last fall is no longer consistent with sustained, non-inflationary economic expansion." When Chile quietly scrapped its 15-year-old currency band system in September, hoping to boost exports, few investors batted an eyelid.

The one area where there was still any serious nail-biting was in a bunch of bonds previously considered just about as safe as emerging markets could get: Brady Bonds and government Eurobonds. The market regarded both as sacrosanct; Bradies were backed by US Treasury bonds, while there was an unwritten but powerful rule that sovereign (as opposed to corporate or regional) Eurobonds were senior to other debt and would always claim first payment in a crunch. No country had ever defaulted on either (although both Poland and Costa Rica had come close on Eurobonds in the early 1980s). In fact, no country had defaulted on any international sovereign bond since the 1930s. But with the finances of more and more countries knocked sideways by the emerging markets crisis, the prospect no longer seemed unthinkable, and a handful of countries – Russia, Ukraine, Pakistan, Ecuador, Romania – seemed to be trapped in a slow-motion race for the unwanted gold medal.

❝ No country had defaulted on any international sovereign bond since the 1930s ❞

Arguments against payment were coming from an unexpected source: the IMF and the Paris Club of government creditors. Fed up of footing the bill in numerous bailouts across the globe over the past two years, they were getting enthused by the idea that private bond-holders should be "bailed in" to rescue attempts and take a share of the pain if a borrower was going under. Not surprisingly, the suggestion provoked fierce opposition among investors, who argued that default would only make things worse for debtor countries by cutting off future lending. Struggling debtor countries were caught in the middle: desperate for IMF help and Paris Club debt rescheduling but realizing that failure to pay up would almost certainly freeze them out of world bond markets for years to come.

Russia looked as though it was leading the race after its domestic debt default raised well-founded questions about its ability (and willingness) to honour foreign debts. The country still faced problems scraping the money together to keep up payments not only on its own sovereign borrowing, in the name of the Russian Federation, but on more than $70 billion of debt inherited from the former Soviet Union. Moscow was at pains to draw a distinction between the two types of debt, insisting it would service its own Eurobonds and IMF loans in full. As for the Soviet-era overhang, it quickly approached government and commercial creditors to ask for partial debt forgiveness and more time to pay.

Sure enough, Russia soon started missing interest payments on former Soviet debt to the Paris Club, and in December 1998 it started slipping into arrears on $32 billion worth of dollar-denominated bonds known as Principal Arrears Notes (PRINs) and Interest Arrears Notes (IANs). The bonds represented Soviet-era commercial debt that had only been restructured and securitized in late 1997 after six painstaking years of negotiations with the *ad hoc* London Club group of creditor banks – the shortest-lived sovereign restructuring in memory. Like GKOs and OFZs, PRINs and IANs were scattered across a wide ownership, so the London Club again took the lead with yet more talks to "re-reschedule" the debt. Investors would have been within their rights to scream for full and immediate payment of the bonds, which were technically in default, but they agreed to wait to see what the London Club could come up with.

This time the wrangling took just over one year. In February 2000 the two sides struck a deal writing off roughly 36 percent of the bond value – a discount similar to the Brady Bond deals of the 1980s and early 1990s – and wrapping up the rest as sovereign Russian Eurobonds. The market was pleased; prices for PRINs and IANs, which had languished for months below 10 cents on the dollar, had already doubled in price in anticipation of a deal, and gained again when the news was confirmed. Cheery Russian officials said they would go for a similar restructuring on more than $40 billion in Paris Club debt.

But this was former Soviet rather than sovereign Russian debt. Despite (or perhaps because of) its on-again, off-again relations with the IMF, by early 2000 Moscow was still up to date on its own Eurobond payments. (The Fund agreed in April 1999 to lend Russia $4.5 billion over 18 months, but disbursement was again disrupted by a series of hurdles, including embarrassing allegations that vast amounts of IMF cash had been syphoned out of Russia in a money-laundering scandal.)

The unwanted honours for the first default on an international sovereign bond since the 1930s went elsewhere: to desperate Ecuador. The Andean country, small by Latin American standards but still the size of Italy and with a population bigger than Belgium's, had never been an economic powerhouse; now it was staggering under what Finance Minister Ana Lucia Armijos admitted was its worst economic crisis for 50 years, with two-thirds of its 12 million people living in abject poverty. Its February currency crunch sparked a run on the banks, and harsh austerity measures aimed at getting the IMF on board were met by strikes and violent protest. With public-sector foreign debt roughly equivalent to its entire annual GDP, and debt-service payments lapping up 42 percent of the national budget, the country was going under.

In late August, President Jamil Mahuad made the fateful announcement: Ecuador would not pay interest coming due on part of its $6 billion in Brady Bonds. The country still had a 30-day grace period to see if it could come up with the money or an alternative solution, but on September 28 it took its place in the history books as the first Brady Bond defaulter, failing to pay the coupon on $1.6 billion of Discount bonds. Many investors saw the hand of the IMF behind the default, although the Fund declined to comment. But it was probably no coincidence that Ecuador clinched a preliminary funding deal with the IMF just days after the August warning.

In October, the country added another dubious trophy to its cabinet by defaulting on its $500 million in Eurobonds, saying it wanted to restructure its entire stock of external and domestic debt. Ecuador's already low prestige as a borrower, and the relatively small amount of debt at stake, meant the wider impact of such a momentous and yet long-expected act was surprisingly limited. Eurobond holders were predictably furious, although Brady bond-holders were rather pleased that Eurobonds would not be treated with kid gloves.

For Ecuador the impact of the defaults was clear: it could say goodbye for a very long time to any further borrowing through the international capital markets. Negotiations with creditors had been due to start in January 2000, but politics got in the way. For months, crippling austerity measures aimed at winning IMF support had been stirring popular revolt. A plan to adopt the dollar as Ecuador's official currency – born of desperation as the economy sank deeper into the mire – was the last straw. Critics said the plan would raise prices while keeping salaries low. On January 21, escalating protest by indigenous Indian groups boiled over into a military coup, which installed Vice President Gustavo Noboa as the country's fifth president in three years. Yet another head had rolled as a result of the emerging market crisis, and the new government put restructuring talks on the back burner until Ecuador's economy improved. Creditors were likely to have a long wait.

Ecuador also set a precedent, blowing apart the cherished market assumption that Eurobonds were in some way senior to other debt and ring-fenced from renegotiation or default. Pakistan, Ukraine and Romania had all been resisting IMF pressure to include private investors in their debt restructuring plans under the new "bail-in" policy, as a precondition for more IMF cash and the prospect of a deal on Paris Club debt. Ecuador opened the door. In November 1999, Pakistan's new military-led regime, which had snatched power the previous month in a popular, bloodless coup, said it wanted to restructure just over $600 million in Eurobonds; in December it became the first country to pull off a successful Eurobond rescheduling, swapping the bonds for new debt. Ukraine followed in January 2000, saying it could not pay its foreign debts and needed to restructure a mixed $2 billion bundle of bonds (including a €500 million Eurobond). The debt markets would never be the same again.

NOTES

1 *Independent*, October 3, 1998.
2 "Global Capitalism: Making it work", in *The Economist*, September 12, 1998.
3 *The Los Angeles Times*, September 4, 1998.
4 Soros, *The Crisis of Global Capitalism*, pp. xi–xii.
5 President's Working Group on Financial Markets, p. 11.
6 President's Working Group on Financial Markets, p. 11.
7 President's Working Group on Financial Markets, pp. 11–12.
8 *Euromoney*, November 1998.
9 *International Bank Credit Analyst*, quoted in *The Economist*, October 10, 1998.
10 *The Economist*, October 10, 1998.

11 Krugman, *The Return of Depression Economics*, p. 133.

12 Krugman, p. 136.

13 IFC, *Emerging Stock Markets Factbook*, 1999, p. 14.

14 Krugman, p. 112.

15 World Bank, *Global Development Finance 1999*, p. 24. (*See also* similar figures from the Institute of International Finance in Chapter 8, pp. 188–189.)

16 Chase Securities International Fixed Income Research, *Emerging Markets Quarterly Outlook*, June 17, 1999.

7

ORDINARY PEOPLE

The meek shall inherit the earth, but not the mineral rights – Attributed to
J. Paul Getty

REAL-LIFE STORIES

"BANGKOK, Thailand – She used to work for a finance company. Now she
services customers in a brothel a few minutes' drive from downtown Bangkok.
Her nickname is Oh, she is in her early twenties, and she was among thousands retrenched when the government closed scores of distressed finance
companies last year.
'I was made redundant about five months ago, in December. They gave me
one month severance pay but it wasn't nearly enough and I couldn't find
another job,' she said.
She won't talk about her new line of work."
(James Mclean, June 29, 1998.)

"OBNINSKOYE, Russia – You do not live to be 79 in Russia by being quick
to cry.
Fyodor Kozachuk survived Stalin, World War Two, the darkest days of
Soviet communism and the last decade of traumatic economic reforms.
Now, with Russia's rouble in sudden freefall and shops running out of
basic supplies, Kozachuk is forced to look away and wipe his eyes.
'Two heart attacks and an ulcer,' he says. 'I don't have enough money
for medicine.'

His wife whispers: 'Don't cry.' He rises proudly to his feet. Using a wooden kitchen chair as a walker, he makes his way into the next room to blow his nose.

'People have been buying up sugar and flour for the winter. What are we to buy it with?'"

(Peter Graff, September 8, 1998.)

"SAO PAULO, Brazil – Hundreds of angry parents were there to greet school director Carlos Giannazi when he threw open the doors of his São Paulo public elementary school for this term.

Mothers and fathers had camped out all night on the sidewalk in the working-class suburb of Capela do Socorro in the hope of securing places for their children in the overflowing classrooms.

'I was looking at a line of some 1,000 people but we only had 70 empty slots. The problem is the government isn't investing,' Giannazi said.

(Shasta Darlington, March 26, 1999.)

HOW MARKETS CAN HURT ECONOMIES

From a market point of view, by mid-1999 the crisis was all over bar the shouting. But just because the markets were happy again, it did not mean the underlying economies were nearly so cheerful. The snapshots above – just three stories among many by Reuters reporters at the height of the crisis – give a glimpse of what the market turmoil did to people far beyond the dealing rooms, government offices and central banks where the high financial drama was played out. The middle classes in the crisis countries were knocked for six, and millions of poor people who thought they might have started getting somewhere in their lives were kicked back into the gutter.

On the face of it, the market rollercoaster may not seem to have a great deal to do with everyday lives in Indonesia or Ecuador. But the knock-on effects of the market turmoil made themselves felt in a multitude of ways. For a start, the collapse or forced restructuring of debt-riddled banks, finance companies and industrial conglomerates in Asia and Russia cost millions of jobs, and a single bankrupt firm could drag down several of its business partners in a tangle of bad debt. Even places with a reasonably sound financial sector, such as Hong Kong or Brazil, had to hike domestic interest rates to please the markets and defend their battered currencies, irrespective of whether their own economic conditions called for such action.

> **Just because the markets were happy again, it did not mean the underlying economies were nearly so cheerful**

Back in the real world, the higher cost of credit threw some previously well-functioning companies into debt and bankruptcy problems of their own, demolishing still more jobs. Those who did manage to stay in work often had to come to terms with smaller pay packets as companies cut back on labour costs. People had less to spend, and consumer demand dropped.

Economic growth tripped over; a host of countries fell into outright recession, and those economies that did not actually shrink experienced a sharp slowdown. Asia's five worst-hit countries – the so-called Crisis Five of Thailand, Malaysia, Indonesia, the Philippines and South Korea – saw their economies wither by a collective 8 percent in 1998 – even worse than government forecasts – with Indonesia's GDP crumbling by more than 13 percent. Hong Kong, too, was badly bruised; regional demand for its banking services and shopping facilities had fallen apart, and the currency board system left no leeway on monetary policy. With interest rates forced sky-high to defend the dollar peg, the territory dived into its worst recession for a generation. Russia's economy slumped by 4.5 percent, although there was one unexpected plus: the country's creaking industry received a shot in the arm as locally made goods started to fill in for costly imports, leading to a GDP rebound in 1999. Brazil's economy also back-tracked, albeit less sharply than predicted. Ecuador, already unbalanced in 1997 by El Niño storm damage that cost an estimated 15 percent of GDP, was tipped into disaster. (*See* Table 1.)

TABLE 1 Real change in GDP (%)

	1996	**1997**	**1998**	**1999**
Thailand	5.9	–1.8	–10.4	4.2
Malaysia	10.0	7.5	–7.5	5.4
Indonesia	8.0	4.5	–13.2	0.2
South Korea	6.8	5.0	–6.7	10.7
Hong Kong	4.5	5.0	–5.1	2.9
Russia	–3.4	0.9	–4.5	3.2
South Africa	4.2	2.5	0.6	1.2
Brazil	2.7	3.6	–0.1	0.5
Argentina	5.5	8.1	3.9	–3.1
Ecuador	1.9	3.5	0.4	–7.0

Source: International Monetary Fund, *World Economic Outlook*, April 2000

The pain did not stop at the main crisis countries themselves. One of the most striking and scary things about the 1997–99 market meltdown was the way it swept over countries which had relatively little to do with Thailand or Russia. South Africa, for example, had to crank up its interest rates to defend the rand, a move that helped crush economic growth to virtually zero in 1998. One of the more concrete channels of contagion was trade: if you depend on selling goods to a country that is in trouble, it is logical to expect trouble yourself. Japan's intensifying recession – the economy shrank by 2.8 percent in 1998 – had a lot to do with the drooping export markets in its Asian backyard. US exports to the crisis countries plunged by 40 per cent.[1] Argentina's tight trade links with next-door Brazil, which bought around a quarter of Argentine exports, were not such a gift when Brazilian demand began to slide. Merchants in the Gulf trading hub of Dubai saw their custom drop off dramatically once Russians were no longer piling in to stock up on duty-free electronics and textiles for resale at home.

Central Europe had turned progressively westwards for its export markets, with countries such as Poland, Hungary and the Czech Republic sending more than 60 percent of their foreign sales to the European Union by 1998; only 2 or 3 percent of their formal trade was with Russia, although informal links (such as trading across the Russian/Polish border) meant the impact was stronger than it would appear at first. Nevertheless, Poland, Bulgaria and the three small Baltic states took quite a knock, with their exports to Russia and other former Soviet republics in the Commonwealth of Independent States (CIS) plunging by between 50 and 70 percent in the first quarter of 1999.[2]

But the worst trade victims of Russia's crunch were in the CIS itself. Most CIS members had remained heavily dependent on exports to their giant neighbour. Small and secluded Moldova, for example, relied on Russia for a huge 63 percent of its exports; little wonder, then, that the Moldovan economy shrank by 8.6 percent in 1998. The vulnerability was magnified by a web of other trade links within the CIS. Belarus sent 59 percent of its exports to Russia and another 15 percent to Ukraine, which in turn depended heavily on Russian markets; the total at stake for Belarus came to the equivalent of more than 40 percent of GDP. While growth across Central and Eastern Europe and the Baltics remained positive, slipping to 2.4 percent in 1998 from 3.6 percent in 1997, the CIS economies bombed by an average of 3.5 percent.[3]

World trade as a whole grew by less than 5 percent in 1998, compared with 10 percent the previous year, as the economic impact of the Asian crisis began to bite. And there was another, wider dimension to the trade effect:

with demand for raw materials for Asian industry on the skids, world commodity prices took a violent tumble. By February 1999 the benchmark Bridge/Commodity Research Bureau Index, which reflects prices for 17 key commodities ranging from foodstuffs to metals and refined oil products, had slithered to its lowest in nearly 24 years. By mid-1998 crude oil prices had slunk to ten-year lows at less than $10 a barrel – a major factor in pushing Russia over the edge. And fears that Russia might sell off some of its gold reserves intensified relentless pressure on the precious metal, which by mid-1998 was around 18-year lows. Any country that depended on selling its commodities for a living, be it Nigerian oil, Chilean copper or South African gold, was facing a huge squeeze. (The picture was so bleak for oil producers that OPEC and non-OPEC countries reached a rare agreement to pull together on production cuts. The deal slammed the price decline into reverse; by April 2000 prices were around $25 a barrel after breaching a heady $30, raising fresh worries for the energy-guzzling US economy.)

In addition, any country fighting the crisis economies directly for export markets faced intensified competition once currencies such as the baht, won or real were devalued. With European Union growth slowing, particularly in Germany, exports to developed markets were also pinched. Poland and Hungary might have been congratulating themselves on reducing their trade exposure to Russia, but with westward exports accounting for between 20 and 40 percent of GDP, they got knocked from both sides.

> Any country that depended on selling its commodities for a living was facing a huge squeeze

Not only does a smaller economic pie mean smaller portions for all but the privileged, but a rising population means it has to be shared round even more people. For a country simply to stand still in development terms, it has to notch up GDP growth equal to population growth, which often runs as high as 2 or 3 percent a year; anything less, and the country inevitably slides backwards. Indonesia's GDP per head crashed 14.6 percent in 1998 and an estimated further 1.6 percent in 1999, according to World Bank figures. South Korea's dropped 6.7 percent in 1998. Brazil's per capita output slid 1.1 percent in 1998 and another 1.7 percent in 1999.

BROKEN BANKS AND TIGHTER CREDIT

The hedge funds and big international banks were not the only ones to get burned by Russia's domestic debt default. A number of Brazilian and South Korean banks had GKO holdings which, particularly in the latter case, could only aggravate any existing weaknesses on the balance sheet.

One big unsung casualty of the Russian default was Latvia, where banks had also stocked up on GKOs and had 8 percent of their total assets tied up in Russia. Several banks collapsed as a result of their Russian losses, including the Baltic country's fifth largest, Rigas Komercbanka, which had 13 percent of its assets in suddenly worthless Russian debt. (The central bank came to Komercbanka's rescue, declaring the Russian default an "act of God" and recapitalizing the institution; it was relaunched in 1999 as First Latvian Commercial Bank.)

Again, bank failures may seem far removed from everyday life – unless you happen to have your savings stashed away in one of the crumpled institutions. Real estate broker Yelena Nartova was just one of the millions of Russians who finally trusted the country's banks enough to deposit her savings of $50,000, gained mostly from the sale of her parents' flat. She chose Rossiisky Kredit – advertising motto: "Strength, reliability and solidity." Its Moscow offices were elegant and plush, and the 15 percent interest rate on dollar accounts was attractive. In August 1998, as rumours swirled of an impending crisis, Nartova managed to withdraw about $8,000. But the near-collapse of the entire banking system cut her off from the remaining $42,000 and left her with a bureaucratic nightmare to try to reclaim the money. "If I get my money back I will never invest a penny again in this country," she told Reuters' Adam Tanner. "I don't want to be robbed again."

It is not only stung savers who have reason to rue bank collapses. The cost of sorting out and injecting new capital into wrecked banking systems is enormous, and it is the taxpayer who tends to foot most of the bill. A large chunk of Asia's banking losses was taken on by governments, which bought up non-performing loans (NPLs) from the banks, most or all of which will eventually have to be written off. In late 1999 the IMF estimated more than half of financial sector loans in Thailand and Indonesia were non-performing, and the Indonesian government might have to borrow $68 billion through bond issues – around 45 percent of the country's GDP – to recapitalize shaky banks and wind up the dead ones. "[C]onsiderable uncertainty – and probably upside risks – surrounds such estimates," it added cautiously.[4] Other estimates of the public cost have been even higher. Credit ratings agency Standard & Poor's said the cost to Indonesia could amount to more than 80 percent of GDP. "Indonesia is suffering the world's worst banking crisis since the 1970s ... and may take up to a decade to fully recover," it said in June 1999. The agency put the cost to Thailand, South Korea and Malaysia at 35 percent, 29 percent and 22 percent of GDP respectively. (To put this in perspective, the US savings and loan crisis of the late 1980s cost US taxpayers only 2–3 per cent of the country's GDP.[5])

At the same time, the shift away from official aid since the 1980s had left many countries highly dependent on international capital markets for the extra finance they needed to fund investment and development, or simply to cover their current-account deficits and roll over existing debt. Quite apart from the destabilizing effect of having billions of dollars pulled out of their markets in one fell swoop (amounting to a swing of more than 10 percent of GDP in several Asian countries, according to the US Treasury Department's Summers), these countries suddenly found themselves having to pay far higher interest on loans and bonds as the crisis drove up the risk premium demanded by the market. That was if they could persuade anybody to lend to them: countries such as Russia and Ukraine, as well as debt-stricken private companies in Asia, were frozen out of the market all together. Even the more respectable sovereign borrowers found it harder, and more expensive, to launch new bonds.

New bond issues plunged to a total of just $500 million a month in August and September 1998, compared with $9 billion a month in the first half of the year, and remained subdued at around $3.5 billion a month in the final quarter. The average spread for newly issued emerging market bonds – the premium paid over comparable US or German government paper – more than doubled from 247 basis points in the first half of 1997 to 616 basis points in the second half of 1998.[6] In other words, an average borrower country was having to fork out a yield of well over three percentage points more than it had done less than two years previously. And although market access improved and spreads narrowed slightly in 1999 as the crisis slackened off, the IMF noted that "the terms and conditions of primary market access for emerging market borrowers … continued to be generally less favourable than prior to the Russian crisis".[7]

It was a dangerous world out there, and the only countries to escape the crisis entirely were those that were already too poor, messed-up and isolated to take much part in the brave new globalized economy: think Haiti, or Somalia, or North Korea. Take just one case – Argentina – which was under pressure as early as 1997 from events thousands of miles away in Asia. Goldman Sachs analyst Alberto Ades identified three distinct stages of Argentina's slide into recession. "The first shock was the Asian crisis, which severely depressed commodity prices. In the 12 months to the third quarter of 1998, the price of Argentina's basket of exports declined 10 percent," he wrote in a research report. "The second shock was the Russian crisis, which reduced the availability of external financing and increased the cost of external borrowing in both the public and private sectors ... Finally, the Brazilian crisis and ensuing recession reduced external demand and further pressured both commodity prices and debt-servicing costs."[8]

Or consider Kyrgyzstan, a country of snow-capped peaks and 4.5 million people nestling between Kazakhstan and China. The former Soviet republic, once touted as the Switzerland of Central Asia, was perhaps the hardest hit in the region. Unlike Kazakhstan or Turkmenistan, it has no oil and gas to fall back on and imports 60 percent of its consumer goods. Gold is its major export, accounting for two-fifths of industrial production. The previously stable som currency lost around half its value in 12 months after Russia devalued, and inflation escalated to 45 percent in 1999. "You want to write about the Kyrgyz economy? Well, there isn't one," said Asylbek, who drives an unlicensed taxi in the capital, Bishkek. "There are no jobs, prices are high, and everything that can be stolen has already gone."

SMALL MERCIES – NO GLOBAL CRASH, BUT PAIN FOR MILLIONS

It was some consolation that the crisis turned out to be slightly less awful than many had predicted when it first broke, at least in duration if not in magnitude. The emergency interest rate medicine administered by the major industrial countries in late 1998 managed to head off the recession that had been threatening the developed world, and that in turn would have choked off yet more demand for developing countries' exports. Asia rebounded far more smartly than most people had dared hope, led mainly by South Korea, where GDP bounced by a handsome 10.7 percent in 1999. Earlier that year the World Bank had been predicting GDP growth of just 0.3 percent in Asia's Crisis Five, while the IMF was forecasting a slightly more optimistic 1 percent. In fact, the five economies together revived by more than 4 percent.

Nevertheless, the practical effects of the turmoil were quite grim enough as they stood. The world as a whole may have swerved away from a rerun of the 1930s, but the crisis dealt Asia and Russia as big a knock as the Great Depression did to Europe and North America, and stalled growth as far away as Africa. Economies will pick up again, but the set-back in terms of efforts to reduce poverty has been huge. The World Bank warned against complacency: "Though less dramatic than early predictions suggested and very heterogeneous, the negative social impact of the East Asian crisis and consequent crises in Russia and Brazil has been enormous," it said.[9]

Even Asia, first into the woods and first to approach the other side, was still very shaky as the new century approached. "While exchange rates have stabilized and clearly the crisis has bottomed out, most of the countries are nowhere near recovery in terms of fundamentals of output, employment, and real wages," World Bank chief economist Joseph Stiglitz told Reuters Television in July 1999. "In general, for the region as a whole, the fact is the recovery is nowhere along so far that one can be complacent."

> It was some consolation that the crisis turned out to be slightly less awful than many had predicted

Some CIS economies are half the size they were ten years ago, with living standards still falling. Russia's economy has staged a moderate rebound, but from an extremely depressed base, and most of its people remain desperately poor. And although Brazil managed to sidestep catastrophe, its problems nudged Latin America as a whole into its first regional recession since the 1980s debt crisis. "In many ways Latin America – or at least South America – is suffering an economic crisis as bad as that in Asia," *Euromoney* wrote in late 1999. "Brazil's devaluation has brought Ecuador and Colombia to the brink of economic collapse, has put untold strain on Argentina's economy, and has even pushed Chile's previously robust economy into sharp recession."[10]

A few IMF calculations, estimating total economic losses as a result of the crisis, tell a startling tale of missed growth and opportunity. In late 1999 the Fund compared actual and forecast growth in several crisis-hit countries with a hypothetical "non-crisis scenario" and calculated how much cumulative output would be lost over four years from the start of the crisis. On this basis, the IMF reckoned Indonesia would forfeit a huge 82 percent of what the economy could have produced in those four years, with Thailand missing out on 57 percent, Malaysia 39 percent, and South Korea 27 percent. (By comparison, the Fund calculated Mexico lost 30 percent of its potential output to the Tequila Crisis, and Argentina only 15 percent.[11])

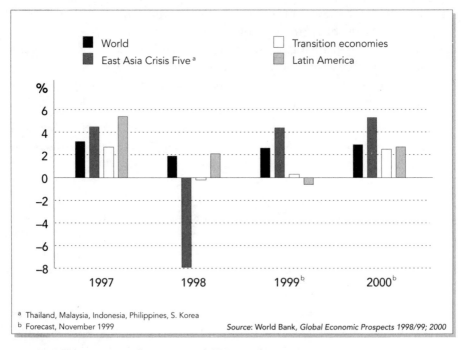

FIGURE 13 The economic rollercoaster: real GDP growth

INFLATION SURGES, JOBS DWINDLE

There was less money to go round, yet at the same time prices were rising. Devaluation automatically upped the cost of anything that was imported, from consumer goods to raw materials for industry, which in turn made locally produced items more expensive. Russia's decision to print more roubles after the devaluation also helped drive up prices, although in the end the central bank was more restrained with the printing presses than many analysts had originally feared. Nevertheless, Russian inflation was running at nearly 85 percent year on year by the end of 1998, and peaked in 1999 at more than 100 percent.

When devaluation struck, Russians dashed to stock up on basic goods such as flour, salt or cooking oil before prices rose. Before the day was out, street pedlars outside Moscow's Kievskaya railway station had already raised their prices for foreign cigarettes by more than 5 percent. Store shelves were stripped and not refilled as importers preferred to hold on to their hard currency rather than buy in fresh goods; besides, the paralysis in the banking system made business transactions difficult or impossible. Before long, imported medicines were becoming scarce.

Within a month, powerful Moscow mayor Yuri Luzhkov and nearly a dozen other regional heads had defied the central government to impose price controls on staple goods, saying they feared hungry crowds might take to the streets (a blatantly political ploy, but no doubt appreciated by consumers nonetheless). And in a strange yet logical twist, many Russians who had a decent quantity of roubles raced to spend them on precious metals, jewellery, cars or other luxury goods before the banknotes became even more worthless.

To make matters worse, Russia's financial meltdown happened to coincide with the country's worst harvest in more than 40 years. There were fears that there might not be enough food to last the winter, prompting the United States to supply 3 million tonnes of food aid. The crash also coincided with the brief summer window when supply ships and barges can get through to the most remote outposts of Russia's frozen north. Britain's *Sunday Times* reported that government cost-cutting meant little money was allocated to transport the supplies in 1998, leaving tens of thousands of people to struggle in the Arctic cold without adequate food or fuel. "The situation in some areas is so desperate that people have been forced to eat dogs," the paper said. "Hundreds of villages appear to have been forgotten by Moscow as Russia struggles to cope with its worst economic crisis since the collapse of the Soviet Union."[12]

Indonesia too was hit by rampant inflation, averaging 60 percent in 1998 – far higher than anywhere else in Asia. The price of rice, the staple food, trebled in one year, and the departure of President Suharto did nothing to stop riots and looting by hungry Indonesians. In mid-1998 there was a fresh explosion of turmoil, with warehouses plundered and food trucks robbed in a desperate attempt to find something to eat. On paper, the country had enough food to go round, and it was preparing to import more, but distribution was in chaos. A report by the US embassy in Jakarta said hoarding, speculation and abuses by the state commodity regulator, Bulog, were also driving up prices. (A former Bulog official was arrested over an alleged scheme to smuggle rice out of the country.) The *Jakarta Post* quoted Food Minister A.M. Saefuddin as saying more than 17 million Indonesian families were facing food shortages, and more than 4 million could afford only one meal a day.

> 66 Indonesia was hit by rampant inflation. The price of rice, the staple food, trebled in one year 99

Latin America, previously a hyperinflation blackspot, also suffered rising prices, but for the most part inflation was unexpectedly contained.

(Brazil's inflation rate topped 8 percent in 1999, more than twice its 1998 level but a far cry from the 60 percent seen in 1995.) Ecuador was the crashing exception, with 1999 inflation of more than 60 percent; in July that year the government was forced to back down on a 13 percent hike in fuel prices, part of IMF-backed austerity measures, after a transport workers' strike and protests by indigenous Indians brought much of the country to a standstill for nearly two weeks. The outlook remained bleak in 2000, with prices spiking up more than 14 percent in January alone – the worst monthly figure for 32 years.

Jobs were slashed across the board. The United Nations' International Labour Organization (ILO) estimated in March 1999 that the crisis had left an extra 20–25 million people unemployed in East Asia alone, with national jobless rates doubling, tripling or even quadrupling between 1996 and 1998. Again, it was Indonesia that suffered most; the ILO said up to 15 million Indonesians lost their jobs, taking total unemployment as high as one in five of the workforce by early 1999.[13] (World Bank data showed a grim but slightly less dramatic picture for Indonesia, with unemployment hitting 5.5 percent in 1998; the Bank said agriculture was able to absorb more jobless people in Indonesia than in the other crisis-hit countries.[14])

Hong Kong's jobless figure soared to a record 6.2 percent in 1998 – three times higher than in the early 1990s. "I have been looking for a job for a long time," said one graduate in business administration, who would previously have expected to stroll into well-paid employment. "I have sent a total of 50 application letters, but have got only four to five inter-views." Mainland Chinese who had been drawn to the previously affluent territory in search of jobs turned back to look for work at home. Malaysia found a nationalist safety valve for its jobs problem, freezing recruitment of foreign workers and then rounding up and repatriating tens of thousands of immigrants – mostly from Indonesia – who failed to show proper papers.

Russia's jobless rose from 9.2 percent of the workforce in 1996 to 12.4 percent in 1998,[15] by far the highest rate since the collapse of the Soviet Union. In Brazil, unemployment doubled to around 8 percent between 1996 and 1998,[16] and there were sharp rises too in Argentina and Chile.[17] Again, Ecuador suffered most in Latin America; unemployment in the Andean country rose to at least 13.5 percent in the first few months of 1999, its highest level of the decade.

Lost employment was not confined entirely to the developing world, despite the West's deft swerve away from recession. Japan, of course, was in deep trouble, with unemployment rising to over 4 percent, its highest since the end of World War Two. But North American and European industry also felt the pinch. British Steel laid off some 1,400 workers in 1998 as the Asian downturn sapped demand and lowered prices for steel. Drooping exports of Asia's popular prestige tipple, Scotch whisky, led to the closure of several distilleries. And some Asian investment projects in Europe ended up on the shelf, such as the computer chip factory planned by South Korea's Hyundai in the Scottish town of Dunfermline. The plant, which would have created 2,000 jobs, was mothballed as Hyundai ploughed into a morass of corporate debt and restructuring, and its future was still uncertain in early 2000.

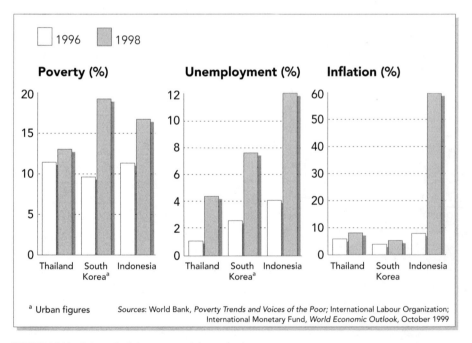

ᵃ Urban figures   Sources: World Bank, *Poverty Trends and Voices of the Poor*; International Labour Organization; International Monetary Fund, *World Economic Outlook*, October 1999

FIGURE 14 Hard times in Asia: poverty, jobs and prices

POVERTY BITES

The crisis hurt a huge range of income groups around the globe, from the elite of the business and financial world, through the middle classes (a relatively new phenomenon in many countries), to the urban poor. Just about the only people who were not affected to any great degree were the ultra-rich and the poorest of the poor, the subsistence farmers who had few links with the global economy. In Asia, Stiglitz said middle-income groups were hardest hit by unemployment, and saw their wages fall by 15–25 percent in real terms. Most of the disappearing jobs were in the manufacturing and service industries, which had been relatively well paid, throwing workers out into poorer, informal-sector jobs or back to the land. Agriculture and extended families managed to absorb many of Asia's jobless and save them from destitution, although these old safety nets had become less solid with the weakening of traditional family ties. But rising prices affected everyone, and it was the urban poor who were most easily tipped over the edge into real penury.

South Korea, the most urbanized of the Crisis Five, had to grapple with a burgeoning number of destitute jobless; the proportion of city-dwellers living below the official poverty line roughly doubled to just over 19 percent. Homelessness, a problem virtually unknown in a country that used to have almost full employment, suddenly escalated.

One Thai former high-roller became a minor celebrity in his new role as street sandwich salesman. Once a millionaire market analyst and fund manager, Sirivat Voravetvuthikun went from riches to rags in August 1997 when the government closed down 56 crippled finance companies. "My ambition is to be known as Mr Sandwich, the same way you go to McDonald's for hamburgers," he told Reuters' Vithoon Amorn in 1998. Other formerly wealthy Thais hawked their valuables at weekend second-hand sales to make ends meet.

> Just about the only people who were not affected were the ultra-rich and the poorest of the poor

Russia's new middle class, which had carved out a comfortable niche between the super-rich tycoons and the working class, was among those that had most to lose. Tens of thousands of upwardly-mobile traders, restaurant and shop owners, bank managers, estate agents, advertising executives and entrepreneurs – Russians who thought they had achieved "normal" Western lives with cars and foreign holidays – lost their jobs or businesses, and many said goodbye to their savings too. Muscovite Lena

Golubeva had a good job with an import firm when she decided to have a baby. She was a single mother, but inflation was low, economic reforms seemed to be bearing fruit, and life felt stable. Then the devaluation slashed the value of her savings, her company took a major hit, and her future suddenly looked very uncertain. "If I had to think today whether I would have a child or not, I'd probably decide against it," she said a month after the devaluation. "Everything seems so terrible now."

Many Russians who on paper should barely be able to afford to eat have traditionally got by by growing their own food on their country plots. For years, Russia's rural economy has revolved more around self-sufficiency and barter than hard cash. But hard cash is still necessary for certain things: extra staples such as milk and bread, and medicine. Until the devaluation, a monthly pension of 650 roubles (about $100) was enough for Fyodor and Alexandra Kozachuk, the Russian pensioners quoted at the start of this chapter. Within a month it was worth about $30, and falling by the hour, while prices rocketed all around.

Wages in Russia fell in real terms by an average of more than 35 percent between August and October 1998; by mid-2000 about 35 percent of Russians were living below the official poverty line, compared with an estimated 21 percent before the crisis.[18] In Indonesia the pay picture was even bleaker, falling by more than 40 percent across the board in real terms during 1998. South Korean wages outside the agricultural sector dropped 10 percent. Thailand saw the biggest fall in rural income, with farm wages slipping nearly 9 percent per head – the result of agricultural prices rising relatively little to compensate for an influx of unemployed workers from the cities.[19]

Increased poverty took a heavy toll, not just in living standards but in terms of social dislocation. "[A]ll [crisis] countries report erosion of their social fabric, with social unrest, more crime, more violence in the home," the UNDP noted.[20] In Thailand, hospitals reported a rise of around 30 percent in mental illness cases. Families were torn apart; some children were even abandoned by desperate parents who were no longer able to care for them. Many South Koreans felt deep shame at having lost their jobs in a Confucian country where a husband's prime duty is to support his wife and children. "We can't go home unless we find the means to make a living," said one man living at a hostel for the homeless. "Do you think wives and children will accept us?"

SQUEEZED BUDGETS, SQUEEZED WELFARE

On top of all this, the belt-tightening prescribed by the markets and the IMF did not only cover monetary policy; crisis countries were also pushed to cut back budget deficits. This usually meant higher tax rates or lower state spending, or both. At the same time, government revenues were being squeezed as depressed economic activity yielded lower tax receipts. The World Bank found that public outlays on education and health fell in most crisis countries, particularly in Indonesia. "Such setbacks can have irreversible effects on human development," it warned.[21] A *Financial Times* survey on Russia in mid-2000 said spending on health and education had fallen 30 percent in real terms since the crisis.[22]

Not only did spending decline, but many parents were forced to pull their children out of school, either because they could not afford it or because they needed extra hands to help earn money. Hundreds of school-age Indonesian children could be found ferreting around the stinking municipal dump on the eastern fringes of Jakarta, looking for debris such as old tin cans and plastic bags to recycle. "This is normal, I am earning money to support my mother," said one eight-year-old boy. "Nobody is supporting me, so I cannot go to school."

In theory, welfare safety nets existed in many countries to cushion the poorest, although with government finances cramped they were often just a drop in the ocean, and came too late to really help. Some governments, such as South Korea's, ran public works schemes to provide basic employment, but these rarely covered all the newly jobless. Hardly any of Russia's poorest received the benefits to which they were entitled in principle.[23]

Thailand's royal family sponsored soup kitchens to feed thousands of people hit by the crisis. "You can imagine how difficult it is now," said Kaew, a mother of three savouring a plate of rice and chilli sambal. Her husband was an unemployed construction worker. "He is out of a job most of the time and when he manages to get one, the wage is cut to 100 baht ($2.50) per day because of the labour glut. We can barely make ends meet," she told Reuters reporter Anchalee Koetsawang in mid-1998. "But I hope the situation will be better next year. My husband will be able to get a more stable job then and we hope to be able to put our own food on the table."

It was not entirely doom and gloom, with people across the crisis zone finding ways to party and forget. In Moscow, young Russians continued to whoop it up at the infamous Hungry Duck and other bacchanalian nightspots; the difference was the absence of well-paid foreigners packing the bar. (The club was closed down in early 1999. The story goes that a group of Duma deputies dropped in just as a male Nigerian stripper was performing for ladies' night, to the strains of the old Soviet national anthem.)

66 Brazil's middle class said goodbye to its days of globetrotting on a strong real, but in Rio the carnival still dazzled **99**

Protests against rising prices and the government's economic management drew moderate attendance, but the general mood across Russia was fatalistic rather than fiery. As well as growing vegetables on their plots outside town, most urban Russians found a variety of ways to supplement their meagre incomes: moonlighting, extra pay slipped under the table, or savings tucked under the mattress. "In the West, you go to your weekend house to rest," said university lecturer Pyotr Akinin. "Our weekend consists of going to the garden to cultivate potatoes."

In Malaysia, a plush new shopping mall opened in May 1998 at the foot of the Petronas Towers, with clowns and uniformed girls handing out balloons and colourful brochures. Auctioneers in Singapore said rich Indonesians were among the most active bidders for fine art and jewels. Brazil's middle class said goodbye to its days of globetrotting on a strong real, but in Rio the carnival still dazzled, albeit with fewer imported feathers and sequins. "We could not afford as much of the shiny paper and glitter because it's imported and more expensive, but we spread it out better and used local materials," one float designer said. "We are artists. That is our job."

MORE POLITICS – EXIT HABIBIE, PRIMAKOV … AND YELTSIN

The crisis was to have still more political repercussions. In Indonesia, anger over escalating food prices exploded again into rage against Habibie's rule. After taking over from Suharto in May 1998, Habibie had gone all-out to try to distance himself from the former regime, promising a free press and free elections. He even held up the suggestion of autonomy for East Timor, the former Portuguese colony occupied by Indonesia since 1975 in defiance of the United Nations. But by September students were back on the streets of Jakarta, and the cities of Bandung and Surabaya, demanding that the new president quit if he could not set the economy straight. In an echo of May's events, Habibie agreed in November to hold elections after student demonstrators were shot dead in the capital.

By now the violence was taking an increasingly divisive twist. Although campaigning for the June 1999 general election went more peacefully than expected, the archipelago slid inexorably into a patchwork of separatist, ethnic and religious violence. Mobs continued sporadically to target ethnic Chinese, but suddenly violence between Moslems and minority Christians exploded in the Moluccas, also known as the spice islands, nearly 2,000 miles east of Jakarta. Within a year the official count stood at 1,500 killed, while human rights groups put the toll at several thousand. Separatist trouble also broke out in Aceh, in northern Sumatra, and in Irian Jaya, the western part of the island shared with Papua New Guinea.

East Timor was in ferment, preparing for a referendum in August in which the territory would choose between independence and wide-ranging autonomy within Indonesia. The result was a resounding "Yes" to independence – and a bloodbath. Led covertly by the Indonesian military, pro-Jakarta militias ran amok, massacring hundreds of people at will in a scorched-earth campaign to leave little standing for the new state. UN-mandated troops moved into the territory in September to restore peace, and an interim UN administration took over. The capital, Dili, was in ruins; in the months that followed, many mass graves came to light.

Meanwhile, the party of Megawati Sukarnoputri, popular daughter of the country's first president, had emerged victorious in the parliamentary election. But it was still the People's Consultative Assembly (MPR) that elected the president, and in October it spurned her in favour of Abdurrahman Wahid, an aged and partly blind Moslem scholar who had been one of her closest allies. Megawati's distraught supporters staged violent demonstrations around the country, and two people were killed when a couple of bombs went off in the capital. With Megawati elected to the vice-president's post, things calmed down, and the outwardly frail Wahid swiftly set about a strongly pro-reformist agenda, including confirmation of East Timor's independence. But his democratic credentials could not stop the country spinning into what seemed like an increasingly centrifugal pattern of violence. In January 2000 fresh religious violence erupted between Christians and Moslems on the eastern island of Lombok, sending a stream of local refugees and tourists fleeing to nearby Bali. The unity of Indonesia looked very fragile in the new century, and the economic crisis had been a catalyst for that threatened fragility.

One hope that cheered many people both inside and outside Russia was that the crash would have finished off the oligarchs, or at least spiked their guns. The banks at the heart of their vast business empires were mostly broke; Russian bank losses were estimated to range from 20 percent of their capital to more than 600 percent in the worst cases,[24] leaving the whole system effectively bankrupt. Russians had joked in the early 1990s about the newly rich; now they made fun of newly poor bankers.

The appointment of Yevgeny Primakov as prime minister was seen as another nail in the coffin of the grey cardinals. Unlike Chernomyrdin, a former head of Gazprom, Primakov had never been close to any of the oligarchs, and hinted at a clampdown. Arrest warrants were issued for two of the biggest fish: Alexander Smolensky of SBS-Agro, formerly Russia's largest bank, and Boris Berezovsky, an oil and media baron with close links to the Yeltsin court. "The crash radically reduced the amount of money that could be made on the state – and thus the power of the corrupt businessmen," wrote Russia specialist Anders Åslund.[25]

But not everyone was so sure. As early as September 1998, *The Economist* had reported on "spectacular looting" in the Russian banking system: transfers going missing, deposits frozen, and blatant manipulation of the exchange rate to sidestep huge losses that the banks stood to make on forward currency contracts with foreigners.[26] Hard-liner Primakov did not last long in the job. In May 1999, Yeltsin, locked in battle with a Duma that wanted to impeach him, confronted his parliamentary enemies by sacking the prime minister and appointing Sergei Stepashin in his place. Very few of the failed banks had their licences revoked, and not one banker was taken to court.

Although most of the oligarchs' banks had collapsed, they quickly devised schemes to transfer business and even to spirit assets away to new operations set up in the shadow of the old. Regulators seemed disinclined or unable to intervene. While creditors were fighting over what was left of Uneximbank, for example – the first Russian corporate to default on a Eurobond – its boss, Vladimir Potanin, was building his recently established Rosbank into one of the top new Russian institutions. Smolensky did the same, creating Soyuz bank on the debt-ridden ashes of SBS-Agro. The oligarchs may have been bloodied, but they were far from bowed.

Russia's political merry-go-round went on. In August 1999, Stepashin was sacked in favour of Vladimir Putin, a former security service boss with little economic experience but the trust of the president. With spectacularly theatrical timing, on New Year's Eve, 1999, Yeltsin announced he was retiring a few months ahead of the presidential election in March 2000. It was plain to see that Putin, who automatically took over as acting president, was his preferred successor. Slamming into a brutal but vote-catching war against Chechen separatists in the south of the country, but playing other policy cards close to his chest, Putin romped home in the polls. Unlike some other crisis leaders, the old fox Yeltsin seemed to have ensured a peaceful and protected future for himself and his entourage.

NOTES

1 Council on Foreign Relations, *Independent Task Force Report*, p. 7.

2 EBRD, *Transition Report 1998*, p. 67.

3 EBRD, *Transition Report 1998*, pp. 73–74.

4 IMF, *World Economic Outlook*, October 1999, p. 57.

5 Council on Foreign Relations, p. 6.

6 World Bank, *Global Development Finance 1999*, pp. 29–31.

7 IMF, *World Economic Outlook*, October 1999, p. 41.

8 *Argentina: Don't Cry for Convertibility*, Goldman Sachs Global Economics Paper No. 16, June 4, 1999.

9 World Bank, *Global Economic Prospects 2000*, p. 47.

10 *Euromoney*, September 1999.

11 IMF, *World Economic Outlook*, October 1999, p. 64.

12 *Sunday Times*, November 15, 1998.

13 ILO news release, *ILO Governing Body to examine response to Asia crisis*, March 16, 1999. (www.ilo.org/public/english/bureau/ inf/pr/1999/6.htm)

14 World Bank, *Global Economic Prospects 2000*, p. 59.

15 EBRD, *Transition Report 1999*, p. 261.

16 World Bank, *Poverty Trends and Voices of the Poor*, p. 12.

17 IMF, *World Economic Outlook*, October 1999, pp. 64–65.

18 *Financial Times*, Russia survey, May 10, 2000, quoting OECD figures.

19 World Bank, *Global Economic Prospects 2000*, p. 57.

20 UNDP, *Human Development Report 1999*, p. 4.

21 World Bank, *Global Economic Prospects 2000*, p. 48.

22 *Financial Times*, Russia survey, May 10, 2000.

23 World Bank, *Global Economic Prospects 2000*, p. 62.

24 *Euromoney*, September 1998.

25 "Russia's Collapse", in *Foreign Affairs*, September/October 1999.

26 *The Economist*, September 19, 1998.

8

RUNNING SCARED

There's no such thing as a free lunch – Attributed to Milton Friedman

JAPANESE BANKS GET FLATTENED

The white-knuckle ride that started in emerging markets and rattled through the entire financial world left the international banks and other major money-movers in deep shock. Many operators were heavily exposed to potential losses, either through direct loans to emerging market companies or through bad market bets. On top of that, many banks (including some that had never dabbled in Indonesian loans, Hong Kong stocks or Russian bonds) were exposed to losses on their business with other endangered financial players – especially the hedge funds. Fear and gloom descended over boardrooms, dealing rooms, sales teams and research departments. The financial world is not generally noted for its spirit of forgiveness towards employees who are judged to have messed up, and it was clear a lot of heads were going to roll.

The first flush of the Asian crisis had left the big Western-based banks relatively unscathed. Many of them were stuck with piles of bad loans to bankrupt Asian companies, and some also made substantial trading losses; Chase Manhattan, for example, disclosed a $160 million pre-tax loss from its trading activities during the global panic of October 1997.

But two of the biggest players in Asia, HSBC and Standard Chartered (both technically British but with strong practical and emotional ties to Hong Kong), had a reputation as prudent lenders with a strong capital base. The turmoil even had its consolations; Standard Chartered said profits on its dealing operations rose 65 percent in 1997 as the extreme exchange rate volatility led to a surge in currency trading. And several Western firms sniffed around Asia's many failed or failing banks, looking for potential bargains to expand their reach on the cheap; France's Banque Nationale de Paris (BNP) and Spain's Banco Santander were among several foreign takers for chunks of Hong Kong's liquidated Peregrine Investment Holdings.

Among Japanese banks, however, there was already blood on the floor. It was bad enough that they had their own domestic crisis to grapple with, but they were also first in the firing line as proportionally the biggest lenders to the rest of Asia. In June 1998 Japanese banks' exposure to Asia's original Crisis Five countries alone – the amount they could lose if all the debt went bad – was estimated at $74 billion, equivalent to 30 percent of the banks' capital. Although European Union exposure to the Crisis Five was greater in absolute terms, at an estimated $116 billion, the total was split between more institutions and accounted for only 14 percent of bank capital. US banks were exposed to the tune of only $17 billion.[1]

The first rumbles of impending doom came in November 1997 when Sanyo Securities and Hokkaido Takushoku Bank went bust, the latter dealing a body-blow to the economy of the northern Japanese island of Hokkaido. But it was the collapse later that month of Yamaichi Securities, Japan's fourth-biggest brokerage, that really sent the financial world into a cold sweat. The century-old institution was brought down not only by shrinking business and Japan's severe credit crunch, but also by revelations that it had hidden massive losses in secret offshore accounts for six years. Its debts exceeded assets by 160 billion yen – then equivalent to nearly $1.3 billion. On November 24, Yamaichi's board of directors fought their way through a throng of reporters into the institution's towering Tokyo headquarters; they took just 45 minutes to decide the game was up. Yamaichi president Shohei Nozawa wept as he begged forgiveness from employees, customers and shareholders alike. Yamaichi's 7,500 workers fumed that they had been kept in the dark until the last minute.

> 66 Among Japanese banks, there was already blood on the floor 99

It was Japan's biggest ever corporate failure, and drove the yen to a five-year low against the dollar. The brokerage was finally declared bankrupt in June 1999, and in March 2000 a Tokyo court convicted two top executives of concealing losses of more than 200 billion yen and making illegal dividend payments to shareholders. Former Yamaichi president Atsuo Miki was jailed for 30 months and former chairman Tsugio Yukihira was handed a suspended sentence; Miki was also found guilty of making illegal payoffs to a corporate racketeer and a leasing company.

Japan's financial sector woes intensified through 1998 as domestic recession and the emerging market crisis squeezed banks and brokerages ever harder. It was clear the government had to do something radical to clean up and shore up the sector, allowing it to clear bad loans and resume lending on a stronger footing, otherwise hopes of economic recovery would remain slim. But government plans to prop up ailing banks with public funds came up against staunch resistance from the parliamentary opposition, which was against using taxpayers' money to bail out rickety financial institutions. Foreign pressure was mounting for urgent action, and in mid-October parliament finally passed laws allowing for the voluntary or compulsory nationalization of problem banks, to liquidate the failed ones and recapitalize the failing. A total of 60 trillion yen – more than $500 billion – was approved to protect depositors and creditworthy borrowers, and to pump fresh funds into the banks that merited another chance.

The nationalization law was promptly put into practice at Long-Term Credit Bank of Japan (LTCB), one of the country's top financial institutions, which for months had been staggering under a mountain of bad debt. Speculation that the bank was on the verge of collapse had slashed its share price to a record low of just two yen by late October, compared to around 900 yen in mid-1996. LTCB, one of three long-term credit banks that helped rebuild Japan from the ashes of World War Two, requested nationalization and went into temporary public ownership until it could be beefed up enough to attract a private buyer. A second, Nippon Credit Bank (NCB), was forcibly nationalized in December, while other institutions, such as Industrial Bank of Japan, sought an injection of public funds without going into public ownership.

To a large extent, the strategy worked. In the heat of the October 1998 panic, the banking sector rescue plan went some way to reassuring the quaking markets that Japan could still pull out of its financial nosedive. And the nationalized banks did eventually attract new buyers, bringing fresh faces to Japan's previously claustrophobic, old-school-tie banking scene. In March 2000, after soaking up 3.6 trillion yen in government funds to cover its debts, LTCB was sold to a consortium led by US investment group Ripplewood Holdings; a high-flying Japanese Internet investor, Softbank Corp, won the go-ahead to buy NCB.

But it was still a hard path for Japan's financial sector, which announced steep losses for the 1998/99 business year after being clobbered far beyond the confines of Asia. The country's remaining big three brokerages were left struggling for survival; the biggest, Nomura Securities, posted a consolidated net loss of nearly $4 billion, including a $670 million hit on Russian bonds and $1.5 billion on US mortgage-backed securities. Daiwa Securities and Nikko Securities chalked up net losses of $1.1 billion and $1.5 billion respectively. And although they all bounced back into the black in 1999/2000, they faced new and potentially dangerous competition from foreign banks stepping on to Japan's more open financial scene.

RUSSIA BATTERS THE REST

The Western banks were not exactly happy to lose money in Asia, but what really got them worried was the Russian crisis and ensuing global market chaos. The figures looked very scary, although estimates of the damage varied widely and it was hard to tell just how bad things would get. As a starting point most analysts turned to figures published regularly by the BIS, detailing lending by developed-country banks. During the panic of September 1998, one Asian-based market strategist sketched out an alarming scenario; using BIS figures, he estimated the world's biggest banks lent the equivalent of nearly 130 percent of their capital to global emerging markets, and about 30 percent of those loans were non-performing. "If it's 30 percent, we've just wiped out half the world's bank capital," he told Reuters, asking not to be identified. James McKay at National Australia Bank calculated in mid-1999 that the non-African emerging market exposure of Europe's banking sector was equal to around 8 percent of European GDP, with Portuguese banks exposed by the equivalent of a staggering 35 percent of national income.[2]

These were estimates covering emerging markets at their widest, but exposure to the core crisis areas alone was still quite enough to keep bankers awake at night. Within a month of Moscow's devaluation and GKO default, credit ratings agency Fitch IBCA published what it admitted was a "highly speculative" estimate that banks and other private investors in Russia could lose more than $100 billion – "the single largest credit loss ever imposed on private sector creditors". BIS-based estimates published by the World Bank showed that the total exposure of European Union banks to Russia in June 1998 had amounted to $67 billion, of which nearly half was owed to German banks.[3] Switzerland's Crédit Suisse group, which owned investment bank Crédit Suisse First Boston (CSFB), admitted a whopping $2.2 billion exposure to Russia, and Germany's Deutsche Bank, Commerzbank and Dresdner Bank were all vulnerable to the tune of 1 billion marks ($590 million) or more.

Then there was the worsening Asian loan picture to consider, and fears that Latin America would follow Russia down the tube. EU banks' combined exposure to Russia, Latin America and Asia's Crisis Five in June 1998 amounted to $388 billion, or 47 percent of their capital; the US and Japanese banking sectors were each owed around $90 billion, amounting to 25 percent and 37 percent of bank capital respectively. (In fact, the chunk of capital at stake was far lower than during the 1980s debt crisis, but few investment professionals were in the mood to take much comfort from such statistics.)

That was not counting losses on the banks' own trading activities. Dutch bank ING Barings, for example, was reported to have moved into GKOs in August 1998 – immediately before the Russian default – while also buying Brazilian Brady Bonds. "This was a game of double or quits and ING ended up doubling its losses," *Euromoney* said, estimating the damage at $500 million; another $500 million of ING Barings' money was believed to have disappeared on loans to Asian and Russian banks.[4]

Leveraged derivatives deals could spirit away sums worth many times the original investment. The World Bank suggested foreign banks could have lost some $15 billion in swap deals with Indonesian corporates alone, and possibly as much as $90 billion on Russian derivatives traded "over the counter", on less formal and less regulated terms than in the official markets. Very often, derivatives deals were not even reflected in the banks' main accounts; they were "off-balance-sheet" transactions that could be funded by limited margin payments, freeing the bank from the need to tie up large amounts of capital. (The World Bank noted that such transactions "often were not subject to adequate scrutiny".[5])

> 66 EU banks' combined exposure to Russia, Latin America and Asia's Crisis Five in June 1998 amounted to $388 billion, or 47 percent of their capital 99

The big banks' potential losses went well beyond their direct emerging market exposure. The wider financial turmoil wrong-footed nearly everyone, and LTCM was not the only outfit to get caught out by unexpected shifts in the major markets. "It's not really about Russia," said one Wall Street analyst. "Much more significant is the incredible volatility in fixed income markets worldwide." And while most banks had relatively small proprietary trading operations relative to their total business, many had also invested in hedge funds, or lent money to them. The LTCM debacle scared everybody witless, and the 14 banks and investment houses that threw in up to $300 million each to rescue the collapsing fund were certainly not acting out of charity; they were heavily exposed to LTCM and directly concerned to minimize their losses. (One of the 14, Merrill Lynch, admitted a massive $1.4 billion exposure to LTCM alone, and a further $600 million to other hedge funds.) "[T]he rescue of LTCM can be seen as an out-of-court bankruptcy-type reorganization ... hoping to salvage as much value as possible," economists Barry Eichengreen and Donald Mathieson wrote in an IMF paper on hedge funds.[6] As it was, the manager of one rival fund reckoned LTCM could have lost more than $14 billion.[7]

Probably the worst casualty of the LTCM affair was Union Bank of Switzerland (UBS), which announced soon after the rescue deal that it would take a charge of 950 million Swiss francs ($700 million) – effectively a loss – as a result of its exposure to the failed hedge fund. UBS's energetic chairman, Mathis Cabiallavetta, quit soon afterwards, along with three other senior executives. An internal document leaked to Reuters journalist Andrew Priest showed that UBS knew LTCM was hugely leveraged, but apparently ignored its own policy guidelines because it felt it had to do business with the fund. The document said LTCM's overall leverage was assumed to be at least 250 times its basic capital (compared with UBS guidelines permitting a maximum of 30 times), but added: "The business imperative is that this is an important trading counterparty for the bank."

Other hedge funds also took a bad hit; press reports suggested Soros' funds lost about $2 billion on Russia, while *The Wall Street Journal* reported that another famous US hedge fund, Tiger Management, lost the same amount when the dollar lurched south against the yen in October 1998.[8] An estimated 40 hedge funds, with some $2 billion in capital, shut down all together.[9] (Tiger Management itself was wound up in March 2000 after further big losses on old-fashioned US "value" stocks that were overshadowed by the high-tech craze.) Some observers, wary of classic hedge fund battle tactics, had initially accused Soros of engineering the rouble's collapse when he urged devaluation in his letter to the *Financial Times*. But the financier strongly denied he had anything to gain from a weaker rouble and was simply issuing a wake-up call to Western governments. "We have no short position in the rouble and have no intention of shorting the currency," he said in a statement. "In fact, our portfolio would be hurt by any devaluation." He later described his stake in Russia's privatized telephone holding company, Svyazinvert, as "the worst investment of my professional career".[10]

There was a loud collective intake of breath. Exposure does not necessarily mean loss, but the banks were forced to make provisions on their balance sheets to cover what they *might* lose. August and September 1998 saw a flurry of profit warnings – official bank announcements alerting share-holders to trouble. CSFB said global market turmoil had cut its net profit for the year to date by about one-third, to around $500 million. Citicorp said its estimated total losses from the Russian chaos would cut its after-tax earnings by about $200 million in the third quarter; its securities arm, Salomon Smith Barney, said it lost $360 million in July and August alone. Morgan Stanley Dean Witter said losses in bond trading and emerging markets would cut its third-quarter net income by about $110 million.

Banking shares plunged, leading the general stock market rout. One index of European banking shares, riding high in July 1998, showed a 40 percent drop by early October;[11] some banks with big interests in emerg-ing markets, such as Spanish rivals Santander and Banco Bilbao Vizcaya (BBV), lost half or more of their market value. Wild rumours swirled that major banks were on the skids; shares in Lehman Brothers, one of Wall Street's leading investment banks, plummeted from $85 to under $30 in less than two months, and the firm was forced to issue a categorical denial that it was filing for bankruptcy.

Unlike some of their Japanese counterparts, Western banks survived, but in the short term their profits were badly battered. By October 1998 global banks and investment houses were turning in a truly awful set of third-quarter results; for many they were the worst figures in years. Bankers Trust lost $488 million, Salomon Smith Barney $325 million, the ING group $169 million, and Merrill Lynch $164 million – its first quar-terly loss in almost nine years. Banks that did manage to stay in the black had their profits slashed. Deutsche Bank, among the most heavily exposed to Russia, saw its net income collapse by more than 80 percent compared with the third quarter of 1997. Announcing the slenderest of profits, US investment bank Donaldson, Lufkin & Jenrette said it had made a $234 million net loss on emerging market securities and junk bonds. Privately owned Goldman Sachs, believed to have been badly burned by its investments in hedge funds including LTCM, postponed plans to go public with a share offering.

INDIVIDUALS FEEL THE PAIN

The crash in asset values also put all sorts of individual investors through the mill. At the rich end of the scale, two senior executives at US securities firm Bear Stearns were reported to have lost up to $9 million each on their individual investments in LTCM;[12] top Merrill Lynch executives said they had $22 million of their own money tied up in the failed hedge fund, and stood to lose an average of $175,000 each. (They denied this had anything to do with Merrill's anxiousness to help in the LTCM bailout.[13])

But Wall Street high-rollers were not the only casualties. The collapsing markets also slashed the value of investments by pension funds, insurance companies and the like, posing a threat to ordinary Westerners hoping to draw a reasonable pension at the end of their working lives. The popularization of market-related investments over the past couple of decades, particularly in the United States and Britain, meant that households from

> ❝ The popularization of market-related investments meant that households from Boston to Bolton had another good reason to fret ❞

Boston to Bolton had another good reason to fret. US households had more of their wealth tied up in the stock market than in their own homes,[14] while widespread share ownership schemes in Britain meant more people than ever before had direct shares in mutual funds or individual companies. Not only pensions and savings but other major financial items, such as market-related mortgage schemes, were at stake; in October 1998 Britain's *Observer* newspaper estimated the global turmoil had slashed the net wealth of every person in the country by an average of £4,000.[15] US television presenter Paul Solman, hosting a programme on the financial crisis, said he had put $3,000 two years previously into a mutual fund that invested in Russia; in late August 1998 he was informed his stake was worth a fraction over $600.[16]

It was not only private-sector cash that was on the line. The EBRD, which for all its investment-banking gloss and marble-clad London headquarters is owned by 60 governments and government-owned institutions, made a net loss in 1998 of nearly $310 million. The development bank had managed to up its operating profit over the year – no mean feat under the circumstances – but this was wiped out by more than $600 million in loan loss provisions, mostly on bad Russian investments.

It was the EBRD's involvement in Russian banking that raised most eyebrows. Roughly a quarter of its total investments were in Russia, of which around 35 percent had gone to the financial sector. Like Russian savers, the EBRD had put too much faith in the country's rotten banks;

despite its supposed regional expertise, critics said it was among the last to recognize the dreadful state of the sector and held on long after others had run for the hills. Its losses included writing off tens of millions of dollars of direct investment in collapsed institutions such as Tokobank and Inkombank. Both had their licences withdrawn in late 1998, and Tokobank was subsequently declared bankrupt. A furious EBRD, which had a 10 percent, $35 million stake in Tokobank, lambasted the bankruptcy process for ignoring creditors' and shareholders' rights. "This particular case is a disgrace," EBRD deputy vice-president David Hexter, formerly with Citibank, told a news conference in Moscow. "It is a model of how not to conduct a liquidation."

In fact, it emerged that the EBRD had held an option to swap its Tokobank equity for debt, making its position more secure, as creditors of a bankrupt outfit are paid off long before shareholders get a sniff at anything that may be left. It had tried to exercise the option in July 1998, but was refused by the management and the Russian courts. EBRD shareholders were angry at the Russians; private-sector investors were angry at the EBRD for apparently negotiating a secret get-out clause while sending a wider signal that it thought Tokobank was a good investment.

Undoubtedly, the EBRD made mistakes. But it was – and remains – in a difficult position: on the one hand it is supposed to operate on sound financial lines to make money, but on the other it has a development mandate in often difficult conditions that a commercial investor would be loath to touch. G7 shareholder governments had urged the EBRD to push cash into Russia in the hope of averting potentially dangerous political instability. EBRD officials said one major reason why the bank invested in Tokobank was because it appeared to be one of the few financial institutions in Russia that was actually lending to real businesses, as opposed to tucking all its cash away in GKOs. "The real difficulty for the EBRD was that it got saddled with opposite aims – to assist transition in risky countries while at the same time making a profit," *Euromoney* wrote.[17]

RUNNING FROM RISK – BANKS FLEE EMERGING MARKETS

A few months after the Russian meltdown the EBRD outlined new lending criteria in a policy paper that marked a fresh and less risky investment strategy, while still insisting it would stay engaged in the shakier countries on its patch. It was part of a collective drawing-in of horns across the financial world, a flight from anything that smelt of any risk whatsoever. The LTCM affair was a seminal moment for the major markets, but many bankers and investors pin the exact turning point down to Russia's GKO default, which shattered two cherished market beliefs: that a country would not default on its domestic debt, and that the international community would not allow the Russian economy to fail. Added to that was the brusque – many would say unjust – way the Russians handled foreign investors. "It was a really dramatic moment," said Merrill Lynch economist Andrew Kenningham. "People's attitude to emerging markets changed because of that."

The swing away from risk was driven partly by very personal factors. Banks often sugar their senior managers' pay with highly lucrative stock options, giving them a strong interest in the financial fortunes of the firm. The slump in banking shares was therefore a direct blow to the net worth of the top bankers themselves. "People are thinking: 'Jesus Christ, I was worth $40 million before Russia and now I'm only worth $15 million,'" said one investment bank employee, who asked not to be named. "There's an obsession with trying to make money without any risk. They're very driven by the bottom line, for themselves and for the company, and they feel like they cannot afford the risk of another major loss due to emerging markets. They're much more prepared to say, 'We'll forego the upside that we might have had.'"

> 66 Net outside investment in emerging markets plunged from $236 billion in 1996 to just $10 billion in 1999 99

Besides, if truth be told, the storming and seemingly endless bull run on the US stock market had been overshadowing emerging market gains for some time. Even before the crash, the promise of outstanding earning and growth opportunities that had lured many investors into emerging markets had begun to pall slightly. In early 1998 the World Bank had already noted that US mutual funds investing in developing-country stock markets had made an average return of 8 percent over the previous five years, while funds investing in the United States and Europe made an average of 19 percent.[18] "You can make huge money on the Dow, so why would people think of throwing money into emerging markets, where even in a good year they can make lower returns than in the US stock market?" said Kenningham.

Figures from the Institute of International Finance (IIF), the main lobbying association for the world financial industry, show that net outside investment in emerging markets (excluding FDI) plunged from $236 billion in 1996 to just $30 billion in 1998 and $10 billion in 1999. Equities investment was virtually halved at a stroke between 1997 and 1998 alone, and bonds saw a similar drop, but the most dramatic pull-out was in bank lending. A $117 billion net inflow of bank cash to emerging market bor-rowers in the peak year of 1996 had already collapsed to $34 billion in 1997 as Asian loans started to go horribly wrong, and in 1998 the direc-tion of the flows switched to a net exodus of $49 billion.[19] (The picture was even worse than it looked, as interest arrears in countries like Russia and Indonesia showed up as positive – albeit involuntary – lending.) And although foreign equity investment stabilized in 1999, the bond picture deteriorated even further and foreign banks continued to haul back more money than they lent to emerging markets. (*See* Figure 15.)

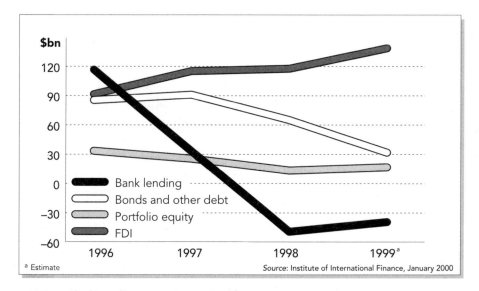

FIGURE 15 The big pull out: net private capital flows to emerging markets

Emerging market bond trading, which in the mid-1990s had attracted some of the brightest and best of the financial world, fell heavily out of fashion. EMTA said annual turnover in the emerging debt market, which peaked in 1997 at $5.9 trillion, slid to under $4.2 trillion in 1998 despite frenzied trading late in the year as investors tried to offload the paper. There was an even steeper drop in 1999, with trading volume almost halving to just $2.2 trillion as hedge funds, banks' proprietary desks and general investors gave emerging markets a wide berth. Trading in Russian bonds, once among the most popular emerging market debt instru-ments, plummeted 82 percent.[20]

The only type of investment that held firm was FDI, which actually climbed over the crisis period, from $92 billion in 1996 to an estimated $139 billion in 1999. This was not just because it is harder to sell a factory in a hurry than a bunch of shares; nor was there necessarily a particular retreat from the countries that were worst hit by the crisis. The United Nations Conference on Trade and Development (UNCTAD) found that FDI to South Korea and Thailand almost doubled in 1998, although Indonesia saw a net divestment for the first time since 1974.[21] Although Russian FDI faltered sharply, dropping by more than two-thirds compared to a booming 1997, the country still took in a respectable $1.2 billion – almost as much as far more highly favoured Hungary – and the EBRD projected a sharp rebound in inflows in 1999.[22]

Many foreign firms that were already established on the ground in developing or transitional economies still saw long-term potential in local consumer markets despite the crisis. "We plan to overcome these complications, not doubting for a second our long-term prospects in this country," Coca-Cola's Russia chief pronounced in late 1998. "Coca-Cola will invest in Russia for the next 100 years." Some firms were able to take advantage of currency devaluations to boost exports from their operations in crisis countries; others took the chance to beef up their existing stakes in local companies while share prices were at rock bottom. A general shift towards encouraging more stable, long-term capital flows in the wake of the "hot money" debacle led to a widespread easing of FDI regulations.

Adrian Simpson, managing director of international risk management firm Drum Resources, said the crisis might even have been a blessing in disguise for Russia, fostering cleaner business practices and encouraging foreign companies to take a long-term view rather than the get-rich-quick mentality he said was common before the meltdown. Russia's lawless business climate was (and to a large degree remains) a minefield for foreign investors, many of whom were taken to the cleaners by unscrupulous Russian partners. At the same time, many foreign companies had avoided paying Russian taxes by operating as offshore firms and doing their business through local intermediaries. "Before the crash everybody was ripping everybody else off," Simpson said. "The crisis has shaken out a lot of the cowboys, Russian and foreign, and forced Western companies to think seriously about Russia."

THE JOB AXE FALLS

In the early and mid-1990s banks, brokerages, mutual funds and other financial houses had fallen over each other to recruit emerging market specialists, often paying extraordinary sums to lure what they regarded as the best talent. Entire trading, sales or research teams were sometimes coaxed en bloc from one bank to another. The Asian crisis started to put a damper on the job market; ING Barings said in February 1998 it would cut 200 emerging market equities jobs, and J.P. Morgan said it would lay off 6 percent of its 1,700 staff in Asia. But there still seemed to be plenty of emerging market posts to be had, especially outside the banks' Asian operations. In the space of a single year, one London-based Eastern Europe analyst was hired by one bank, immediately poached by another, became unhappy and left for a third operation which promptly went bust, and walked into a fourth job straight away. (He was still there in early 2000.)

The Russian meltdown slammed the hiring spree abruptly into reverse. It was hardly surprising that emerging market operations were first in the firing line, but they were not alone. In the fraught climate of late 1998 few people working in any market-related area were entirely sure they would still have a job when they turned up for work in the morning. Scarcely a bank emerged unscathed. Merrill Lynch announced it would cut 3,400 jobs – 5 percent of its workforce – and dispense with a further 900 full-time external consultants, most of them working on technology projects. The axe fell most heavily on the bank's bond, or "fixed income" staff, who were pruned by about one-fifth. It was Merrill's biggest cull since the late 1980s, when it cut 18 percent of its workforce after the 1987 crash. ING Barings said it would lose 1,200 jobs – a hefty 12 percent of its workforce – and in February 1999 the parent ING group announced a far-reaching shakeup at the investment bank, toning down its traditional emphasis on emerging markets. Santander chopped 300 fixed income and equities staff covering Asia, Eastern Europe and the Mediterranean rim; France's Banque Paribas cut 50 emerging market equities jobs; Morgan Stanley fired 60 bond traders in New York and London. BBV, BNP, Robert Fleming ... like the financial losses, the list of job cuts went on.

> 66 The Asian crisis started to put a damper on the job market. The Russian meltdown slammed the hiring spree abruptly into reverse 99

A rash of major mergers sweeping the banking industry added fuel to the fire. Thousands of jobs were already on the block, to cut out duplication of tasks and personnel, and the crisis no doubt persuaded managements to be a little more ruthless than they might otherwise have been. Citicorp and financial services giant Travelers Group, which were in the process of joining to become Citigroup, said they would cut 8,000 jobs, or 5 percent of their workforce, by the end of 1998; they blamed not only the merger, but the global economic turmoil.

Some operators axed whole departments. The Australia and New Zealand Banking Group cuts its emerging markets operation to the bone, and then sold what was left. German state bank Westdeutsche Landesbank clipped the wings of its London-based emerging markets subsidiary, West Merchant, reeling it in as a division of the parent firm. Daiwa Europe, part of Daiwa Securities, dismantled virtually all its fixed income section in London. Bankers Trust's investment banking arm, BT Alex Brown, closed down its emerging market equities desk in London. Merrill ditched nearly all its business related to Russia and the rest of the CIS, deciding it was not worth the candle.

Offices in far-flung countries – especially Russia – were especially vulnerable. CSFB cuts its 300-strong Moscow team by a third; so did Warburg Dillon Read, at its Russian joint venture, Brunswick Warburg. Austria's Creditanstalt uprooted its whole Russian trading operation, moving some of it to London and liquidating the rest. BankBoston said it would close offices in India, Japan, the Philippines and Taiwan.

It is very hard to pin down exactly how many people were affected, but it was certainly the biggest investment industry clearout in recent memory. One estimate in late 1999 suggested the emerging market herd had shrunk 20–30 percent from its heyday in early 1997.[23] "We've returned to a more realistic world," said Bruce Berringer, managing partner at London headhunters Heidrick & Struggles, as the dust settled. "We'll never see the same number of people employed in the industry as 18 months ago." Reuters' emerging market correspondents in London suddenly saw their list of valued contacts shrink before their eyes as one City analyst or trader after another was suddenly reported by colleagues or office switchboards to be "no longer with the company". "We are going into a major market downsizing," said one disconsolate emerging market strategist who had just lost his job. "I'm going on holiday. I'm not going to beat the pavement in this market. That's a wretched situation to be in."

Those who survived could look forward to smaller bonuses and a less expansive lifestyle, as their employers slashed spending on travel and entertainment. Forex traders in Brazil grumbled that the floating of the real had put an end to their long lunches and leisurely work patterns. "Now I am forced to spend most of the day in the trading room," complained one senior dealer in São Paulo – not a sentiment that would receive a great deal of sympathy among his hard-pressed New York or London counterparts.

But it was not all tears. Redundancy payments were often substantial and went a long way to softening the blow. "I've become a teenager from hell, sloping around the house. It's wonderful," said one laid-off economist who was not rushing to find another job. Even some recent bank arrivals did well out of the situation. "One bank was offering two-year guaranteed salaries in mid-1998," said another London analyst. "I know two guys who went there. A week or two later they lost their jobs, but they still got their two years of salary."

Did they all deserve the sack? Certainly individual recklessness and incompetence played their part in a lot of bad investment decisions. So did inexperience, as (in Jeffrey Sachs' words) "naive 25-year-old investment bankers . . . happy to be in Bangkok and Seoul for the first time" rushed off to do their deals.[24] Many of the banks' research departments were hauled over the coals for failing to predict the storm. But the culture of the banks themselves also had a lot to do with the crisis. Insiders describe an ego-driven atmosphere where office politics is paramount, people are reluctant to admit they could be wrong, and competent analysts are not always free to say what they really think. "The reason things got so bad is because most banks and most economists were in denial," said one Russia analyst in London, who recounted how his bosses had been unwilling to hear anything negative about the country before the devaluation and default – not least because the bank had bought heavily into GKOs. "I wrote a piece on why it wouldn't be so bad if Russia did devalue," he went on. "It got absolutely pummelled internally – the whole final document was altered. Then later on, the same people who made me change it used the new version against me."

Banks are market players, and an analyst who smells danger in certain countries or assets may well be leant on to keep quiet if the bank is up to its neck in those investments, or if a sales or syndication team is trying to drum up related business, or if lucrative ties with touchy countries might be damaged. "It's very frustrating. I think Brazil's in a real mess, but I'm not allowed to write that in my external reports," one US-based Latin America specialist complained in late 1998. "Research tends to be used to sound the trumpet and attract investors. Objectivity is not valued." Asian governments, in particular, can be notoriously prickly; Morgan Stanley was once forced to apologize publicly to China over negative comments made by one of its strategists, while the same fate struck Dresdner Kleinwort Benson in Malaysia.

Some notable heads did not roll. Not one senior EBRD official was sacked or resigned over the bank's huge Russian losses. Even more startling, the banks that rescued LTCM decided to keep John Meriwether and his team on board, despite their manifest failure. It was not that they liked the LTCM crew, *Euromoney* explained, but rather that they were afraid firing them could make things even worse. "If there were any nasty surprises still hidden on or off LTCM's balance sheet they would know where to find them," the magazine said. "Too many derivatives firms had suffered shocks after the departure of managers who had left behind positions whose full complexity only they knew how to unscramble."[25]

ALL'S WELL THAT ENDS WELL –
WESTERN BANKS REBOUND

Luckily for the world financial system – and thanks partly to the LTCM bailout – the worst did not come to the worst. The IIF estimated total private-sector losses in the Asian and Russian crises at $350 billion – not exactly small change by anyone's standards. But this sum was spread across a huge number of banks, funds and individual investors. The recovery on major markets patched up many of the mutual and pension funds, avoiding the personal wealth crisis that had threatened Western households. Banks do not like losing money, but the scale of the actual losses was not as damaging as it might have been a few years previously, before the prolonged bull run on Western stock markets allowed banks to build up their capital. Big, diversified financial groups had other business lines that could offset losses related to the emerging market crisis. The Crédit Suisse group, for example, reported surging profits of over $2 billion in 1998, despite a $150 million net loss at CSFB. ING's group profits for 1998 told a similar story, rising 21 percent in spite of trouble at ING Barings. Even some operations that had been directly in the firing line emerged surprisingly swiftly from the mire; Morgan Stanley's fourth-quarter profits leapt 51 percent year on year to a record $1.2 billion.

66 Luckily for the world financial system the worst did not come to the worst 99

By early 1999 nearly everyone was starting to smile again, with a slew of firms, from Citigroup and Salomon Smith Barney to Morgan Stanley, Merrill Lynch, Lehman Brothers and Goldman Sachs, reporting record first-quarter profits. Goldman went ahead with its postponed plans for a public share offering. The Dow's big break in March above the 10,000-point milestone underlined the new mood of optimism.

Western banks also got off relatively lightly in many ways. For a start, IMF-led rescue packages for the crisis economies helped to minimize the knocks that foreign investors could have suffered. On top of that, foreign bankers demanded (and often received) full guarantees from Asian governments to back many of the banks' bad loans to the private sector. Roughly nine out of ten foreign lenders to Thai finance companies, for example, were paid off by the Thai government.[26] "Russia's the only country where foreigners who were interested in a risky punt ended up taking a hit," said economist Paul McNamara at Julius Bär Investments. "In Asia one of the first things a lot of governments did was guarantee the debt, and pump more money into the system to allow firms that were basically bust to service their debt. If you look at Thailand or Indonesia, you could argue foreign creditors have taken much less of a haircut than they really deserved."

Focusing on banks' and investors' large short-term losses also diverts attention away from even bigger gains they may already have realized on those same troublesome investments. In many cases they ended up ahead of the game in the long run. LTCM, for example, had made fat profits for its investors before it ran aground. "If an individual or institution invested $10 million in 1994, it would have received $18.2 million at the end of 1997," the *Washington Post* noted in September 1998. "The remaining interest in the fund would have been worth an additional $10 million at the beginning of the year." Although most of that remaining stake was wiped out, the earlier profits were intact.[27] Italian state auditors confirmed in 1999 that the UIC, which had a $100 million stake in LTCM and had also lent the hedge fund $150 million, had made considerably more money out of its investments over time than it lost in September 1998. The LTCM saga had an even happier ending for the 14 banks that staged the bail-out; by the end of March 1999 the fund had already gained more than 20 percent in value.

Similarly, a bond restructuring may be unwelcome, but it is not necessarily the terrible news it might seem. If you purchased the bonds at face value (for example, if you bought Russian GKOs at a Treasury bill auction) and you are subsequently offered a few cents on each dollar you invested, you have every reason to be upset. But most emerging market bonds trade at a discount on the secondary market, and as the crisis wore on some of those discounts became extremely deep – to the point where the price reflected market expectations of a default. If you bought Russian PRINs at "default levels" of under 10 cents on the dollar, and they were restructured into sovereign Eurobonds at a value of around 64 cents, it could well be cause for celebration. Even better, many banks had written off all PRINs and IANs as a total loss in the dark days of 1998; the price rebound and subsequent restructuring came through on their books as pure profit.

BACK TO THE BOOM? CAUTION RULES

After two years of doom and gloom, many investors were astonished to see some emerging market assets take off again like rockets in 1999. Russia was an improbable star; Russian bonds offered returns of more than 130 percent over the year, and stocks screamed up 255 percent in dollar terms (although the IFCI Russia index was still roughly 40 percent short of where it had been in March 1998). The broad IFCI Composite emerging market stocks index ended 1999 a very respectable 63 percent higher. Turkish stocks did even better than Russia's with a 255 percent dollar rise, China and South Korea notched up gains of more than 100 percent, and sick Indonesia was not far behind. Even bond investors who stuck cautiously to J.P. Morgan's benchmark EMBI+ index reaped rewards of around 20 percent, in a year that saw the first ever Brady Bond and Eurobond defaults.

Of course, such extravagant gains simply illustrate the extreme volatility (some might say the craziness) of emerging markets, with countries derided one year and adored the next. The difference was that this time few people were suggesting the rip-roaring days were back. "The get-rich-quick school had its undoing," said Surojit Ghosh, a managing director at CSFB. "Now you should see a more sensible process of dedicated investors betting on long-term growth."[28] Hedge funds remained conspicuous by their absence; most still had little appetite for high-risk positions, and towering leverage was firmly out of fashion. Small investors also tended to find emerging markets a little too spicy, entrusting far less of their nest-eggs to the sector than they had a year or two previously. Although emerging market bond yield spreads over US Treasuries had calmed down to average less than 800 basis points by January 2000 – a huge improvement on the 1,700 seen in September 1998 – they were still some 350 basis points higher than their pre-crisis best, reflecting a continued nervousness. Many analysts said the size of the market gains owed more to their previously depressed state than to their inherent merit – a classic example of "starting from a low base".

The IIF forecast a solid rise in emerging market investment during 2000, projecting a doubling in portfolio equity flows and a smart rebound on the debt front. Of course, there are always investors ready to seek bargains at the bottom of a market – so-called contrarians who buy when others are selling (or vice versa). "Suffice it to say, 1998 was a less than stellar year for emerging markets *performance* but a wonderful year of *opportunity* because stocks were fabulously cheap," wrote Mobius, who prides himself on taking a long-term investment view. (Among his "Mobius Rules" he lists: "Wait for the panic. Then, calmly, buy."[29]) But there were signs that the asset class might never be viewed in quite the same light again – or at least not for some time.

For most investors who were prepared to creep back into the water, the new watchwords were caution and selectivity. Average emerging market bond yield spreads remained nervously above 800 basis points over US Treasuries in early 2000, compared to less than 400 before the crisis. Many banks launched urgent reviews of their risk assessment techniques, to see how they could have gone so wrong. The employment tide began to turn gently as financial institutions saw new mileage in certain regions or sectors of the emerging markets realm; within a year, many of the banks that had slashed staff levels in late 1998 started picking up modest numbers of fresh employees, sometimes in the very areas they had deserted. ING Barings, Merrill Lynch and Salomon Smith Barney were among a number of banks reported to be looking for more Asia staff; others, such as J.P. Morgan and BBV, were expanding in Latin America. But the numbers were very far from the wild, pre-crisis recruitment scene.

To some extent, selectivity had already shown itself during the crisis, with the stronger economies of Central Europe faring better on the markets front than their weaker neighbours to the east. (Applications by ten former communist European states to join the European Union had been fuelling an EU "convergence play" for some time, particularly in the five countries at the front of the queue, with investors betting on economic stabilization, falling interest rates and a lucrative future in trade and aid.) The new emphasis on moderating risk reinforced the tendency to play safe on Poland, Turkey or recovering South Korea, rather than taking a long shot on Kazakhstan or Vietnam. "The era of colour-blind investors is over," Bank of Israel Governor Jacob Frenkel said. "You are going into an era of selectivity ... a world of beauty contests where each emerging market must show investors that we are better."

> 66 For most investors who were prepared to creep back into the water, the new watchwords were caution and selectivity 99

But by early 2000 it also looked as though the financial industry was starting to cut the entire investment pack in slightly different ways, dividing the emerging market cards into new piles and shuffling them in with some major market assets. On the one hand, the race for technology stocks began to attract some major-market fund managers to countries they would never traditionally have considered. Some new cash, rather than dedicated emerging market funds, started moving not only into Taiwanese and South Korean semiconductor firms, but also into sophisticated

Indian software companies and Israeli flat-panel display technology. Telecommunications stocks, such as Poland's TPSA and Hungary's Matav, were also in vogue. "I think it's in line with a broad trend of globalization in investors' outlooks – people see a particular type of stock in the United States, then look at Europe, then look at the rest of the world," said Jacob Rees-Mogg, a fund manager at British-based Lloyd George Management.

On the other hand, with emerging market debt in disgrace immediately after the crisis, a new, broader buzzword, "high-yield", began to do the rounds. Banks began to consider credit risk on more of a case-by-case basis – comparing, say, a BB-rated sovereign bond from an emerging market borrower with a BB-rated US corporate bond, rather than with higher or lower rated emerging market issues. Bankers covering the higher ranked transitional and developing economies, such as Poland or Mexico, have increasingly found themselves working next to more mainstream market colleagues, blurring the distinction between major and emerging markets. "We now treat emerging markets as just the high-yield end of a global spectrum rather than a distinct area in its own right," said one banker at a major US house. A logical extension of this approach came in October 1999 when Fleet Boston Corp cut BankBoston's emerging markets team by a third and then folded the rest into its high-yield group. It remains to be seen whether such changes will stick, or whether they will prove to be another passing fad in the financial fashion parade.

NOTES

1   World Bank, *Global Development Finance 1999*, p. 9.

2   "Is Systemic Risk Heading for Europe?", National Australia Bank, *Emerging Market Weekly*, July 19, 1999.

3   World Bank, *Global Development Finance 1999*, p. 9.

4   *Euromoney*, May 1999.

5   World Bank, *Global Development Finance 1999*, pp. 39–40.

6   Eichengreen and Mathieson, *Hedge Funds: What Do We Really Know?* p. 12.

7   *The Economist*, October 3, 1998.

8   *The Wall Street Journal*, October 9, 1998

9   *Institutional Investor*, February 28, 1999.

10   Soros, *The Crisis of Global Capitalism*, pp. 162 and 167.

11   *The Economist*, October 10, 1998.

12 *Daily Telegraph*, October 6, 1998.

13 *The Times*, October 3, 1998.

14 Council on Foreign Relations, *Independent Task Force Report*, p. 7.

15 *Observer*, October 11, 1998.

16 Transcript of PBS broadcast *Newshour with Jim Lehrer*, August 26, 1998, at www.pbs.org/newshour/bb/economy/july-dec98/markets_8-26.html

17 *Euromoney*, April 1999.

18 World Bank, *Global Development Finance 1998*, p. 18.

19 IIF news release, January 24, 2000. World Bank figures for long-term net inflows to 1998 show a similar pattern (*See* Chapter 6, p. 152).

20 EMTA news releases, February 22, 1999 and February 14, 2000.

21 UNCTAD news release, March 4, 1999.

22 EBRD, *Transition Report 1999*, p. 79.

23 *FT.com*, November 12, 1999.

24 *The Economist*, September 12, 1998.

25 *Euromoney*, November 1998.

26 Krugman, *The Return of Depression Economics*, p. 88.

27 *Washington Post*, September 27, 1998.

28 *Institutional Investor*, May 19, 1999.

29 Mobius, *Passport to Profits*, pp. 6 and 102.

9

RECRIMINATIONS AND REFORMS

Speculators may do no harm as bubbles on a steady stream of enterprise. But the position is serious when enterprise becomes the bubble on a whirlpool of speculation – John Maynard Keynes, *The General Theory of Employment, Interest and Money*

THE FINGER OF BLAME: COUNTRIES VS MARKETS

The dust of the market crisis had barely started to settle when the finger-pointing began. Who was to blame for the havoc that had brought the world so close to the brink of financial disaster? A loud and sometimes bitter debate exploded in official, academic and financial circles, raking over the evidence against a wide line-up of possible culprits: crony capitalism, bad corporate governance, pegged currency regimes, excessive leverage, hedge funds, bad IMF advice, irresponsible lending, market panic ... The list of suspects was lengthy.

At one extreme, some pinned the responsibility for the meltdown entirely on the countries themselves. Typically, this school of thought focused on Asia's crony capitalism, reckless corporate borrowing and asset price bubbles, on Russia's corruption, mismanagement and tax evasion, on Brazil's fiscal laxity. "There is genuine evidence that countries that faced currency crises ultimately showed key policy inconsistencies *ex-ante*," wrote analysts at Deutsche Bank. "In Asia, capital inflows provided the impetus for excessive risk taking based on inflated asset values ... [I]n Brazil and Russia, benign conditions in international capital markets disguised urgent domestic economic problems. The lack of progress on pressing domestic policy issues was solely responsible for the crash."[1]

Certainly, few would pretend the crisis countries were blameless paragons of virtue. The Asian collapse blew out of the water any notion that the "Asian system" and "Asian values" were inherently superior to other economic or cultural paths; there was even an element of private gloating in some Western circles that the not-so-tiger-like Asians had got their comeuppance. On a less knee-jerk note, a handful of economists, including Krugman, had been arguing for some time that Asia's rapid growth was down to "perspiration rather than inspiration"[2] – that it was not being matched by a corresponding rise in productivity and was generated by very high investment levels that were ultimately unsustainable.

But that was not to say that the fundamental signals were especially negative in every country. Most were running a comfortable budget surplus, and although Thailand and Malaysia had hefty current-account deficits, the external gap in Indonesia or South Korea was fairly moderate. (Indonesia's current-account deficit in 1996 was just 3.4 percent of GDP – smaller that Australia's and less than half that of Thailand.) The IMF itself agreed that Malaysia, for all its big current-account gap and inflated asset prices, had a healthy budget surplus, low inflation, relatively low external debt and a stronger banking system than some of its neighbours.[3] Besides, Asia's large current-account deficits had widely been viewed as acceptable, because (in contrast to Mexico in 1994) they were fuelling investment rather than consumption. On the other side of the coin, Singapore and Taiwan had substantial current-account surpluses, yet they too came under currency attack in the panic of late 1997. Then there was Hong Kong. By general consensus, the territory was well run, well regulated and showed little sign of cronyism before the crisis, yet it was plunged into its worst recession in years.

> ❝ If terrible Asian policies were so obvious, and entirely to blame, how come the shift in market sentiment was so sudden? ❞

If terrible Asian policies were so obvious, and entirely to blame, how come the shift in market sentiment was so sudden? Or as the World Bank's chief economist, Joseph Stiglitz, put it: "If the problems were so severe, how was it that the region outperformed the rest of the world for a third of a century?" Russia, true, was in a bad mess, and Brazil had large budget and current-account deficits. But it seems just as implausible to say there was a clear thread of wrongdoing running through all the crisis economies, as to argue that each country was dragged down by unique circumstances of little relevance to the rest of the world.

Yes, there were fundamental economic problems in all the countries laid low by the crisis; the question is whether they were sufficient in themselves to set off such all-embracing international turmoil. Most analysts suggest they were not, and that the market itself also has a serious case to answer. "[T]he most important cause of the [Asian] crisis was a sharp deterioration in confidence, not of macroeconomic fundamentals, which were mostly extremely strong," wrote Stephany Griffith-Jones.[4]

THE STAMPEDING HERD

Just as there were analysts (mainly in the financial world) who laid the fault squarely at the door of national policy, so at the other extreme there were those who lashed out exclusively at the international markets. Malaysia's Prime Minister Mahathir Mohamad remained their most vociferous critic, continuing to issue scathing condemnations of speculators in general, and currency traders in particular. "I don't understand why there is this reluctance to curb currency trading," he told a business conference in mid-1999. "If you have a gangrenous leg you chop it out, and I think this is a gangrenous cancer and we need to chop it off."

Few took such a hardline approach, however; even Mahathir himself was sometimes prepared to accept that the right kind of longer-term international finance could bring benefits as well as problems. At its best, foreign money can boost productive investment by supplementing sometimes meagre local savings, and can bring new technology and know-how in its wake. Even the bogey of "speculation" has its place, on the grounds that it provides liquidity to keep the market turning – though few beyond the corridors of the big investment banks would go quite as far as Neville Bennett of New Zealand's Canterbury University, who argued approvingly that: "Speculative flows ... fulfil the role of predators in an ecosystem."[5]

Nevertheless, it was clear that the way the international markets had behaved in the crisis had been anything but constructive. The picture that emerged was one of "panic, ignorance and greed", as one top Wall Street trader summed up the forces that drive the financial markets.[6] Most of all, it was back to the problem of self-fulfilling prophecies: the investors who pile out of a market because they are afraid it will fall are the very people who ensure its descent. Alan Greenspan, not given to incautious comment, remarked on "the violence of the responses to what seemed to be relatively mild imbalances in Southeast Asia in August and September of 1998".

66 Players are human; they can panic, and a panicky herd will stampede 99

"History tells us that sharp reversals in confidence happen abruptly, most often with little advance notice," he told a Fed symposium in August 1999. "These reversals can be self-reinforcing processes that can compress sizeable adjustments into a very short time period ... What is so intriguing is that this type of behaviour has characterized human interaction with little appreciable difference over the generations. Whether Dutch tulip bulbs or Russian equities, the market price patterns remain much the same."

The herding instinct of the financial markets has some logical basis. Fund managers have a direct motivation for staying comfortably in line with the market, as their performance is measured not in absolute losses or gains but against the performance of their competitors. A canny investor knows that the actions of the herd will directly affect price movements, and may stick with the herd for that very reason.

But emotion also plays an enormous role. Players are human; like any of us, they can be greedy, stupid or ill-informed. They can panic, and a panicky herd will stampede. It was this that blew the crisis up out of all proportion to the underlying cause, knocking economies over like skittles. "The increase in [national economic] vulnerabilities does not fully account for the spread and depth of the crisis," the World Bank found. "The severity of currency and stock market declines and the few warnings from market participants indicate that a self-fulfilling loss of market confidence played an important role."[7] Berkeley economist Brad DeLong put it more simply. "[T]he sudden change in opinion reflected not a cool judgment of changing fundamentals but instead a sudden psychological victory of fear over greed," he wrote.[8]

As Greenspan said, there is nothing new about the market's propensity to bolt. (Keynes, drawing on his inter-war experience, also noted how: "Loose funds may sweep around the world disorganising all steady business."[9]) But the 1997–99 crisis was exacerbated by the huge size and lightning speed of the modern global marketplace. The force of the global markets is immense; typically, developing countries may have foreign reserves of a few tens of billions of dollars, compared with a global forex market turnover of around $1.5 trillion every day. Panicky markets overshoot, so that currencies, stocks and bonds plunge well below the point where they would in normal times be considered fairly priced. To take a fairly moderate example, analysts canvassed just before the real was floated estimated it was overvalued by around 15–25 percent, implying it should depreciate to between 1.5 and 1.7 to the dollar; in fact, it soon tumbled beyond 2.0 to the greenback and has only briefly touched 1.7 since then, much less 1.5. Most crisis currencies overshot far more wildly; in early 2000 Indonesia's rupiah was still some 70 percent weaker than before the meltdown.

Added to that was the time-honoured problem of moral hazard, where a person decides how much risk to take on the basis that he or she will net the potential gains, but someone else will bear the losses if things go wrong. "Financial markets ... resent any kind of government interference but they hold a belief deep down that if conditions get really rough the authorities will step in," said Soros – who should know.[10] For all the financial community's complaints that debtor countries behaved irresponsibly, most analysts agree that investors regularly stuck their necks out on the assumption that IMF-led rescue packages would protect their money if anything went awry. The World Bank argued that the private sector was more prone than governments to moral hazard, as the political headaches that accompany a financial crisis are big enough to make national leaders think twice before banking on an international bailout. "[L]ending to Russia despite unsustainable policies was based in part on expectation of support from the international community," the Bank said.[11]

A FLAWED TRANSITION

Not that local banks and businesses in the crisis countries were exactly innocent of recklessness and moral hazard as they borrowed dollars up to their eyeballs or loaded up on shaky GKOs. How could they have been allowed to do it? The spotlight swung not only on to the inadequacies of local supervision and regulation, but also on to the way developing and transitional economies had rushed – or had been rushed – into throwing themselves open to international capital before they were ready for it. The Washington Consensus had dictated that an open economy was a good economy, and countries had lined up to reap the advertised benefits of globalization. As recently as April 1997 an IMF committee had been recommending that full capital-account convertibility should be a formal goal for all member states; in other words, the IMF was well on the way to requiring its members to drop all controls on the free movement of international capital.

But even the staunchest free-marketeers were forced to admit there were two glaring omissions on the Asian casualty list – India and China, which between them accounted for nearly 40 percent of the world's population. No one could say the two regional giants were run on impeccable lines; China, in particular, was a hot-bed of corruption and cronyism, with a bad-debt problem that made some of its neighbours' creaking banking systems look creditworthy by comparison. But this was not just a lucky escape. China had strict and sweeping limits on who could exchange yuan, and for what purpose; as a result, it was extremely difficult to speculate against the currency. Despite nearly a decade of startling economic reforms, India had not removed all its curbs on capital-account transactions. In other words, both countries were protected by two closely related market heresies, technically distinct but often referred to interchangeably: exchange controls and capital controls.

China's survival through the crisis, and its refusal to devalue the yuan in spite of its own drooping export growth, was a pillar of support for the rest of Asia. (Some political analysts read a subtle but distinct shift in regional power relations as a result of the crisis, with China claiming the moral high ground in its perpetual jostle for supremacy over a badly weakened Japan. "[T]he mantle of leadership in Asia began to shift from Tokyo to Beijing," wrote Jonathan Story. "Beijing rejected devaluation of the yuan as its contribution to stabilizing currency relations in Asia … Japan missed the bus to world eminence."[12]) China and India apart, it also seemed that countries such as Taiwan, which had strict limits on foreign share ownership and kept a subtle but insistent hand on the forex market, had fared rather better than their more open neighbours.

Debate began to focus on the sometimes indecent haste with which many countries had offered themselves to the international markets, exposing themselves to the full force of global finance before they were robust or flexible enough to take the knocks. Thailand, for example, had even set up its own offshore financial market, the Bangkok International Banking Facility, which played a key role in funnelling foreign dollars to Thai banks and finance companies. With hindsight, this looked like a very bad idea. "East Asia's crisis has shown that the IMF's existing model of financial liberalization, predicated upon free capital flows, foreign portfolio investment and short term foreign currency denominated borrowing, is unstable and vulnerable to movements in the exchange rate," wrote public policy analyst Thomas Palley.[13]

> 66 The doors were thrown open before reforming countries had a chance to develop solid rules and regulatory bodies to keep players in line 99

There was also much breast-beating about the way the former communist countries of Europe and Central Asia were railroaded into free-market economics. The EBRD admitted it had not paid enough attention to key differences between countries such as Russia, which had seen more than 70 years of central planning, and Poland or Hungary, which had communism imposed on them nearly three decades later.

The doors were thrown open before reforming countries had a chance to develop solid rules and regulatory bodies to keep players in line. "Financial sector supervision in East Asia generally has been weak, and regulations relatively lax," the World Bank said. "These problems were exacerbated by the rapid liberalization of financial markets without a commensurate strengthening of supervision and regulation."[14] The central lesson of the crisis, the EBRD said, was that markets could not work properly without establishing the rule of law and a decent tax and regulatory framework.[15] "There's an assumption that it's enough just to liberalize and privatize. The missing element is institution-building," former Polish Finance Minister Grzegorz Kolodko told delegates at the annual EBRD meeting in 1999.

IMF UNDER FIRE

With all the flak that was flying, the IMF could hardly expect to come off unscathed. Critics across the political spectrum laid into the Fund, accusing it of arrogance, secrecy and bad economics. Some said it was nothing more than a tool of G7 interests. Others – especially the Republican congressmen who for months blocked $18 billion in US contributions to the IMF – slammed it for pouring good money after bad as one rescue package after another failed to halt the contagion. The Russian bailout in July 1998 drew particular vitriol; Ariel Cohen of Washington's conservative Heritage Foundation think-tank called it one of the IMF's "most spectacular failures".[16] (Suggestions in mid-1999 that IMF cash might have contributed to billions of dollars allegedly spirited out of Russia in a money-laundering scam did little to improve the Fund's image, despite strenuous rebuttals.)

The Fund also came under fire, mainly in academic quarters, for the advice it pressed on the crisis countries. This charge was led by Harvard's Jeffrey Sachs, who argued that Asian countries should simply have been allowed to let their currencies depreciate when they came under pressure, making their exports more competitive, rather than cranking up interest rates to crippling levels to defend pegs that were ultimately unsustainable. "[I]nvestors do not gain confidence when short-term rates are pushed to dozens of percent," he wrote. "It is neither worthwhile nor feasible to twist monetary policy to soothe panicky investors, especially at the cost of internal depression."[17]

Sachs and others noted that the IMF was used to dealing with crises provoked by governments living beyond their means – a situation calling for higher interest rates to push down the budget deficit and dampen inflation. But Asia was different; the problem lay in the private sector. Governments were running budget surpluses and inflation was low; in fact, their economies were slowing down. As for forcing countries like Thailand or Indonesia to close down weak banks, Sachs said, this could only intensify investor panic. "Once export growth starts to pick up, then panicked money managers will begin to remember why they were there until recently singing the praises of the region," he wrote in *The New York Times* in late 1997. "The region does not need wanton budget cutting, credit tightening and emergency bank closures. It needs stable or even slightly expansionary monetary and fiscal policies to counterbalance the decline in foreign loans."[18]

Others were singing the same or a similar tune, that to insist on higher interest rates and government spending cuts in countries that were threatened with recession (and in some cases were even running a budget surplus) was a recipe for disaster. Stiglitz, on loan to the World Bank from his professorship at Stanford University, raised hackles in Washington in late 1997 by openly suggesting IMF policies could lead to turmoil in Indonesia. An increasingly public rift formed between the two sister institutions, with Stiglitz playing the main gadfly, accusing the Fund of inflicting "pain for its own sake". "When exchange rates are trashed by the market, the monetary authorities need to stand up and resist it," IMF chief economist Michael Mussa told a conference in September 1999. "Do you want to kill the economy in order to save the exchange rate?" Stiglitz flung back. "The answer is patently no." Few were surprised when Stiglitz announced in November 1999 that he was leaving the Bank to return to academia. "Quite frankly, a student who turned in the IMF's answer to the test question 'What should be the fiscal stance of Thailand, facing an economic downturn?' would have gotten an F," he wrote in a parting shot.[19]

MIT's Paul Krugman said the IMF had been sucked into playing a "confidence game" with the markets, trying desperately to get countries to do what it thought investors wanted them to do in the hope of stopping the attack. In the process, it turned its back on the kind of Keynesian remedies (such as lower interest rates) that might have halted the slide into full-blown recession – remedies that were promptly adopted by the Fed and other central banks in late 1998 to head off a slump in the major Western economies. "Why did these extremely clever men [in the IMF and US Treasury] advocate policies for emerging market economies that would have been regarded as completely perverse if applied at home? ... The short answer is 'fear of speculators'," he wrote. "[I]nternational economic policy ended up having very little to do with economics. It became an exercise in amateur psychology."[20]

Others said the Fund had even failed in this narrow aim. They suggested that in imposing austerity policies that were bound to meet heavy popular resistance in countries such as Indonesia and South Korea, the IMF helped to stir up the very unrest that would spook the markets. "Investor confidence plummeted instead of being bolstered by the Fund's orthodox shows of force; outsiders can recognize a depressed economy and social unrest when they see them," wrote Lance Taylor of New York's New School for Social Research.[21] Soros said the IMF's understanding of how financial markets operate "left much to be desired".[22]

The IMF rebuffed its critics, arguing that keeping interest rates down would have caused even more disastrous currency collapse and led to massive debt and inflation problems. It was also anxious to stress that it later allowed considerable policy loosening in Asia; some officials even cautiously admitted they might have misjudged the situation at first. "Had we known, when the Thai programme was signed in August 1997, that Asia, including Japan, was heading for major economic slowdown, less fiscal contraction would have been recommended," wrote first deputy managing director Stanley Fischer.[23]

For the most part, however, the IMF was unrepentant. The Fund's prescriptions in Asia had "worked less well than hoped" for two main reasons, Fischer argued: countries had not implemented them promptly enough, and Japan's recession worsened the external climate. He also defended bank closures, saying it was vital to attack the financial problems at the heart of the crisis. And as the crisis economies began to recover, the Fund was quick to claim the credit. "The bitter IMF medicine has been tried on people, and people have found it good," Michel Camdessus boasted at the close of the annual IMF and World Bank meetings in September 1999. "We are ready to help other people in the ward benefit from our kind of medicine."

LOOKING FOR SOLUTIONS – THE RUSH TO REFORM

"No event of the past 50 years has generated more calls for a re-examination of the institutions, structures, and policies aimed at crisis prevention and resolution than the Asian/global financial crisis that began in Thailand in July 1997," began the report of an independent task force put together by the New York-based Council on Foreign Relations, charged with examining how to protect the world financial system.[24] The task force, which pulled together eminent persons from various walks of life, from corporate chiefs to academics and labour leaders, was the brainchild of President Clinton; conceived in the fearful days of September 1998, it was part of an explosion of meetings, studies and new groupings that would try to stop the same thing happening again. "If one car runs off the road, maybe the driver's attention lapsed," remarked Stiglitz. "But if car after car runs off the road at the same corner, maybe it's time to redesign the road."

Back in 1997, anxious Asian nations had already started looking for ways to curb the excesses of the market – most memorably with Mahathir's angry call to ban currency trading (a stand he later softened, proposing that the IMF should supervise forex markets along rules to be laid down by the WTO). But it was not until the second half of 1998, with the entire world financial system on a knife edge, that politicians in the West really began to take seriously the idea of reforming the "global financial architecture", as the high-minded phrase went.

> 66 After months of apparent apathy among Western leaders, there was a sudden merry-go-round of top-level crisis meetings 99

After months of apparent apathy among Western leaders (many of whom, as Soros recounts, were away on holiday and out of touch when the Russian crisis struck[25]), there was a sudden merry-go-round of top-level crisis meetings: G7, G8 (the G7 plus Russia), European Union, US–Japan, Britain–Japan, China–Japan, and so on. Clinton called for a new IMF facility that would make emergency funds available up-front to countries struggling to avoid being sucked into an international financial crisis. Britain, which held the G7 presidency, wanted a global regulatory watchdog. Germany's new, left-of-centre government wanted "target zones" for the world's major currencies. France wanted more political clout for the Bretton Woods bodies (and, implicitly, less US influence over them).

In October the G7 unveiled what was hailed at the time as a sweeping reform plan, endorsing Clinton's IMF idea and aiming to keep a closer eye on hot money flows. "We must do more to build a modern framework for the global markets of the 21st century and to limit the swings of boom and bust that destroy hope and diminish wealth," G7 leaders said in a statement. Privately, officials acknowledged the plan skirted round any concrete moves to curb capital flows. "Behind these ideas are almost no details; and almost none looks workable," commented *The Economist*.[26]

New talking shops were created to debate the reform process. As well as the Council on Foreign Relations task force, Clinton rallied the great and the good of the US financial world into a President's Working Group on Financial Markets. The specialist Financial Stability Forum, made up of national and international regulators, was charged with examining practical ways to improve the global financial system. On a more political level, another "G" group of nations, the G20, was set up; throwing together the G7 and emerging market giants such as Brazil, China, India, Russia and South Africa, it aimed to give major emerging market countries a bigger say in steering the world economy.

Inevitably, the wheels turned slowly. The G7 summit of June 1999, nicknamed the "architecture summit", was heralded as a pivotal moment, but in reality all the hardest hitting proposals were defused in the polite, watered-down language of the final communique. "The problem is in the words: 'We encourage, we recommend, we favour, we welcome,'" said one academic closely involved in the reform proposals, complaining that the communique lacked either the carrot of incentives or the stick of clear penalties for non-compliance.

There was lots of talk, but by early 2000 many observers felt not a great deal had come of it. Many of the more challenging or off-the-wall proposals – from abolishing the IMF at one extreme to giving it vast new powers at the other – had been swept under the carpet. A note of complacency set in as world economies rebounded. "The recovery is still fragile. But a lot of the restructuring one might have hoped for – the momentum for change – is waning a bit," said one official at the Financial Stability Forum. Some suggested the politicians' calls for a shake-up of the world financial framework amounted to little more than a cynical fig-leaf, to make it look as though they were doing something constructive.

And yet there *have* been changes – albeit mostly more conceptual than practical so far. "It's an approach to reform that looks more like a plumber fixing leaky pipes than an architect trying to devise a grandiose new world order," wrote Adam Zagorin in *Time*.[27] But the world also needs plumbers; crafting new regulatory frameworks is a tedious and painstaking task, and some results have started to see the light of day. To run through the entire reform agenda in detail would take a book in itself – indeed, several such books can be found in the bibliography of this volume – and an account like this cannot hope to do more than sketch out some of the major themes. (As one BIS study pointed out: "Thinking about how to make the international financial system more stable has almost turned into an industry in itself.") What is clear is that the crisis has not only stirred up some fresh ideas on how the world financial system should be run, but has also forced a reappraisal of two of the financial world's most cherished assumptions – that capital controls are automatically a "Bad Thing", and that Eurobond holders will always get repaid in full.

COOLING HOT MONEY – THE REHABILITATION OF CAPITAL CONTROLS

With so much criticism of the role that the international capital markets played in the crisis, it was inevitable that much of the reform debate would centre on how to calm their excesses. Speculative attacks are not confined to emerging markets, as the assault on the pound amply illustrated in 1992. But developing and transition economies – often smaller and usually more fragile than their developed cousins – can be particularly vulnerable. (Former Fed chairman Paul Volcker likened small countries exposed to financial market volatility as "rowboats on the ocean".[28])

Asia decided it was time to beef up its collective defences against any future currency attacks. In May 2000 the "ASEAN-plus-three" group – ASEAN's ten members plus Japan, China and South Korea – agreed in principle to expand a web of finance lines between their central banks, so that they could come to each others' aid in an emergency. It was a firm statement of political will, intended to convince the markets that any country would be able to draw on enough combined fire-power to see off its attackers. Details were scanty, however, and sceptics doubted other countries would really risk their own reserves to shore up a neighbour's currency.

The crisis of 1997–99 was clear evidence that for all the potential benefits of foreign investment, the costs could outweigh the advantages. When foreign capital suddenly turns tail, the results are all too plain. But it is also possible to have too much of a good thing; a rush of investment into a small economy can cause distortions, inflating stock market or property bubbles and buoying up the national currency to an uncomfortably strong level. Exports suffer; at the same time, people feel richer and buy more foreign goods. The current account starts to suffer, and the seeds of reversal are sown. "The negative effects of highly mobile capital can, paradoxically, be strongest for economies that either are – or are perceived as about to become – highly successful," Griffith-Jones wrote.[29]

Everyone but the hardest-boiled free-marketeers agreed some way had to be found to stop, or at least discourage, the extreme fickleness of short-term international investment. There were ample suggestions on how to do it, including renewed support for an idea first proposed by economist James Tobin in 1972 that an international tax should be levied on all foreign exchange dealings. Advocates of the idea, which draws particular support in academic and non-governmental circles, say this "Tobin tax" would be tiny – perhaps 0.1 percent – but would serve to dampen repeated, short-term speculative movements. Critics say the plan is unfeasible in today's frontier-free, split-second forex market.

But the main focus turned to capital controls, a policy option that had been common among major Western countries as recently as the 1970s, but had since fallen heavily from grace. For countries that had not yet dismantled controls on their capital flows, the official message suddenly switched; it was no longer "Open up this minute," so much as "Hasten slowly." "The domestic markets and financial infrastructure for portfolio investments in equities and debt instruments are not well developed in many emerging market countries. Creating the domestic infrastructure is necessary before these markets can be opened internationally," said an IMF paper published in February 1999, whose authors included Mussa. "Given the particular problems associated with short-term foreign debt, there may also be a case for liberalizing longer-term flows, particularly foreign direct investment, ahead of short-term capital inflows."[30]

> 66 For countries that had already opened up their economies, the issue was whether to close them again 99

For countries that had already opened up their economies, the issue was whether to close them again. Malaysia's bold decision to clamp controls on capital outflows in the midst of the turmoil became a test case. "The atmosphere of insult and counter-insult in which they were imposed gave Malaysia a profile higher than China or India, which had quietly maintained controls throughout the Asian crisis," wrote Peter Montagnon and Sheila McNulty in the *Financial Times*.[31] Rarely has the outcome of a single economic policy been so keenly awaited, with supporters lauding the country's nerve and critics predicting economic disaster in the financial wilderness.

The main principle behind capital controls to stem outward flows is that they free a country from the need to keep interest rates high to protect an embattled currency. The downside, apart from discouraging some "good" as well as "bad" investment, is that they can become an invitation to graft and evasion. Few economists advocate their use as anything but a temporary measure, and most say they will not work in the longer term unless the breathing space they provide is used to press on with economy-strengthening reforms. Krugman (who wrote a controversial piece in *Fortune* advocating exchange controls in Asia just before

Malaysia introduced them) likens them to "a sort of curfew on capital flight while calm is restored … [J]ust as the right to free speech does not necessarily include the right to shout 'Fire!' in a crowded theater, the principle of free markets does not necessarily mean that investors must be allowed to trample each other in a stampede."[32]

In the end the Malaysian experience was all rather inconclusive: its economy rebounded pretty much in line with those of its neighbours, and as the figures started to improve, foreign investors thought better of ostracizing the country. There was no great exodus of pent-up cash when the controls were eased a year later; the IFC reinstated Malaysia in its main emerging markets indices in late 1999 and by early 2000 foreign investment was pouring into Malaysian stocks once again. (Local dealers said hedge funds were among the buyers.) Mahathir claimed credit for rescuing the whole of Asia, arguing that speculators had toned down their activities for fear of getting caught if other countries followed his lead. The IMF claimed credit for floating Malaysia off the rocks by raising the Asian tide with its own policy prescriptions.

What really seems to have happened is that Malaysia shut the stable door just after the horse had bolted. In retrospect just about everyone, from the IMF to Krugman, agreed that the flood of capital leaving the country had practically run its course when the shutters came down. "I think currency controls have worked, but more by luck than good judgment," said one Western diplomat in Kuala Lumpur.

But Malaysia's take on capital controls was not the only option. Rather than erecting high barriers on the road out of its markets, Chile was feted as a country that had managed to slow down hot money by building speed bumps on the way in. The scheme required up to 30 percent of investment funds entering the country to be deposited in a non-interest bearing account at the central bank for one year. (Colombia had similar rules on foreign loans.) This amounted to an effective tax on inflows and a deterrent to short-term investment, as the money on deposit was forced to lie idle for 12 months.

Ironically, Chile lowered the compulsory deposit to 10 percent in mid-1998, and to zero soon afterwards, hoping to attract more foreign funds to bolster its waning peso as the emerging market crisis started to bite. Some critics of capital controls claimed the country had seen the error of its ways, although the mechanism itself remained in place, including the requirement that capital must stay in the country for at least a year. Nevertheless, the fact that Chile and Colombia seemed to have weathered both the Tequila Crisis and the chaos of 1997–99 rather better than most of their Latin American neighbours gave weight to the argument that the system – or some other way of cooling inflows – could work.

The idea, far from new itself, captured the imagination of the shell-shocked financial world. Suddenly many economists, bankers and officials who would previously have reacted with horror to any suggestion of capital controls were able to utter the phrase without wrinkling their noses in disgust. The Council on Foreign Relations task force recommended that emerging economies with fragile financial systems should take "transparent and non-discriminatory tax measures to discourage short-term capital flows and encourage less crisis-prone, longer-term ones, such as foreign direct investment".[33] The EBRD said governments "should explore market-based means of constraining the volatility of short-term capital flows as long as serious deficiencies remain in reform".[34]

A Commonwealth Expert Group chaired by former South African Finance Minister Chris Liebenberg went further. "While the Group prefers the use of market-based measures to regulate capital inflows, it believes that it may be necessary for countries to consider capital controls [on outflows], on a temporary basis, in the event of a serious crisis where the costs of any resulting distortions are likely to be lower than the alternative of an economic slump," it said.[35]

Even the IMF, which only months before the crisis had been advocating full capital-account convertibility across the board, started to give cautious signs that controls were no longer anathema. Although it firmly ruled out Malaysian-style curbs on outflows, it let it be known as early as September 1998 that it was talking with South Korea about the possibility of controlling inflows, probably through taxes on foreign exchange deposits. "It is important that they should not proliferate into general capital controls," stressed the Fund's Asia-Pacific director, Hubert Neiss. "They should act to prevent excesses and abuses." Caution notwithstanding, it was a sea-change in financial attitudes.

PEGGING OUT – SEMI-FIXED CURRENCY SYSTEMS FALL FROM GRACE

Naturally enough, considering the origin of the crisis, another theme that gained ample attention was currency regimes. Having seen one currency peg after another turn into a target for speculators, there was a growing (if incomplete) consensus that currency bands and crawling pegs had had their day. The Council on Foreign Relations task force urged countries to "just say no to pegged exchange rates".[36] It was one thing on which both Stiglitz and Fischer could agree. "Increasingly unrestricted capital mobility and the consolidation of trade blocs should prompt countries in emerging markets ... to move towards free floats or strict pegged regimes such as currency boards," wrote analysts at Santander Investment.[37]

Sure enough, emerging market governments and central banks have tended to gravitate to one end of the spectrum or the other. By the turn of the century only a handful of major emerging market countries – among them Hungary, Turkey and Venezuela – still managed their currencies through a trading band and/or a crawling peg system. (In a sign of the times, Poland switched to a free float in April 2000.)

At the other end of the flexibility scale, currency boards seemed to have proved their credentials in Argentina, Hong Kong, Bulgaria and a scattering of other countries. But economists warned it was not a panacea, requiring a number of preconditions to be successful. Analysts at Merrill Lynch pinpointed five such requirements, including a credible government, adequate reserves and a solvent banking system.[38] Small wonder that no new countries submitted themselves to its discipline during the crisis, despite proposals in Indonesia and Russia.

> 66 There was a growing consensus that currency bands and crawling pegs had had their day 99

One country, Ecuador, has gone a stage further since the crisis – not just tying its currency to that of another country, but deciding to adopt it wholesale. In March 2000 Ecuador's Congress voted to press ahead with plans to adopt the dollar as the national currency, placing its faith in the greenback to save the shattered economy, despite public concern that it would fuel already rampant inflation. The move is not as unusual as it might seem; nearly 30 countries, including Panama, Liechtenstein and a host of Pacific islands, already use other nations' currencies. It is also a fashionable idea, slotting into wider debate on the possibility of major global currency blocs following the birth of Europe's single currency. But its success in Ecuador seems far from assured; even Steve Hanke, a prominent proponent of currency boards and dollarization, said the country was going about it the wrong way, rushing in with a vague and overambitious bill. The jury is out.

RULES AND REGULATIONS

With so much evidence of irresponsibility, moral hazard and outlandish leverage, there were loud calls to fortify the international regulatory framework governing developed and emerging markets alike. The great crashes of the past had yielded certain lessons; limits on leverage in the US stock market (although not on bonds and forex) were brought in after 1929, and circuit-breakers were introduced on major Western stock markets after 1987 to force a cooling-off period when bear markets turn too panicky. But the crisis demonstrated gaping holes in the net.

One of the more concrete responses from officialdom was a new framework of banking rules put forward by the international Basle Committee on Banking Supervision. The committee, which as recently as 1997 had put out 25 commandments for good banking in its "Core Principles for Effective Banking Supervision", set about improving that structure. Among its proposed revisions, the most eye-catching was a radical change in the rules on capital provisioning – the amount of money banks are required by law to put aside to offset potential losses. Existing rules stipulate different levels of provisioning according to the type of borrower; if a bank buys a bond issued by a sovereign state (even a shaky one), it is obliged to put less cash aside than if it buys a top-grade corporate bond issued by one of the world's most solid companies. The regulations can also perversely favour short-term over long-term lending, a factor that contributed in no small measure to the crisis. The proposed new rules, put out for consultation in June 1999, aim to force banks to make a more realistic assessment of risk by tying their provisioning to credit ratings, drawn either from external ratings agencies or the banks' own risk assessment models. Of course, this raises a fresh problem: the distinctly shaky record of both these groups in spotting trouble ahead. Full and effective enforcement of the rules around the world is a further headache. But the hope is that the proposals, due for final agreement in July 2000, could at least help to discourage reckless lending to countries that look likely to get into payment trouble.

Few institutions aroused greater ire as a result of the emerging markets crisis than the hedge funds, which many people saw as a – or even *the* – major villain in the piece. A number of studies have indicated that they may not have taken nearly as big a role in the emerging markets turmoil as popular imagination suggests; one IMF report, for example, concluded that the baht was the only Asian currency in which hedge funds collectively had taken significant short positions.[39] A defence was also raised (by Soros and others) that hedge funds could actually help to counterbalance violent market swings, because they

> 66 Few institutions aroused greater ire as a result of the emerging markets crisis than the hedge funds 99

often stuck their necks out on positions that were contrary to the market as a whole. (Soros admits, for example, that he sold the ringgit short at the beginning of 1997, but says he started buying the Malaysian currency mid-year when others were rushing to sell.[40]) "[R]ecent history is far from clear that hedge funds, on balance, do more harm in precipitating the fall of asset prices than they do good by helping break the free fall that can afflict oversold markets, including markets for currencies," the IMF report said.[41]

On the other hand, one critic of the IMF study, Michael Howell of London-based consultancy CrossBorder Capital, said its authors completely underestimated the size of hedge fund activities and leverage. "Hedge funds in London made most of their money in 1997 by shorting Asian currencies," he told *Euromoney*.[42] In his detailed account of the Asian currency crisis, Henderson said hedge funds attacked not only the baht but the Philippine peso, ringgit and rupiah too.[43]

Whether hedge funds really are the unacceptable face of capitalism or just glossy but fallible money-churners, there is no question that some of their activities – from the two-pronged attack on the Hong Kong currency and stock market to the LTCM fiasco and the gut-wrenching dollar/yen sell-off – played a deeply destabilizing role. There were persistent demands for action to rein them in with tighter regulation. But in testimony to a congressional banking committee in October 1998, Greenspan pointed out a fundamental difficulty: many hedge funds already operated offshore, and a crackdown in the United States was likely to drive even more of them on to less regulated pastures. "The hedge funds, as far as I can see, cannot be regulated directly in this country," he said. "In my judgment ... really the only significant, effective means that we have to make certain that ... that group of hedge funds does not create a problem, is by making certain that the banks and others who lend them money have direct supervision themselves."

This, in the main, seems to be the direction the reforms are taking. In its recommendations in March 2000, the Financial Stability Forum stopped short of urging direct regulation of hedge funds (such as imposing capital adequacy requirements), although it did not rule it out as a future option if other steps proved inadequate. But it did demand less secrecy, saying hedge funds with capital over $1 billion should be required to meet strict disclosure requirements, and urging offshore financial centres to close international reporting and regulatory loopholes.

As for the hedge funds themselves, anecdotal evidence suggests they became more open with their own investors and cut their leverage levels right back in the aftermath of the crisis – though for how long, who can say? Soros said he was toning down the size of his bets and taking a more conservative investment line after his Quantum and other funds made further big losses by missing the boat on technology stocks. There was talk he had lost his Midas touch, but plenty of younger fund managers are eager to assume his crown.

Pressure has also grown on banks to limit the extent of their own leveraged exposure, be it through hedge funds or on their own account. As the IMF pointed out in 1998, the capital wielded by hedge funds is actually quite small in relation to the investment world as a whole; in late 1997 total hedge fund capital was estimated at around $100 billion, compared with more than $20 trillion at the disposal of institutional investors in the developed markets alone.[44] The President's Working Group on Financial Markets said banks and other publicly owned companies should be required to reveal their exposure to any "significantly leveraged institutions".[45] "Banks have lost money on hedge funds, but their exposures are tiny relative to their capital, or to their own trading losses," *The Economist* argued. "For banks and their regulators alike, it is more important to take a long hard look at how banks manage their own financial risks, and at the rules for allocating capital against their loans."[46]

Regulators and reformers have also increased the emphasis on transparency and information across the board. Although many of the danger signs were public (and disregarded) before the crisis, other vital facts were either unavailable or misleading. (Official South Korean debt figures, for example, put non-performing loans at less than 1 percent of total lending in 1996, while outside estimates ranged from 15 to 30 percent.[47] And knowledge of Thailand's hidden forward currency positions could have saved a lot of people a lot of money.) The Financial Stability Forum said governments and banks alike should keep much closer tabs on build-ups of potentially dangerous debt exposure, requiring better access to details such as currency and maturity. The Commonwealth Expert Group said existing market systems for reporting large futures positions should perhaps be extended to currency trading.[48] And the IMF made noises about strengthening its Special Data Dissemination Standard, which sets guidelines for the publication of national statistics.

"BAILING IN" – THE IMF GETS TOUGH ON BOND-HOLDERS

Moves to keep a closer eye on private capital, if not necessarily a much tighter rein, have gone hand in hand with a far more explosive development: the determination of major industrial countries and the IMF to make private portfolio investors share the cost of rescue efforts and debt forgiveness when emerging market economies get into hot water. In its most basic sense, the IMF phrase "bailing in the private sector" meant getting it to play a part in bailout packages – "i.e., get[ting] it to roll over its debts or provide new money rather than rushing for the exit", as Fischer put it.[49] While not exactly welcome in the financial world, this idea was not especially controversial. Willingly or unwillingly, international banks had already reached agreements in several crisis countries to roll over or repackage commercial debts; their agreement in February 1999 to refinance trade credits to Brazil was crucial in heading off a far greater debt crunch. Some banks were even involved in preventive plans to bring private cash to the rescue in an emergency; for an up-front fee and using government bonds as collateral, Argentina was able to cut a deal that guaranteed it access to up to $6.7 billion in bank credit if it should need the money in a crisis.

> 66 A new front was opened in the war on moral hazard: bond-holders who assumed they had an automatic right to get all their money back should think again 99

What really got the financial industry up in arms, however, was a far more contentious suggestion: that not only banks, but individual bond-holders should take a direct share in the pain when a country is unable to pay its debts. A new front was opened in the war on moral hazard: Eurobond or Brady bond-holders who assumed they had an automatic right to get all their money back ahead of banks or government lenders should think again. The IMF was generally loath to say out loud it had pushed Ecuador to default on its sovereign bonds, or that it might do the same with other countries such as Romania or Ukraine. "We are not saying …'Pay this one, don't pay that one.' This is a decision for the country to take," Camdessus told a news conference in April 1999. The Paris Club of government creditors was more explicit, making its own debt relief for Pakistan conditional on the country seeking an unprecedented Eurobond restructuring. There was firm backing from the Council on Foreign Relations task force, which said: "In extreme cases where rescheduling of private debt is needed to restore a viable debt profile, the IMF should require as a condition for its own emergency assistance that debtors be engaged in 'good faith' (serious and fair) discussions on debt rescheduling with their private creditors."[50]

Publicly, the financial industry was outraged, arguing that it had already taken its share of the pain when bond markets crashed around the world. But in private many analysts admitted something had to be done to stop portfolio investors assuming taxpayers would bail them out through official rescue packages when default was in the air. The main counterargument was that squeezing bond-holders would penalize debtor countries (and by extension, other emerging markets), which would suddenly all find it harder and more expensive to borrow on the international capital markets. "Although rescheduling bonds may be inevitable in some cases, the bond markets are among the most stable source of financing available to Emerging Markets countries, and great care should be taken to ensure that this flow of funds is encouraged, and not driven away," the EMTA said. "We continue to urge that, in the interest of all concerned, rescheduling must be approached on a case-by-case basis and only as a last resort."[51] The IIF took a similar line, stressing that voluntary solutions such as roll-overs should take precedence over restructuring. "Concern about moral hazard from official support is understandable, especially after Russia," IIF managing director Charles Dallara wrote in a letter to the IMF's Interim Committee of finance ministers and central bank governors in April 1999. "However, seeking to extract specific forms and amounts of financial support from the private sector would be misguided."

Even bankers who agreed private investors ought to take a share of the pain were annoyed that existing Eurobond contracts had been broken. "Changing the rules half-way through is very unfair," one complained. "The nature of the bond market is that the investor wants to know exactly how much he's going to get paid. If he's a risk-taker he'll go to the equities market." Pressure mounted to change contracts for future bond issues, to make rescheduling easier and give purchasers a clearer idea of the risks they might run – perhaps by formally requiring a country's assets to be shared among all creditors in the event of default. Similarly, contracts might allow any restructuring to be agreed by majority rather than unanimous vote, a move that would speed up negotiations and prevent a minority of recalcitrant holders from stalling the process.

In early 2000 it was still unclear whether such radical and controversial changes in the bond market would be widely accepted. But Ecuador, Pakistan and Ukraine were vital test cases for the new "bail-in" ethos, and the official sector was sounding adamant. "It is not appropriate for the official sector to mandate the terms of debt contracts between countries and their creditors. But lenders and borrowers alike must recognize that if they choose contractual arrangements that are costly and inefficient in the event of failures, the official sector will not be prepared to shoulder the consequences," US Treasury Secretary Lawrence Summers warned in a speech at the London Business School in December 1999. Another thing was for sure, however: without arm-twisting, no country would want to be the first to introduce a contract acknowledging even the slightest possibility of default.

BRETTON WOODS UNDER SCRUTINY

Although many of the more sweeping proposals to transform or abolish the Bretton Woods institutions quickly fell by the wayside, the crisis seems to have caused more of a shakeup in attitudes at the IMF and World Bank than they had seen for years or even decades. Faith in the IMF fell to an all-time low after its costly international rescue plans, which mobilized more than $180 billion for five countries, failed to block the contagion. The IMF and its allies retorted that the countries that bounced most quickly out of the mire – Thailand, South Korea and Brazil – were those that stuck most closely to IMF prescriptions, while Russia and Indonesia paid the price for failing to follow through on its advice.

Some critics said the Fund needed even more money to mount bigger, better rescues and act as a true, international lender of last resort – a role for which it was not originally designed, but which many people now expected it to perform. Others, including Sachs, said big IMF bailouts should be a thing of the past. Some, including the Council on Foreign Relations task force, wanted the two Bretton Woods bodies to shift back to the tasks they were built for, with the IMF taking care of the big financial picture and the World Bank concentrating on development lending.

In a small way, the Fund's ability to respond to crises has been strengthened by the creation of a new Contingent Credit Lines (CCL) system, the fruit of Clinton's original idea to provide the proverbial "stitch in time". "Critically, it enables IMF support to be provided in a *preventive* rather than in a *reactive* mode," Fischer said.

Both institutions have also been at pains to emphasize that future rescue programmes must pay greater attention to social welfare and the needs of the poor. In November 1999 the IMF replaced the Enhanced Structural Adjustment Facility (ESAF), its central lending mechanism for poor countries, with a "new" Poverty Reduction and Growth Facility, designed to "include an explicit focus on poverty reduction in the context of a growth oriented strategy". Under the new initiative, countries are to present their own strategy for cutting poverty, in consultation with their own people. Cynics doubted whether the IMF, or indeed governments, would really listen to the poor, but others saw it as a step in the right direction.

The crisis also gave new impetus to the IMF and World Bank's Heavily Indebted Poor Countries (HIPC) initiative, a sluggish process in which the major creditor nations have been shuffling towards substantial debt relief for some of the world's poorest countries. In the wake of fresh global debt turmoil, the G7 agreed in June 1999 to a slight easing in the strict qualifying conditions for HIPC, increasing the number of countries that might benefit from relief on a mixture of official and commercial debt. The United States and Britain announced unilaterally sweeping write-offs. Debt campaigners were delighted, but said the HIPC needed to go much further towards lifting the debt burden that has crushed dirt-poor countries such as Vietnam, Bolivia or Chad for two decades or more. Perhaps it takes one tragedy to focus attention on another.

NOTES

1   Liliana Rojas-Suarez and Gustavo Cañonero, "Does Globalization Help or Hurt Emerging Markets?", in Deutsche Bank Global Emerging Markets Research, *Global Emerging Markets*, May 1999.

2   Krugman, *The Return of Depression Economics*, p. 33.

3   IMF, *World Economic Outlook*, October 1999, p. 54.

4   Griffith-Jones, *Stabilising Capital Flows to Developing Countries*, p. 35.

5   *National Business Review*, December 12, 1997.

6   Fay, *The Collapse of Barings*, p. 44.

7   World Bank, *Global Development Finance 1998*, p. 30.

8   DeLong, p. 5.

9   Keynes, *The Post-War Currency Policy*, quoted in Michie and Grieve Smith, p. 228.

10   Soros, *The Crisis of Global Capitalism*, p. xv.

11   World Bank, *Global Development Finance 1998*, p. 44; *1999*, p. 94.

12   Story, *The Frontiers of Fortune*, pp. 217–218.

13   Palley, *International Finance and Global Deflation; there is an alternative*, in Michie and Grieve Smith, p. 103.

14   World Bank, *Global Development Finance 1998*, p. 36.

15   EBRD, *Transition Report 1999*, p. 5.

16   *The Heritage Foundation Backgrounder, Russia's Meltdown: Anatomy of the IMF Failure*, October 23, 1998. (www.heritage.org/library/backgrounder/bg1228.html)

17   *The Economist*, September 12, 1998.

18   *The New York Times*, November 3, 1997.

19   *The New Republic*, April 17, 2000.

20   Krugman, pp. 104 and 112–114.

21   Taylor, *Lax Public Sector, Destabilizing Private Sector: Origins of Capital Market Crises*, in UNCTAD, p. 148.

22   Soros, p. 147.

23   *The Economist*, October 3, 1998.

24   Council on Foreign Relations, *Independent Task Force Report*, p. 3.

25   Soros, p. 163.

26   *The Economist*, October 3, 1998.

27   *Time*, October 4, 1999.

28   *Euromoney*, June 1999.

29   Griffith-Jones, p. 35.

30   Eichengreen, Mussa *et al.*, p. 9.

31   *Financial Times*, August 4, 1999.

32   Krugman, p. 164.

33   Council on Foreign Relations, p. 8.

34   EBRD, *Transition Report 1998*, p. 77.

35   Commonwealth Secretariat, *Protecting Against Volatile Capital Flows*, p. 6.

36   Council on Foreign Relations, p. 8.

37   Santander Investment, *Fixed-Income Strategy*, July 1–15, 1999.

38   Andrew Kenningham and Eric Lindenbaum, in Merrill Lynch research note *Currency Boards: Five Preconditions for Successful Implementation of a Currency Board*, September 1, 1998.

39   Eichengreen and Mathieson, p. 10.

40   Soros, pp. 136–137.

41   Eichengreen and Mathieson, p. 15.

42   *Euromoney*, February 1999.

43   Henderson, p. 127.

44   IMF, *World Economic Outlook*, May 1998, pp. 4–5.

45   The President's Working Group on Financial Markets, p. 33.

46   *The Economist*, October 17, 1998.

47   *The Economist*, September 12, 1998.

48   Commonwealth Secretariat, p. 14.

49   *The Economist*, October 3, 1998.

50   Council on Foreign Relations, p. 8.

51   EMTA, *1998 Annual Report*, pp. 1–2.

NEVER AGAIN?

There can be few fields of human endeavor in which history counts for so little as in the world of finance – J.K. Galbraith, *A Short History of Financial Euphoria*

A CLOSE SHAVE

More than 1.3 billion people – about a quarter of the world's population – live in the two dozen or so countries that were worst hit by the global markets crisis of 1997–99. If you count China (which you probably should, as its economy has also been rocked by the Asian storm despite its insulated markets), the number almost doubles. The eight core crisis countries alone – Asia's Crisis Five, Japan, Russia and Brazil – count around 850 million citizens. That is an awful lot of economic misery.

True, the spectre of another Great Depression was averted. To this day, most Westerners remain blissfully unaware of how close they came to a major slump. No country has suffered the catastrophic downturn that the United States went through from 1929 to 1933, when its economy shrank by 30 percent. The impact on world output has not been as great as the oil shocks of the 1970s; IMF estimates in April 2000 showed global growth chugged along rather better than expected, at 2.5 percent in 1998 and 3.3 percent in 1999. But a sequence of events that can cause economies from one corner of the globe to another to shrink by 5, 10 or even 13 percent in a single year is up there with the biggest collapses in modern history. (The sharpest US recession since World War Two, in 1982, pales by comparison; the economy shrank by a mere 2.1 percent.)

In early 2000 the recovery appeared to be consolidating, with Asia's Crisis Five returning to buoyant growth (if not the regular 8 or 9 percent a year that they previously took for granted). Deflationary pressure in Japan and China seemed to have eased off, most of Latin America was on the up and even laggardly Russia was showing some spark. Thailand confidently said it could do without the last $3 billion of its international rescue package. But not everything in the garden was rosy. Asia was still swamped by bad loans, and its banking reforms had a long way to go before the region would have anything like a solid financial sector. "Without vigorous corporate and financial restructuring, the return to sustainable growth will likely take longer, the fiscal costs of the crisis could rise, and the economies will remain vulnerable to new external and internal shocks," the World Bank warned in December 1999.[1] The IMF said Russia's upturn was built on weak foundations and Latin America's recovery was still at the mercy of the markets. "Access to international finance remains the principal vulnerability of the region," it said. "Latin America's current-account deficits are large compared with the pool of external financing projected to be available for the emerging markets."[2]

> **66 To this day, most Westerners remain blissfully unaware of how close they came to a major slump 99**

The ups and downs of the market rollercoaster have been hair-raising. From its apex in 1997 to its nadir in 1998, the Russian stock market plunged more than 93 percent – a bigger percentage fall in a few months than Wall Street's 86 percent collapse in the great crash of 1929–33.[3] Most big Asian and Latin American stock markets lost over 60 percent of their value from peak to trough, with Malaysia shedding nearly 80 percent. And in the marketplace, the West was not immune. "Public capital markets in the United States virtually seized up," Alan Greenspan told an IMF and World Bank audience without a trace of exaggeration in September 1999. Then came the rebound, with most major and even some emerging markets touching new record highs at the turn of the 21st century before succumbing to jitters over high-tech stocks. Investors who bought or held on at the right time were pretty happy.

But the legacy of poverty will linger long after the markets have rebounded and growth rates improved. Studies on real wages and employment in financial crises show that it takes them years to recover to pre-crisis levels. Some of the ground lost in health and schooling may never be made up; malnutrition slows children's mental development and kids taken out of school may never complete their education.[4] "The financial turmoil of the last two years has dealt a blow to the expectations we had for reducing poverty," World Bank President James Wolfensohn said in mid-1999. "Just a short time ago, we had confidence that the international development goal of halving poverty would be met in the next 20 years in most areas of the world. Today, countries that until recently believed they were turning the tide in the fight against poverty are witnessing its re-emergence along with hunger and the human suffering it brings."[5]

MARKETS RULE, OK

The crisis-hit countries made mistakes – some minor, some major. Some errors were innocent, others venal. Some were a matter of economic dispute. The IMF may have made things better or worse. But what turned a handful of brush fires into a global conflagration was the immense power and unpredictability of the international financial markets. "The world financial markets had, in effect, become judge and jury of the world economy," writes Jonathan Story. "Nothing escaped their attention. National economic performance was judged in the foreign exchange markets. Government policies were assessed through the bond markets. Corporate returns were measured through the world's integrated corporate bond and equity markets … Some governments, currencies or firms were treated with more respect than others, for most of the time, but if governments did not respond to the markets' policy prescriptions, the markets' sanction was to withdraw confidence. They could not impose policies on sovereigns who refused to comply, but they could make the cost of non-compliance very high."[6] (This attitude is overtly betrayed in at least one investment bank research paper, which referred to markets as "disciplinary devices".[7])

The markets are essentially amoral. They do not pretend to have a charitable mandate, nor (despite numerous conspiracy theories to the contrary) do they generally set out with the intention of wrecking a country. Their central purpose is to make money, and whether they coincidentally do good or bad in the process is largely irrelevant to them. Veteran emerging markets investor Mark Mobius lays it on the line while describing Estonia's attempts to get the best price it could in its telecoms privatization: "Now the problem with that is if you don't go a little soft on foreigners, we'll find a government that will. It may not be nice to say it, but that's just the way it is. I mean, we can stick our money in a second flat just about any darn place in the world, so why would we stick it in Estonia, of all places, unless we think we're going to make a killing on it?"[8]

The speed with which money changes hands in today's frenzied, computer-dominated marketplace is breathtaking, and the sheer size of the capital flows can swat down a nation's financial defences in a twinkling. "No matter how manicured your pond is in normal times, once the elephant arrives everyone begins to flee and you have a real problem," Hong Kong Finance Minister Donald Tsang told *Euromoney*.[9]

Textbook economics says the market is an entirely neutral and logical price-setting mechanism that will naturally tend towards equilibrium. The theories of rational expectations and efficient markets suggest that all relevant information will be factored into prices and that it is therefore impossible to make a speculative killing. Unfortunately, this view ignores a crucial fact: the people driving this technology-fuelled juggernaut are human. "The *a priori* assumptions of rational markets and consequently the impossibility of destabilizing speculation are difficult to sustain with any extensive reading of economic history," wrote Charles Kindleberger.[10]

Despite the blizzard of information blowing across their screens, market players cannot know everything – especially when the industry's hire–fire tendency means those at the cutting edge are often extremely young and inexperienced. Dealers are deluged with news and data, little of which they can be expected to remember for much longer than it takes to execute a trade. The people who are paid to take the long view – the analysts and strategists – do not always get it right, and even if they do, they are not always able to speak their mind. Historical perspective is a rare luxury, and financial fashions change. "If you go back a year or two, yield was the thing," said one experienced trader handling Central European currencies. "Everyone was hunting yield – forget the fundamentals, just look at the yield. Now it's 'Forget the fundamentals, look at the direct investment flows,' real or otherwise."

> ❝ The sheer size of the capital flows can swat down a nation's financial defences in a twinkling ❞

Markets often see only what they want to see, and they can get it very wrong. In mid-1997 they saw a glittering Asian future. In mid-1998 they saw riches in Russia. Arrogance, recklessness, incompetence, well-meaning error – all this is human. So, unfortunately, is panic. The herd mentality, the amount of money being played with and the danger of self-fulfilling prophecies can magnify mistakes to the point where entire economies can be steamrollered. "Once you take the possibility of self-fulfilling crises seriously, market psychology becomes crucial – so crucial that within limits the expectations, even the prejudices of investors become economic fundamentals – because believing makes it so," says Krugman.[11]

Markets are bigger, faster, more powerful and potentially more frightening than they have ever been. Japan's "Mr Yen", Eisuke Sakakibara, says the centre of the world's economy has shifted into cyberspace. "These cybercapitalism convulsions drove the world ... to the verge of a great depression in September and October 1998," he writes. "In physics it is widely known that the faster the information feedback of a system, the more unstable it becomes. Likewise, the cybercapitalism that is starting to take shape is likely to become an extremely unstable and risky system."[12] Others have made even direr predictions. "To put the matter simply market forces, if they are given complete authority even in the purely economic and financial arenas, produce chaos and could ultimately lead to the downfall of the global capitalist system," Soros warns.[13]

LIMITED OPTIONS

The crisis showed how horribly limited a nation's options can be nowadays when confronted with a hostile market. Ironically, countries such as Thailand, South Korea and Brazil got so badly burned precisely because they had obeyed the tenets of free-market globalization and thrown their economies open to international capital. When it turned against them, it seemed they could do little to calm it. Malaysia went out on a limb by slapping controls on capital outflows and managed to defy predictions that it would become a market pariah. At about the same time, Chile was slackening its controls on hot money inflows, anxious that it was suddenly not getting enough cash coming in. Some former Soviet states (including Russia) eased off on liberalization and even back-tracked slightly with steps such as price controls. "For many countries, progress in transition [in 1998] ... has been slower and more erratic than at any time since the fall of the Berlin Wall," noted the EBRD.[14] Ecuador looked to the dollar for salvation, but few expected it to be saved.

Probably the most successful counter-attack was mounted by Hong Kong, which saw off speculators by appearing to turn away from the free-market ethos to buy up its own stock market. It worked extremely well, partly because it was so unexpected from that paragon of capitalist values. (It was also a determinedly short-term ploy; a year later the Hong Kong government was preparing for a gradual sell-off of its $26 billion stocks portfolio through a unit trust scheme.) But for all its vulnerability to the vagaries of the market, Hong Kong was in a relatively privileged position: it was sitting on huge foreign reserves and had Beijing in the background if it needed reinforcement. Many other crisis countries, such as South Korea or Russia, were far too strapped for cash to be able to pull off such a move. Most seemed to have little choice but to keep their economies more or less open, swallow (with varying enthusiasm) the IMF's policy prescriptions, and pray the markets would calm down.

The turmoil sparked far less of a backlash against liberalization and global-ization that many analysts had expected – at least on the government side. Demonstrators on the streets of Seoul or Jakarta may have forced some political change, but ultimately they could do little to alter the course of economic events. Anti-capitalist activists in London or Seattle have made lots of noise and good headlines, but they have scarcely chipped the edi-fice they are trying to bring down, delayed WTO talks notwithstanding. Most countries in the world are now so locked into the global economic system that it would be extremely hard to turn their backs on it, even if they wanted to. The progressive whittling away of official aid since the 1980s has left many developing and transitional economies highly depen-dent on international capital markets for the extra finance they need to fund investment and development.

And there is no denying that at its best, foreign capital can bring genuine benefit – which is why developing and developed countries alike fight to attract it. But for small or fragile economies it is like a dangerous and addic-tive medicine: in the right dosage it works wonders, but an overdose can be very risky and a sudden halt in supplies pro-vokes violent withdrawal symptoms. The crisis fostered a growing feeling that – contrary to the more extreme interpretations of the Wash-ington Consensus – not everything can be left to the markets. "The challenge of globalization in the new century is not to stop the expansion of global markets," argued the UNDP. "The challenge is to find the rules and institutions for stronger governance – local, national, regional and global – to preserve the advan-tages of global markets and competition, but also to provide enough space for human, community and environmental resources to ensure that glob-alization works for people – not just for profits."[15]

> **❝ Most countries are now so locked into the global economic system that it would be extremely hard to turn their backs on it ❞**

THE NEED FOR CHANGE

To be sure, none of the reforms to the "global financial architecture", proposed or actual, represent the end of the Washington Consensus that some had hoped for. But it has been dented; some ideas that were previously anathema to the world financial establishment have not only had an airing but have been met with cautious approval. "The result is less a bold new financial architecture than a subtle shift in the old consensus," remarked *Institutional Investor*. "There is a growing sense that the strict free-market orthodoxy should be softened. And there is an increasing push for more countries outside the Group of Seven – notably developing nations – to have a voice in the critical decisions that will shape their future."[16]

On a practical level, the overhaul of international rules governing the way banks and markets should behave is painstaking, tedious and perhaps too conservative for some people's taste. But if it manages to prevent at least some of the abuses and excesses of the crisis from being repeated, it will have been worthwhile. Howard Davies, chairman of Britain's Financial Services Authority, calls it a "quiet revolution in international financial regulation", arguing that for the first time, the expertise of the world's regulatory bodies is being married with the power of the international financial institutions to make sure the rules are followed. There is also a crying need to take the needs of ordinary people into account, even – indeed, especially – in the throes of financial meltdown. "Those who bet wrongly in financial markets should suffer losses. And borrowers should repay their debts, even when they are onerous. But citizens who take no part in the game should be shielded from the consequences of financial collapse to the maximum extent possible," writes Princeton's Alan Blinder.[17]

All of this depends on governments in emerging and developed economies alike mustering the political will to see through any reforms that are agreed – never a foregone conclusion. The economic rebound carries a real risk that complacency could overtake the urgency of late 1998. Ever since Asia started to crawl out of the pit there have been warnings that its commitment to sorting out its corporate and banking tangle may have slipped. (In April 2000 the IMF held up a $400 million disbursement to Indonesia, saying it was falling badly short in several areas including the restructuring of state banks.) The same goes even more strongly for Russia's rotten business scene. At an international level, bright new regulations will not be worth the paper they are written on if they are not enforced around the globe, from London to Bangkok to the Cayman Islands. "If we don't do more, then we'll be just as vulnerable as we have been," writes Stiglitz.[18]

The international banks got a few very nasty shocks from the developments of 1997–99, but they are well able to look after themselves. "The crisis wasn't so much a threat to the banks as to the market system itself," said Isaac Tabor, chief economist at Westdeutsche Landesbank's emerging market arm in London. "Banks are fairly resilient. They take their losses and after a short while they start looking for new opportunities. People who invested in emerging markets knew they were taking a risk. They were greedy, as we all are, and they probably expected the countries to manage themselves better from the macroeconomic point of view. Hard luck." The main blow to the banks, once the sharp but short-lived losses were put behind them, was the damage the crisis did to their business relationships, curbing the chance to make future revenue from bread-and-butter activities such as brokerage. And although emerging markets activity remained subdued compared to the boom years, with most investors still preferring to keep their distance, banks that held on to certain assets (including Russian debt) netted huge profits in 1999.

"Bailing in" private investors – forcing them to take the rough with the smooth – is a concrete development. "It means that investors who are paid well to take risk suffer if their bet is a bad one," said one analyst at a US investment bank. But the arguments in favour of the change of tack by the IMF and the Paris Club go beyond the purely moral or vindictive. True, it may well damp down private lending to emerging market countries through bank loans and bonds, and those countries will probably have to pay a slightly bigger premium for the privilege of borrowing. But there are plenty of people both outside and inside the financial industry who think this may be no bad thing, helping to curb the extremes of hot money that have done so much damage. "In the long run it's probably quite healthy if there's not a return to the kind of boom period we saw in '97," said Andrew Kenningham at Merrill Lynch. "One of the problems for the countries at the receiving end is that one year everyone's trying to throw money at them, and the next year nobody's going to touch them with a bargepole. If the result of all this is that spreads are going to stay wider but be less volatile, then that would be a good thing for the emerging markets themselves."

A SAFER WORLD?

One can only hope the market system will get a little safer as the financial world learns from its near-fatal mistakes of the late 1990s. Sadly, it probably will not. With the best will in the world, financial regulators cannot close every loophole. Even if they could, the sheer weight of the global financial markets would still remain a colossal force to be reckoned with. Most crucially, markets have always been desperately forgetful, and they are getting even more amnesiac as technology spins the wheels ever faster. "When everything is speeded up, the world has a shorter memory," writes Thomas Friedman. "Mexico stiffs creditors in 1995 and by 1998 it's the darling of international investors again. Who remembers 1995?"[19] Or as Krugman put it in *Time*: "When magazines like this start declaring that 'Asia is back', just remember how good the press clippings were back in 1996."[20]

Despite the currently subdued levels of cash flowing back into emerging markets, some specialists in the field fear the exuberant gains in some asset prices (including Russian stocks and bonds) during 1999 suggest history could repeat itself – though they may not want to say so publicly for fear of upsetting their employers. "I think there is every chance of the boom–bust cycle being repeated, despite the talk about transparency, a new architecture, reforming the IMF and so on," said one gloomy City analyst.

> Markets have always been desperately forgetful, and they are getting even more amnesiac as technology spins the wheels ever faster

But there are potentially far bigger and more immediate dangers than the emerging markets on the world's financial doorstep. By general consent, by early 2000 the US stock market – accounting for more than half the value of the world's equity markets – was looking increasingly bubble-like and riding for what could be a heavy fall. Turmoil in high-tech stocks, which wiped 25 percent off the technology-heavy US Nasdaq index in a single week in April, set stomachs churning. US households have around a quarter of their net wealth tied up in the stock market; a crash in the main index, the broader Dow, would rock consumer confidence and wipe out many investors who have borrowed heavily to buy into the boom. Although it presented a generally benign picture in its April 2000 outlook on the world economy, the IMF also faced up to a bleaker possibility. "Very high valuations, particularly in the technology and bio-tech sectors, continue to pose the risk of a large market correction and a sharper economic slowdown later," it said, warning that a 25 percent fall in the Dow could knock the dollar down 20 percent against other major currencies, bring US growth to a virtual halt, throw Japan back into the doldrums and slice nearly a full percentage point off world growth.[21]

The emerging markets crisis of 1997–99 was the first really spectacular illustration of what globalization really means, warts and all. The fact that the world financial system scraped out of serious danger by the skin of its teeth does not necessarily mean central banks and governments can perform the same conjuring trick again. Wherever you live, hold on to your hat. And never trust anybody who tries to tell you the markets always set a fair price.

NOTES

1   Executive summary of World Bank, *Global Economic Prospects*, 2000. (www.worldbank.org/prospects/gep2000/sumeng.htm)
2   IMF, *World Economic Outlook*, April 2000 (advance web site version), pp. 18 and 73.
3   Wall Street figure in Soros, *The Crisis of Global Capitalism*, p. 145.
4   UNDP, *Human Development Report 1999*, p. 4; World Bank news release, "Latest World Bank poverty update shows urgent need to better shield poor in crises", June 2, 1999. (www.worldbank.org)
5   World Bank news release, June 2, 1999.
6   Story, *The Frontiers of Fortune*, pp. 62–63.
7   Deutsche Bank Global Emerging Markets Research, *Global Emerging Markets*, May 1999.
8   Mobius, *Passport to Profits*, p. 84.
9   *Euromoney*, July 1999.
10 Kindleberger, *Manias, Panics, and Crashes*, p. 22.
11 Krugman, *The Return of Depression Economics*, p. 110.
12 *Yomiuri Shimbun*, August 4, 1999.
13 Soros, p. xxvii.
14 EBRD, *Transition Report 1998*, p. 22.
15 UNDP, *Human Development Report 1999*, p. 2.
16 *Institutional Investor*, September 10, 1999.
17 Blinder, *Eight Steps to a New Financial Order*, in *Foreign Affairs*, September/October 1999.
18 *Fortune*, September 27, 1999.
19 Friedman, *The Lexus and the Olive Tree*, p. 110.
20 *Time*, June 21, 1999.
21 IMF, *World Economic Outlook*, April 2000 (advance web site version), pp. 37–39.

ROLLERCOASTER CHRONOLOGY

1982 **August** – Mexico announces it cannot meet its impending foreign debt obligations, trigggering the 1980s debt crisis.

1987 **February** – Brazil unilaterally suspends interest payment on $110 billion in medium- and long-term debt, including $83 billion owed to foreign banks, prompting similar moves by other heavily indebted countries.

1989 **March** – US Treasury Secretary Nicholas Brady proposes new plan to tackle LDC debt problem, shifting the emphasis away from new bank lending to debt reduction.

June – Mexico becomes the first country to restructure its troubled bank loans into tradable Brady Bonds – the first time private banks agree to any debt forgiveness.

November – Berlin Wall is pulled down, symbolizing the collapse of communism in Central and Eastern Europe and paving the way for a reunited Germany.

1991 **December** – The Soviet Union is dissolved, leaving more than a dozen newly independent nations.

1994 **January 1** – Zapatista rebels launch peasant uprising in Mexico's southern Chiapas state.

March 23 – Mexico's presidential heir apparent, Luis Donaldo Colosio, is assassinated, triggering further market panic.

August 21 – Ernesto Zedillo is elected Mexican president.

September 29 – The secretary-general of Mexico's ruling party is shot dead, intensifying political worries.

December – Zapatista rebels resume armed conflict after a ceasefire.

December 20 – Mexican government broadens the peso's trading band; the currency falls 13 percent against the dollar to its new limit. Market panic continues.

December 22 – Mexico scraps its crawling peg system and floats the peso. The currency plunges a further 18 percent and sets off turmoil in emerging markets worldwide.

1995 **January 31** – President Clinton announces the biggest international rescue package to date, pledging Mexico nearly $50 billion including a controversial $20 billion from the US Exchange Stabilization Fund. It marks turning point in so-called Tequila Crisis.

1996 **July 3** – Russian President Boris Yeltsin is re-elected for second term, reassuring investors the country is on free-market path.

November – Russia taps international capital markets for the first time since the 1917 revolution with a $1 billion Eurobond issue, the biggest ever debut by a sovereign state.

1997 **January 23** – Leading South Korean steelmaker Hanbo Steel Corp. defaults on loans, the first of a string of major corporate failures in 1997.

March/April – Russian President Boris Yeltsin completes a major cabinet reshuffle, putting reformers in key positions.

May 14–15 – Thailand's baht comes under attack by speculators. Thailand and other regional monetary authorities intervene jointly to support the currency.

May 26 – Czech central bank abandons its currency trading band and floats the crown after two weeks of relentless market pressure. The currency quickly weakens 10 percent.

June 30 – Thai Prime Minister Chavalit Yongchaiyudh assures the nation in a televised address there will be no devaluation.

July 2 – Bangkok announces a managed float of the baht and calls on the IMF for "technical assistance". The currency is effectively devalued by 15–20 percent.

July 8 – Malaysia's central Bank Negara has to intervene aggressively to defend the ringgit. In Indonesia, the rupiah starts to crumble.

July 11 – Jakarta widens its rupiah trading band from 8 to 12 percent. The Philippine central bank says it will let the peso move in a wider range against the dollar. Both currencies tumble.

July 14 – The IMF offers the Philippines almost $1.1 billion in financial support under fast-track regulations drawn up after the 1995 Mexican crisis.

July 24 – Asian currency meltdown. Rupiah, baht, ringgit and peso slump as confidence in region deteriorates. Malaysian Prime Minister Mahathir Mohamad launches bitter attack on "rogue speculators". Hong Kong later reveals it spent $1 billion on intervention during two-hour period on an unspecified day in July.

August 5 – Thailand unveils austerity plan and complete revamp of its finance sector as part of IMF-suggested policies for a rescue package.

August 11 – IMF unveils rescue package for Thailand, the biggest since Mexico's 1995 bailout, totalling $17.2 billion.

August 14 – Indonesia abolishes its exchange rate band. The rupiah plunges.

September 20 – Malaysia's Mahathir tells delegates of IMF/World Bank conference in Hong Kong that currency trading is immoral.

September 22 – Ringgit slumps to 3.12 to the dollar, its weakest since 1971, following Mahathir's remarks.

October 6 – Russia signs agreement with London Club of creditor banks to restructure more than $30 billion of defaulted former Soviet debt, mainly into new bonds called PRINs and IANs.

October 8 – Indonesia says it will ask the IMF for financial assistance.

October 20–23 – The Hong Kong stock market suffers its heaviest drubbing ever, shedding nearly a quarter of its value in four days.

October 27 – Asian jitters spill over on to world stock markets. The Dow plunges 554 points, its largest single-day point loss ever.

October 28 – The Dow rebounds 337 points, its biggest ever single-day point gain to date.

October 30 – The South Korean won hits lowest permitted level of 984.70 within daily trading band.

October 31 – Indonesia's IMF package is unveiled, providing for $42.3 billion.

November 4 – Thai government collapses as Prime Minister Chavalit Yongchaiyudh resigns. The baht rises on the unpopular premier's departure.

November 9 – Thai opposition leader Chuan Leekpai is appointed new premier.

November 10 – Brazil promises $18 billion in tax increases and spending cuts to ease investor concerns about its budget deficit (most of cuts are not implemented). Won closes at 999.00 to the dollar, with traders targeting 1,000.

November 17 – South Korea's central bank says it will no longer try to defend the won at current levels. The currency immediately falls its daily limit down to 1008.60.

November 19 – South Korea widens its daily band limit on the won to 10 percent; next day it plunges to new limit.

November 21 – South Korean finance ministry official says Seoul is discussing details of a bailout package with the IMF. The won and Seoul stock market rally.

November 24 – Japan's oldest brokerage, Yamaichi Securities, announces it will shut down, burdened by a severe credit crunch, shrinking business, and a racketeering scandal.

December 3 – IMF announces international rescue package for South Korea, which will total $58.2 billion – the biggest ever.

1998 **January 6** – Indonesia unveils wildly optimistic 1998/99 budget, out of kilter with IMF austerity targets. Rupiah loses half its value against dollar over five days, breaking briefly through 10,000, on rumours Jakarta might declare a debt moratorium.

January 12 – Peregrine, one of Asia's largest independent investment banks, collapses under a mountain of bad loans to Indonesian borrowers. Shares fall sharply in Hong Kong, China and Singapore.

January 15 – IMF Managing Director Michel Camdessus and Indonesia's President Suharto sign agreement strengthening economic reforms.

January 22 – The rupiah collapses a week after IMF package shows no signs of easing Indonesia's debt and confidence crisis, hitting a record low of 17,000. Recovers to 11,800 on central bank intervention.

January 28 – International creditor banks and South Korea say they have agreed plan to exchange $24 billion of short-term debt for new, longer-term loans. In Indonesia, mobs attack shops owned by ethnic Chinese over rising food prices.

February 11 – Indonesian Finance Minister Mar'ie Muhammad says the government is preparing for a currency board system. The rupiah rises to 7,200 to the dollar.

February 14 – IMF threatens to halt bailout funding over Indonesia's currency board plans. Police detain 154 people in riots over rising prices that leave at least three dead.

March 6 – IMF says its board will not discuss Indonesia's economic reform programme before April, effectively delaying a $3 billion payment initially expected by March 15.

March 10 – Suharto re-elected president for a seventh five-year term by the 1,000 member People's Consultative Assembly. Thousands of students hold protest rallies.

March 20 – Indonesia says has decided to drop currency board idea for the time being.

March 23 – Yeltsin sacks loyal Prime Minister Viktor Chernomyrdin and entire Russian cabinet, saying reforms have not been dynamic enough. Names virtually unknown energy minister Sergei Kiriyenko as acting prime minister.

April 10 – Russia's State Duma (lower house of parliament) rejects Kiriyenko as prime minister in first of three votes, sending markets into new whirl of uncertainty.

April 17 – Duma rejects Kiriyenko again. Markets react negatively.

April 24 – Duma finally approves Kiriyenko.

April 29–May 5 – New Russian cabinet packed with reformers is introduced. Markets recover slightly but downturn soon resumes.

May 11 – India stuns world with announcement of three underground nuclear tests.

May 12 – Coal miners in Russia's Arctic north start protests over unpaid wages.

May 14 – Mobs rampage through Jakarta and students demand Suharto's resignation. Several Asian markets suffer sharp losses.

May 21 – Suharto resigns and is succeeded by former vice president, Jusuf Habibie.

May 27 – Russian central bank triples key interest rates to 150 percent after shares tumble 11 percent and Treasury bill yields soar to 18-month highs. Asian markets are also hammered as the yen falls against the dollar.

May 28 – Pakistan conducts nuclear tests.

May 29 – The dollar rockets to seven-year high of 139 yen on fears of possible nuclear arms race in Asia and news that Japanese unemployment is at highest since end of World War Two. Recession looms in much of Asia.

June 1 – Pakistani stocks plunge 12.38 percent as traders get their first chance to react to sanctions imposed after the country's nuclear tests.

June 4 – Russian central bank cuts key interest rate to 60 percent from 150 percent in a sign of growing confidence.

June 5 – International lenders and Indonesian companies reach a deal to reschedule massive corporate debt.

June 10 – China's central bank governor warns weak yen is having severe impact on Beijing's foreign trade, raising fears that China may devalue its yuan currency. Markets across Asia tumble, led by a near 5 percent fall in Hong Kong. Taiwan dollar hits new 11-year lows.

June 12 – Japan says its GDP fell by an annualized 5.3 percent in the first quarter, signalling recession. Yen dives towards 145 to the dollar.

June 17 – United States joins Japan in buying yen, taking markets by surprise. Yen rises to high of around 134 at one stage.

June 18 – IMF delays expected $670 million instalment of its $9.2 billion loan to Russia, citing problems with implementing reforms.

June 19 – Russia seeks extra $10–15 billion credit package from IMF and other lenders.

June 23 – Yeltsin and Kiriyenko present anti-crisis plan consisting mainly of tax laws. Yeltsin warns Duma to pass them quickly, citing "social and political dangers".

June 25 – IMF approves the release of its $670 million instalment to Russia, but fails to impress markets. Indonesia and the IMF sign another letter of intent – the fourth.

June 29 – For the first time, South Korea closes banks, shutting five ailing operations in a major step towards meeting mandate of IMF rescue package.

July 1–2 – Siberian miners start new pickets of railways, demanding wage arrears and resignation of Yeltsin and his government.

July 12 – Japan's ruling LDP is trounced in Upper House elections. South Korea imposes involuntary restructuring on *chaebol*.

July 13 – Japanese Prime Minister Ryutaro Hashimoto announces his resignation. IMF and other foreign lenders agree to $22.6 billion bailout package for Russia.

July 14 – Tens of thousands of South Korean workers down tools to protest against wage cuts and layoffs.

July 15–17 – Russia's Duma guts government anti-crisis plan, rejecting large part of revenue-raising measures.

July 20 – Workers' protests begin at Hyundai factory in south-east Korean city of Ulsan.

July 23 – Record 7.0 percent unemployment in South Korea, with more than 1.5 million unemployed.

July 30 – Japanese parliament formally names LDP's Keizo Obuchi as prime minister.

August 13 – International financier George Soros advises Russia to devalue rouble and adopt currency board. Stocks plunge to lowest in more than two years and short-term Treasury bill yields soar well above 100 percent.

August 14 – Hong Kong government intervenes in local stock market, buying stocks to squeeze out investors accused of playing currency and interest rates against the stock market. Hang Seng index soars 8.47 percent. Yeltsin rules out Russian devaluation, but some banks have trouble paying each other and dollars become scarce on streets.

August 17 – Russia shifts and widens rouble trading band, setting new lower limit of 9.5 to dollar for rest of 1998. Government orders 90-day moratorium on repayments of some foreign bank debt, and says $40 billion of rouble-denominated debt will be restructured. Exchange rate on the street collapses and Russians line up in frantic search for dollars.

August 23 – Yeltsin sacks entire Russian government, calling back Chernomyrdin as acting prime minister.

August 25 – Hyundai workers at Ulsan return to work after a union-brokered agreement to limit number of layoffs.

August 28 – Rouble trading is suspended indefinitely on main Moscow Interbank Currency Exchange (MICEX). Official rate remains about 7.90 to dollar but small amounts of dollars actually available on street are sold at around 12 roubles.

August 31 – Duma votes overwhelmingly against Chernomyrdin as premier. Yeltsin renominates him for second vote. Wall Street suffers second-largest point loss in history, plunging 6.37 percent and sparking another series of stock market routs in Asia.

September 1 – Wall Street stages its second-largest comeback in history, sparking a rally in Asian markets. Malaysia imposes new foreign exchange and capital controls to contain speculation.

September 2 – Russian central bank abandons support for the rouble. Malaysia announces ringgit will be fixed at 3.80 to the dollar indefinitely.

September 4 – Federal Reserve Chairman Alan Greenspan says United States cannot remain "oasis of prosperity" amid global economic stress. Ukraine effectively devalues hryvnia, shifting trading band sharply lower to 2.50–3.50 from 1.80–2.25 per dollar.

September 7 – Duma rejects Chernomyrdin a second time. Rouble falls to 18.90 to dollar.

September 10 – Yeltsin nominates Foreign Minister Yevgeny Primakov as prime minister, giving up trying to win approval for Chernomyrdin.

September 11 – Parliament approves Primakov as prime minister. He signals more conservative approach to economic reforms than his predecessors. Brazil hikes market interest rate to nearly 50 percent in desperate bid to check capital outflows.

September 14 – President Clinton says balance of risk in world economy has shifted away from inflation, and priority is to spur growth.

September 15 – Brazil says it is talking with the IMF.

September 23 – Fed brokers $3.6 billion commercial bank bailout for hedge fund Long-Term Capital Management, on brink of collapse as result of world market turmoil.

September 29 – Fed cuts key interest rate by 25 basis points, to 5.25 percent. Canada follows suit. World markets are disappointed the cut is not bigger.

October 1 – Slovakia abandons its currency band and floats crown.

October 3 – Japan announces $30 billion Miyazawa Plan to help Asian neighbours rebuild their economies.

October 4 – Fernando Henrique Cardoso is re-elected Brazilian president after pledging tough austerity measures to save economy.

October 5–8 – Dollar plunges 18 percent against the yen as hedge funds unwind leveraged market positions.

October 6–14 – Interest rate cuts in Spain, Britain, Denmark, Portugal, Ireland and Greece.

October 15 – Fed announces surprise interest rate cut of further 25 points, without waiting for next policy-makers' meeting. Canada also cuts rates. US Congress agrees to unblock long-delayed $18 billion in funds for the IMF. World markets start to pull out of tailspin.

October 16 – Japanese parliament finally passes measures providing $500 billion of public money to support country's crumbling financial system.

October 26 – Italy adds to tide of interest rate cuts.

October 28 – Brazil unveils plan to save $84 billion by 2001 via tax increases, budget cuts and other measures.

November 13 – IMF and rich nations announce a loan package totalling more than $41 billion for Brazil to avoid financial meltdown in Latin America.

November 17 – Fed cuts interest rates by further 25 basis points – its third cut in less than two months. World markets celebrate.

December 3 – All 11 euro zone countries cut rates simultaneously.

1999 **January 6** – Governor of Brazil's Minas Gerais state, former president Itamar Franco, declares 90-day moratorium on debt payments to central government in defiance of Cardoso's anti-crisis austerity drive. Move blows apart Brazil's fragile market calm.

January 13 – Brazil effectively devalues real by nearly 8 percent by scrapping tight mini-band in which it traded. News rocks financial markets around the world.

January 15 – Brazil's central bank scraps support for the real and allows it to float.

January 29 – Real sinks below psychological two-per-dollar barrier for the first time ever.

February 2 – Brazil stuns markets by naming Arminio Fraga, aide to billionaire speculator George Soros, as new central bank president.

February 12 – Ecuador abandons its currency band system and floats the sucre.

April 28 – IMF agrees to lend Russia $4.5 billion over 18 months, but insists Duma must pass several reforms before money is released.

May 12 – Yeltsin rocks financial markets by sacking Primakov and appointing Sergei Stepashin as acting prime minister.

June 30 – Fed raises its main interest rate by 25 basis points, indicating it thinks global crisis is easing.

September 28 – Ecuador becomes the first country to default on Brady Bond, saying it will not pay interest due on $1.6 billion of Discount bonds.

October 25 – Ecuador defaults on $500 million of Eurobonds, the first country ever to do so.

December – Pakistan carries out the first successful Eurobond restructuring.

2000 **February 13** – Russia and London Club of creditor banks agree to reschedule nearly $32 billion of Soviet-era debt, swapping PRINs and IANs for new Russian Eurobonds. Deal paves the way for Russia's return to international capital markets.

February 29 – Ecuador's Congress approves bill to scrap sucre and adopt dollar as national currency.

GLOSSARY

(The definitions below cover the sense in which the terms are used in this book; some may have alternative senses in a different context.)

Bank Negara: Malaysia's central bank.

basis point: one-hundredth of a percentage point – the standard market measure for interest rates and bond yields.

bearish: expecting prices to fall.

BIS: Bank for International Settlements, the Swiss-based international clearing agency and consultation forum for central banks of the major industrial countries.

Brady Bond: one of a variety of financial instruments born out of the 1980s debt crisis, which restructured distressed foreign bank loans into tradable bonds involving some kind of discount on the amount owed, often with US **Treasury bonds** as collateral. (Named after then US Treasury Secretary Nicholas Brady.)

bolsa: Spanish and Portuguese term for stock market.

bullish: expecting prices to rise.

Cetes: Mexican peso-denominated **Treasury bills.**

chaebol: major South Korean business conglomerate.

coupon: fixed interest rate on a bond.

crawling peg: currency system which allows a gradual depreciation or appreciation in an exchange rate, usually to adjust for inflation.

Crisis Five: the five countries worst hit by the Asian crisis – Thailand, Malaysia, Indonesia, the Philippines and South Korea.

currency basket: bundle of foreign currencies gathered on a weighted basis into a single unit, against which an exchange rate can be set.

currency board: strict exchange rate system in which a country pegs its currency firmly to another (such as the dollar or euro), and fully backs its monetary base with foreign currency reserves.

debt-service ratio: the proportion of a country's export earnings needed to cover principal and interest payments on its debt.

dollarization: adoption of the US dollar either formally, as the national currency, or informally, as the main currency across large parts of an economy.

Dow: the Dow Jones Industrial Average, the main benchmark US stock market index.

exposure: in banking, the amount a lender stands to lose in the event of default.

EBRD: European Bank for Reconstruction and Development.

ECLAC: United Nations Economic Commission for Latin America and the Caribbean.

EMBI (and **EMBI+**): Emerging Markets Bond Index and Index Plus – benchmark bond market indices produced by investment bank J.P. Morgan.

EMTA: Emerging Market Traders Association, a bond industry interest group.

EMU: Economic and Monetary Union, the single currency pact initially joined by 11 European Union countries.

ERM: Exchange Rate Mechanism of the European Monetary System, the first stage in moves towards a single European currency.

Eurobond: bond issued by a country or company through the **Euromarket**, in a currency other than its own.

Euromarket: pool of offshore currency deposits held in banks outside their country of origin.

FDI: foreign direct investment in business, implying long-term involvement, a degree of managerial control and possibly technical input; the complement of **portfolio investment**.

Fed: US Federal Reserve, the system of 12 regional Federal Reserve Banks that constitute the US central bank.

float: currency system in which exchange rates are set by the market.

FOMC: Federal Open Market Committee, the **Fed**'s policy-making body.

forex: abbreviation of "foreign exchange".

G7: the Group of Seven major industrialized countries, comprising the United States, Japan, Germany, France, Britain, Italy and Canada.

G8: G7 plus Russia.

GATT: General Agreement on Tariffs and Trade, the international trade treaty that preceded the **WTO**.

GDP: gross domestic product – the total value of goods and services produced in a country in a given period.

GKO: short-term, rouble-denominated Russian **Treasury bill**.

GNP: gross national product – similar to **GDP**, but includes income from abroad.

hedge fund: private investment fund which typically aims to produce high returns from rapid, short-term market movements; often located offshore for tax and regulatory reasons.

HKMA: Hong Kong Monetary Authority, effectively Hong Kong's central bank.

IAN: Interest Arrears Note, a dollar-denominated Russian bond created in 1997 to repackage Soviet-era commercial debt (*see also* **PRIN**).

IFC: International Finance Corporation, the World Bank's private-sector lending arm.

IFCI: the IFC's Investable emerging stock market indices (now called the S&P/IFCI), which measure in dollar terms the performance of markets deemed reasonably open to foreign investors. The **IFCI Composite** is the broad, all-region benchmark.

IMF: International Monetary Fund.

IIF: Institute for International Finance, a global association of banks and other financial institutions.

ILO: International Labour Organization of the United Nations.

intervention: trading by a central bank in the open market, aimed at influencing exchange rates or stabilizing market conditions (**intervention band:** *see* **trading band**).

junk bond: high-risk, high-yield corporate bond.

Keynesian: following the economic precepts of British economist John Maynard Keynes (1883–1946), notably the use of government spending and low interest rates to stimulate demand during recession.

LDCs: less developed countries – a financial forerunner of the term "emerging markets".

lender of last resort: one of the key functions of a central bank, which must be able to lend to the country's banking system at all times, allowing banks to smooth over temporary cash-flow shortages and maintaining confidence in the financial system.

leverage: increasing investment capital by using borrowed funds, or by making small **margin** payments.

London Club: *ad hoc* group of commercial bank creditors involved in renegotiating problem debt.

long bond: 30-year US **Treasury bond**, a key international bond market benchmark.

LTCB: Long-Term Credit Bank of Japan.

LTCM: Long-Term Capital Management, Connecticut-based hedge fund.

margin: small, up-front payment to secure an asset.

market capitalization: total value of all the shares listed on a stock exchange.

MICEX: Moscow Interbank Currency Exchange.

moral hazard: key financial concept that players have a weaker sense of responsibility for their actions if they know someone else will bear any potential losses.

NAFTA: North American Free Trade Agreement, linking the United States, Canada and Mexico.

NPL: non-performing loan, on which the borrower has failed to make payments in full or on time.

OECD: the Paris-based Organization for Economic Co-operation and Development, which loosely speaking groups the world's rich nations; it includes a handful of emerging market economies such as South Korea and Mexico.

OFZ: rouble-denominated Russian Treasury bond.

OPEC: Organization of Petroleum Exporting Countries, effectively the oil producers' cartel.

Paris Club: group of major Western creditor governments involved in renegotiating problem debt. (Formally speaking, the "Group of Ten" countries that first signed the IMF's General Agreement to Borrow in 1962.)

portfolio investment: collecting a range of shares and other assets on a long- or short-term basis for investment purposes only, implying no managerial involvement in the companies concerned; the complement of **FDI**.

PRIN: Principal Arrears Note, a dollar-denominated Russian bond created in 1997 to repackage Soviet-era commercial debt (*see also* **IAN**).

real growth (or **growth in real terms**): rise in GDP or GNP after adjusting for inflation.

securitization: packaging loans or other non-tradable financial items into tradable instruments, or "securities", such as bonds.

SELT: Russia's electronic interbank currency market.

shorting (or **going short**): selling borrowed assets in the expectation that their price will fall before they have to be bought back and returned (the opposite of "going long").

spread: normally the difference between the buying price and selling price of an asset, or between borrowing and lending rates, by which a financial intermediary makes profits; in bond markets, also the difference between the yield on a particular bond and on benchmark bonds of similar maturity (such as US **Treasuries**).

Tesobonos: Mexican **Treasury bills** denominated in dollars but settled in pesos.

trading band (or **intervention band**): formal exchange rate parameters within which a government or central bank allows its currency to trade without **intervention**; sometimes coupled with a **crawling peg**.

Treasury bills/bonds (or **Treasuries**): short-term/long-term government bonds.

UIC: Italian Exchange Office, an agency of Italy's central bank.

UNCTAD: United Nations Conference on Trade and Development.

UNDP: United Nations Development Programme.

UNICEF: United Nations Children's Fund.

WTO: World Trade Organization, founded to supersede the **GATT** and encourage international trade liberalization.

yield: percentage return on an investment; in bond markets, a high yield reflects a perception of high investment risk. Bond yields are usually expressed to reflect market price as well as **coupon** rate, so that yields rise as prices fall.

BIBLIOGRAPHY

Bairoch, Paul, and Lévy-Leboyer, Maurice (eds), *Disparities in Economic Development Since the Industrial Revolution*, London: Macmillan, 1981.

Brady, Rose, *Kapitalizm: Russia's Struggle to Free its Economy*, New Haven: Yale University Press, 1999.

Branford, Sue, and Kucinski, Bernardo, *The Debt Squads: The US, the Banks, and Latin America*, London: Zed Books, 1990.

Bulmer-Thomas, Victor, *The Economic History of Latin America Since Independence*, Cambridge: Cambridge University Press, 1996.

Colclough, Christopher, and Manor, James (eds), *States or Markets? Neoliberalism and the development policy debate*, Oxford: Clarendon Press, 1993.

Commonwealth Secretariat, *Protecting Against Volatile Capital Flows*, London: Commonwealth Secretariat, November 1998.

Council on Foreign Relations, *Independent Task Force Report: Safeguarding prosperity in a global financial system*, New York: Council on Foreign Relations, 1999. (www.foreignrelations.org/public/pubs/IFATaskForce.html)

Dawson, Frank Griffith, *The First Latin American Debt Crisis*, London: Yale University Press, 1990.

Delamaide, Darrell, *Debt Shock*, London: Weidenfeld and Nicolson, 1984.

DeLong, J. Bradford, *A Review of Paul Krugman, The Return of Depression Economics*, May 1999. (www.j-bradford-delong.net/Econ_Articles/Reviews/krugman_depression.html)

Economic Commission for Latin America and the Caribbean (ECLAC), *External Debt in Latin America: Adjustment Policies and Renegotiation*, Boulder, CO: Lynne Rienner, 1985.

Economist Publications, The, *The World in 1997; The World in 1998* (annual), London: The Economist Group, 1996, 1997.

Eichengreen, Barry, and Mathieson, Donald, "Hedge Funds: What Do We Really Know?", *Economic Issues, No. 19*, Washington: IMF, September 1999. (www.imf.org/external/pubs/ft/issues/issues19)

Eichengreen, Barry, Mussa, Michael, *et al.*, "Liberalizing Capital Movements: Some Analytical Issues", *Economic Issues, No. 17*, Washington: IMF, February 1999. (www.imf.org/external/pubs/ft/issues/issues17)

Emerging Markets Traders Association (EMTA), *1998 Annual Report: There's Life in the Emerging Markets*, New York: EMTA, 1999.

European Bank for Reconstruction and Development (EBRD), *Transition Report* (annual) 1994–99, London: EBRD.

Fay, Stephen, *The Collapse of Barings: Panic, ignorance and greed*, London: Arrow Books, 1996.

Friedman, Thomas L., *The Lexus and the Olive Tree*, New York: Farrar Straus and Giroux, 1999.

Fuentes, Carlos, *A New Time for Mexico*, London: Bloomsbury, 1997.

Galbraith, John Kenneth, *A Short History of Financial Euphoria*, New York: Whittle Books/Penguin, 1994.

Galbraith, John Kenneth, *The World Economy Since the Wars: A personal view*, London: Sinclair-Stevenson, 1994.

Garran, Robert, *Tigers Tamed: The end of the Asian Miracle*, St. Leonards: Allen & Unwin, 1998.

George, Susan, *The Debt Boomerang*, London: Pluto Press with the Transnational Institute, 1992.

George, Susan, *A Fate Worse Than Debt*, London: Penguin Books, 1994.

Griffith-Jones, Stephany, "Stabilising Capital Flows to Developing Countries", in *IDS Bulletin, Vol. 30, No. 1, 1999*, Brighton: University of Sussex Institute of Development Studies.

Henderson, Callum, *Asia Falling: Making sense of the Asian Crisis and its aftermath*, New York: BusinessWeek Books/McGraw-Hill, 1998.

Hirst, Paul, and Thompson, Grahame, *Globalization in Question: The international economy and the possibilities of governance*, Cambridge: Polity Press, 1996.

International Finance Corporation (IFC), *Emerging Stock Markets Factbook* (annual), 1998, 1999, Washington, IFC.

International Finance Corporation (IFC), *Investment Funds in Emerging Markets*, Washington: IFC, 1996.

International Monetary Fund (IMF), *World Economic Outlook* (bi-annual), May 1999, October 1999 and April 2000 (advance web site version), Washington: IMF. (www.imf.org)

Keegan, William, *The Spectre of Capitalism: The future of the world economy after the fall of Communism*, London: Vintage, 1993.

Kindleberger, Charles P., *Manias, Panics, and Crashes: A history of financial crises*, New York: John Wiley & Sons, 1996.

Krugman, Paul, *The Return of Depression Economics*, London: Allen Lane/The Penguin Press, 1999.

Leeson, Nick, with Whitley, Edward, *Rogue Trader*, London: Warner Books, 1997.

Michie, Jonathan, and Grieve Smith, John (eds), *Global Instability: The political economy of world economic governance*, London: Routledge, 1999.

Mobius, Dr J. Mark, *Mobius on Emerging Markets*, London: Financial Times/Pitman Publishing, 1996.

Mobius, Mark, with Fenichell, Stephen, *Passport to Profits: A guide to global investing*, London: Orion Business Books, 1999.

O'Rourke, P.J., *Eat the Rich: A treatise on economics*, London: Picador, 1999.

Pastor, Robert A. (ed), *The Debt Crisis: A financial or a development problem?*, Boulder, CO: Lynne Rienner Publishers, 1987.

President's Working Group on Financial Markets, *Hedge Funds, Leverage and the Lessons of Long-Term Capital Management*, Washington, April 1999. (www.ustreas.gov/press/releases/docs/hedgefund.pdf)

Posner, Mitchell, *Profiting from Emerging Market Stocks*, Paramus, NJ: New York Institute of Finance/Prentice Hall, 1998.

Sachs, Jeffrey, and Huizinga, Harry, *US Commercial Banks and the Developing Country Debt Crisis*, National Bureau of Economic Research Working Paper 2455, Cambridge, MA: December 1987.

Sachs, Jeffrey, Tornell, Aaron and Velasco, Andrés, *Financial Crises in Emerging Markets: The Lessons from 1995*, Cambridge, MA: National Bureau of Economic Research Working Paper 5576, May 1996.

Skidmore, Thomas E. and Smith, Peter H., *Modern Latin America*, New York: Oxford University Press, 1992.

Soros, George, *The Crisis of Global Capitalism: Open society endangered*, London: Little, Brown and Company, 1998.

Spero, Joan Edelman, *The Politics of International Economic Relations*, London: Routledge, 1994.

Story, Jonathan, *The Frontiers of Fortune: Predicting capital prospects and casualties in the markets of the future*, London: Financial Times/Prentice Hall, 1999.

United Nations Children's Fund (UNICEF), *The Progress of Nations 1993*, New York: UNICEF.

United Nations Conference on Trade and Development (UNCTAD), *International Monetary and Financial Issues for the 1990s, Volume X*, Geneva: United Nations, 1999.

United Nations Development Programme (UNDP), *Human Development Report* (annual), 1997, 1999, New York: Oxford University Press.

World Bank, *The East Asian Miracle: Economic growth and public policy*, New York: Oxford University Press, 1993.

World Bank, *Adjustment in Africa: Reforms, results and the road ahead*, New York: Oxford University Press, 1994.

World Bank, *World Development Report* (annual), 1983, 1996, 1999, New York: Oxford University Press.

World Bank, *Global Development Finance* (annual), 1998, 1999 (latter in web site version, www.worldbank.org), Washington: World Bank.

World Bank, *Global Economic Prospects and the Developing Countries* (annual), 1998/99, 2000, Washington: World Bank, 1999.

World Bank, *Poverty Trends and Voices of the Poor*, Washington: World Bank, December, 1999. (wb.forumone.com/poverty/data/trends)

INDEX